n+1

ISSUE 27

WINTER 2017

n+1

DEEP END

THE INTELLECTUAL SITUATION

POLITICS

FICTION

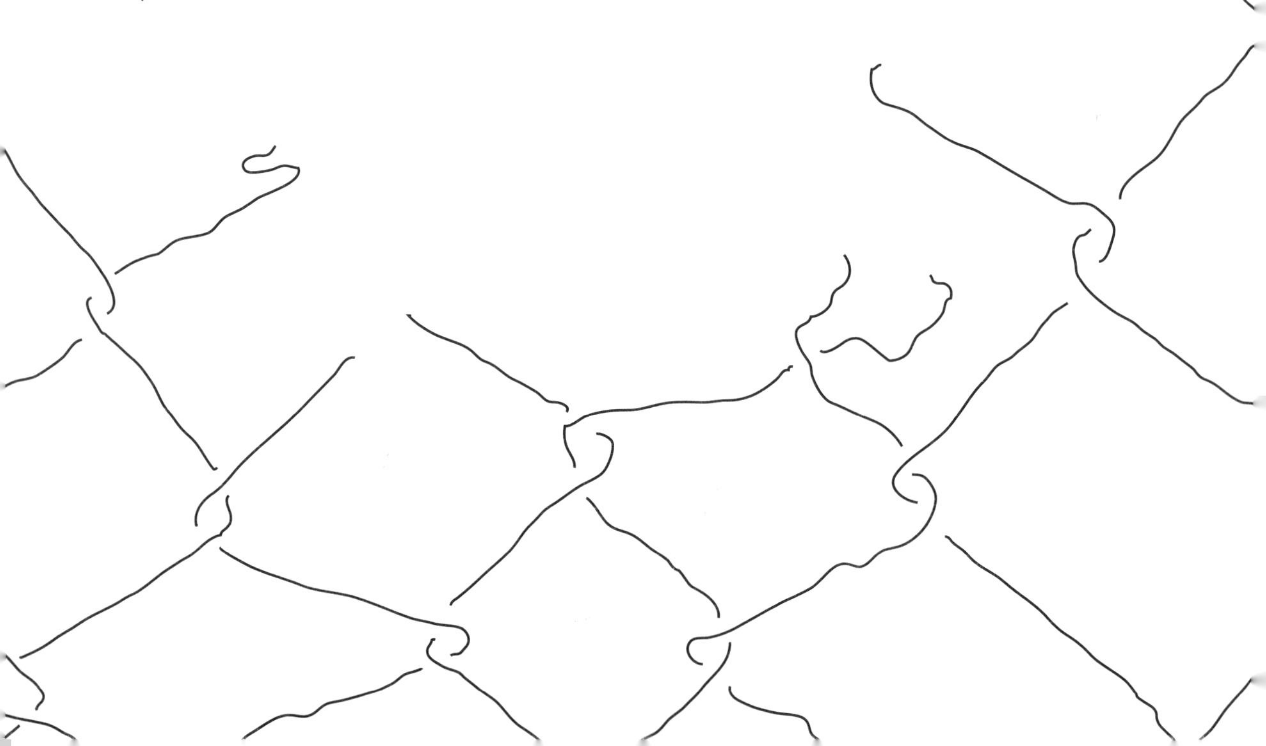

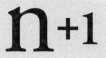

ISSUE 27
WINTER 2017

ESSAYS

REVIEWS

LETTERS

n+1

n+1 is published three times a year by n+1 Foundation, 68 Jay St. #405, Brooklyn, NY 11201. Single issues are available for $14.95; subscriptions for $36; in Canada and other international, $55. Send correspondence to editors@nplusonemag.com. *n+1* is distributed by Ingram and Ubiquity, Disticor in Canada, and Antenne in the UK and Europe. To place an ad write to ads@nplusonemag.com.
n+1, Number Twenty-Seven

ISBN 978-0-9970318-3-6.

WWW.NPLUSONEMAG.COM

THE INTELLECTUAL SITUATION

A Diary

No President

Tuesday in Philadelphia

AT THE CAMPAIGN OFFICE WITH THE OVERworked field staff and their whiteboards, snack packs, coffee cups, Adderall, we're picking up packets of turf for Clinton. We call it "bitter realist" canvassing, but we have good reasons for knocking on doors. Here in Pennsylvania there's a tight race for a crucial senate seat. Up in one northeastern district, where the majority are registered as Democrats, an immigration lawyer is running against a longtime Republican incumbent for state representative. PHILLY LOVES A FIGHTER the posters say, showing the lawyer slamming a punching bag (like Rocky, you see). The Republican's handouts are more forthright, showing images of who this nasty lawyer defends: the bearded, brown faces of "TERRORISTS." Elsewhere, Republican bigot Martina White, who introduced legislation to punish Philadelphia for being a sanctuary city, tries to hold her statehouse position against another Democratic challenger. A billboard on I-95 reads VOTE WHITE.

In Port Richmond, where some churches still hold mass in Polish, we walk up and down Aramingo Avenue, which divides the neighborhood like a wall: white people on one side, black and brown people on the other. A nervous woman passes us in the crosswalk wearing an oversize hoodie advertising the Achieving Independence Center—a halfway house. Pumpkins and dirty couch cushions sag on the porches. Some doors advertise that the occupants are busy watching the Eagles: PLEASE DON'T DISTURB. Through the windows, we catch families gathered around the TV, quietly scrolling on their phones. Farther up, toward Tioga: Fraternal Order of Police stickers, WE SUPPORT THE POLICE signs. Outside one house, a large American flag flies with a difference—among the red stripes, there's a thin blue one.

"I'm not voting," a thirtysomething white man says through his screen door. "Both candidates are garbage. Anyway, I never vote." Why? He pauses. "Because"—slowly, druggily—"I don't like it." A younger black man, a veteran, holds us in a long, wonkish conversation in which he says he's 51–49 Clinton. "I'm a fiscal conservative. I'm worried about her spending plans." Well, we say, Trump's tax cuts are going to tank the deficit—but he cuts in. "Look, if Bernie Sanders were running, this would be no problem. He'd have my vote in a second." It makes no sense (a "fiscal conservative" for Sanders?) but we don't press. At the next door, a middle-aged Latina woman answers, and just when we think it's going well she mentions she's undecided on the presidency. "What's important to you this election?" we ask. "Fidelity to the Bible," she says. "Specifically regarding abortion." We thank her for her time.

Northwood, on the smart side of the elevated rail tracks, is full of trees and stately homes built of Wissahickon schist. These were once the homes of industrial bosses; they're now diverse, poorer but stable, the last vestiges of an otherwise decrepit working-class ideal. We try to persuade a middle-aged black woman who organized with the civil rights movement that the immigration lawyer is worth her time; she has to kick the Republican incumbent out. "You shouldn't be talking to me about some 'progressive Democrat,'" she huffs. "We should be talking about a *revolution*, like what Bernie Sanders was talking about." What about the presidency? "Oh, I'm voting for her. I'm not happy about it. I remember Sister Souljah, I remember 'super-predators.' The Clintons are racists, too. But election time is always about choosing the lesser racist. You've got to *weigh* your racists."

Down the street, a man with a Muslim name. "I can't decide, I can't stand the corruption," he says. From Trump, he means? "No, from Hillary!" But—anxiously—isn't he worried about racism, about violence? After all, listen to what Trump's been saying! "Nah, it's Hillary who's the problem. Read the WikiLeaks!"

Another door, another challenge. "Tell me," a young man says. "Who elects the President: the people or the electoral college?"

"Well, technically, the electoral college . . . "

"That's why I'm not voting."

Most people aren't home. Most people, as usual, won't vote.

ON TUESDAY NIGHT, some of us are in the living room, watching the returns, rapt, as we would be anyway. A few more are in the kitchen, cutting the flag cake into smaller pieces, making bad electoral-college jokes, or wondering whether flag eating will also be banned under Trump alongside flag burning and national-anthem protests. The friend who baked the cake nearly severed a finger in the process and wound up in the hospital. What's an American flag without a little blood baked in?

A group prefers to stay in the garden, smoking, small-talking. Our friend E. is speaking at length about Edward P. Jones's novel *The Known World*. He's just discovered it and wants to let everyone know. He identifies strongly with one of the characters: would you believe they have the same name! We laugh over this, a little too loudly, and he mentions a parallel between a scene in the novel and *Sentimental Education*. We discuss going to bed while the revolution roils the streets outside and nominate acquaintances for the role of Sénécal, the friend who joins the secret police. Who will be the one to betray us to Trump's Gestapo or shoot us on the barricades?

A helicopter circles in the distance. The returns are getting worse, the news from Michigan, North Carolina, Pennsylvania. Our wise friend, when asked what to tell the children, speaks of the need for a resilient message: "We keep fighting, we don't run away and hide when we lose a game. The world doesn't end when the other team wins." We nod. "Of course that's a little simplistic," she adds. "If I feel my family is threatened, we're getting out."

In the corner, a former data wonk for the Sanders campaign is gently knocking his head against the wall. Someone from the TV room says, "Oh fuck, oh fuck, oh fuck." Everyone left looks ashen, subdued, older, exhausted. The world-weary friend speaks to the wise friend about life under authoritarian dictatorships: there are Russians, Turks, Chinese—they too survive. Their lives are blighted, embittered, limited, but they get by. We are simply joining the new world order.

Beneath the shock, guilt creeps in alongside the sense of failure. Everyone here has volunteered for the Democratic Party. Could we have done more? Should we have done more? Pushed harder, launched ourselves more fervently and earlier into more difficult places? One's sense of agency begins to weaken. This is a room of doers, achievers, people used to seeing their efforts rewarded. We begin to feel like the young white woman we spoke to earlier. She'd voted for Trump, she admitted, but we shouldn't worry, she always gets everything wrong, her life a succession of bad choices. She doesn't know how to pick a winner. "Yeah, he's an asshole," she said, "but I just don't like Her." While she talked, her toddler, cashew-toned, blue-eyed, biracial, played happily with other darker-skinned children in the front yard. We wanted to tell her that her choices hadn't let her down as much as she thought, but that she had let herself and those choices down when she voted.

We want to tell ourselves this, too. Not the voting part: the part about our decisions not having been the wrong ones. We'd put aside whatever rancor, envy, knowingness we felt in order to toil, however reluctantly, in the name of Hillary Clinton, and we did not feel like losers. But part of the disaster of Trump's victory is that our best actions come to seem like mistakes. When society rewards a man whose level of bad childishness even debases the word *child*, our work to become—not just *act like*—adults feels pointless, squandered. The superego becomes a voice of punishing desublimation: If only you hadn't believed the adults when they told you that something was just a game, that there was more to life than competition, that kindness was a virtue. The failure to remain true to your preadolescent self stings. Maturity feels like failure.

Fifty-three Percent

THE NEXT DAY, in the private glow of our computer screens, we try to draw lessons. We read articles about exit polls, try to remember where the rust belt starts and stops, weigh gender against race. The first lesson is the deceptiveness of data. Knocking on doors turned voters—like magic!—into real people, people whose collective opinion is in no way coherent or conclusive. The social world does not fit the statistical world.

And yet we cling to the statistics; for the moment, they're all we have. Fifty-three percent of white women voted for Trump. Why, how? We hadn't expected them to throw their weight unanimously behind the first woman President, but we'd expected more than this. Surely many voted for whiteness above all else, consciously or otherwise. Others didn't trust her, a rich career woman who couldn't speak to or for the poor. At least some favored Trump because he reminded them of their husbands and boyfriends—arrogant chauvinists of exaggerated confidence—and they were sticking by their man. In the tea leaves we read a failure of feminist infrastructure. Maybe this is what happens when all you have are Planned Parenthood and gender-studies departments. There are many, many women in the United States to whom feminism has never been available.

Perversely, we look at Melania Trump and see a woman who needs feminism. We look at Ivanka Trump—perhaps the most privileged woman in America, the beneficiary of an international domestic-labor market that frees her from housework by leaving it to underpaid women from Asia, Africa, and South America; a woman who hardly pays her factory workers in Dongguan for sixteen-hour days making Ivanka Trump shoes; who poses for *Vogue* while her Chinese nanny, Xixi, watches her three children—we look at this woman and think even she needs feminism. What else could compel her to change? Segregation of the sexes is especially stark among the rich, and if there's any form of oppression Ivanka knows, it's sexism. No matter how many women she ignores, undermines, or exploits, she will never be a man. And she will injure many women she will never know and never see.

Racism, nationalism, and patriarchy belong to a common project. All nationalist programs reduce women to breeders for the nation, expelling, degrading, or killing those they don't want. Nationalism is not kind to gays, lesbians, or gender nonconformists, either. At best, women can hope to be exceptions—honorary men granted the privilege of oppressing other women. The respect, pride, and affection benevolent patriarchs have for women is similar to the sort they have for their dogs. The difference is not in degree but kind: the love of masters for their pets can be deep, but it's not the love of equals.

If political progress resembles the movement of a train, the front car chugging toward a still-distant horizon of possibility, reaction attacks the station, the point of entry where people linger, hesitate, and imagine getting on board. We thought we could take the entry point of feminism for granted, believe in the permanence of its basic achievements: the franchise and representation in government, the right to pleasure and the right to solitude, 100 cents on the dollar for our labor, the freedom to decide when and whether to have children. We assumed our own generation's fight would be for new and better things, for ways of being and thinking not available in the past—not for the achievements won by our mothers and grandmothers. But while we had our eyes on the horizon, the rear car was derailed, the station besieged. The challenge, now, is to expect nothing but still demand everything: to fight our mothers' fight and our own at the same time.

Adieu au prolétariat

DAYS PASS, AND we remind ourselves: nearly two million more Americans voted for Clinton than for Trump. This helps with morale, if not with policy. More Americans voted for Gore than for Bush in 2000, but that didn't prevent the Bush Administration from implementing a maximalist agenda the moment it took office. Trump may have been incoherent and inconsistent in his campaign promises (one day he's building a wall and banning Muslims, the next he's building bridges and, at Ivanka's urging, paying for everyone's child care), but he has been consistent in his choice of advisers. They constitute a small right-wing criminal class within the larger corrupt American political class—a mixture of white supremacists, "law and order" fascists, and the inevitable finance-industry revanchists. Until a few weeks ago, those looking for a sliver of common sense pinned their hopes on the chair of the Benghazi hearings and the guy who shut down the George Washington Bridge to punish a disloyal mayor. There is every reason to expect the worst. We should prepare for an increase in deportations, further militarization of our borders and police forces, cuts in social programs (with particular damage to minority communities), and an increase in hate crimes. Democracy itself may well be at stake.

Online, writers launch blithely into essays about what the vote represents, what the voters want, as if this were some normal election to be analyzed in the usual mode. It's like Vox trying to figure out the victory of the 1938 *Anschluss* referendum in Austria ("Surprising turnout numbers in the

Salzburg suburbs") and missing the *Wald* for the *Bäumen*. We read and parse in a manic, useless way until a friend's email forces us to recognize the waves of feeling we've been pushing aside every half hour. The feeling is of strangeness, of failed recognition. We were wrong about what was going to happen: now the analysis defers the inevitable recognition of what *has* happened. Even the phrase "President-Elect" doesn't compute. When the TV announcers say it, it sounds like a mistake.

WE DO FEEL READY to blame someone. Clinton's campaign was doomed from the start. "Not our President"? Not our Party either. The Democrats—festooned this season with celebrities and capitalists to an unthinking degree—rarely talked about what workers and the dispossessed needed to build their lives. Most voters could hardly name a thing Clinton was *for*. Instead, the campaign piped into every swing-state living room a nonstop stream of American success, the sunshine pabulum of the DNC: "America is great because America is good," "America is already great." Anger, loss, and economic trauma could be overcome by a genial disposition, an endless exhibition of proper behavior with an extra helping of negative ads correcting Trump for his crude (never "criminal") actions.

If voters didn't know what Clinton was for, they knew what she was against: Donald Trump, and people who did things like him. Her strategy was "disqualification." Clinton ran on "competence": She was, as her supporters never ceased to remind us, "the most qualified presidential candidate in history." The message was engineered to resonate with white-collar women familiar with being passed over for senior-level jobs. But it put a new twist on the politics of '60s neoconservatism, combining it with the meritocratic strain that's ruled the Democratic Party since the '80s. No need for a straightforward, easily intelligible ideological call—the people versus "the billionaire class," say. Just: *Trust us. Our policies are healthy and good for you.*

This story about the ultimate triumph of the most talented may well have sounded familiar to voters struggling to stay above water. It may even have prompted many of them not to vote. When they lost their jobs, or struggled to stay afloat as incomes stagnated and costs rose, they were repeatedly told that their misfortune was their fault. They didn't have the right skills, they had failed to keep up. Why did they stay in "sunset" industries? Why couldn't they just go to college and get a "good job" like the meritocrats? The working class didn't lose out because politicians considered them expendable. They lost, they were told, because they were not competent.

It was this rhetoric that moved Trump beyond criticism. If the trouble with Trump was that experts called him incompetent, or that he should have been disqualified for saying things that, while terrible, could be spun as "honest," then the trouble with Trump was the trouble with the struggling voters themselves. They, too, had been told that they were incompetent, that they were unqualified. To turn against Trump would be to turn against oneself. To embrace Trump was to embrace a particular version of oneself, to give free rein to impulses that on other occasions—four and eight years ago, for instance—had been restrained. One does not need to sympathize with this logic to understand its force.

Enemy of the Republic

IT IS FAR BETTER TO "overreact" to a moment that sets up the means for tyranny than not to react. Better to seize hold of the abnormal than turn violation into the normal.

If the polity is not the state but its citizens, the most important thing individual Americans can do is deny Trump aid, collaboration, agreement, and acceptance. Not accept, not adjust, not adapt, not appease, not conciliate. There is something sinister in the media's "ten-step plans" to adjust to a President-Elect Trump, as if this were a personal upset needing therapy rather than a question of democratic legitimacy itself.

For the time being, many Americans may have to be political to an unusual degree, and political in a new way. One should consider citizens' capacity to resist and disobey. To what extremes of disobedience and resistant behavior do peaceful Americans know how to go? The ordinary, unromantic, and vilified forms of disobedience may turn out to be most needed. Refusal of allegiance. Refusal of participation. Not showing up. Leaving key government jobs, or staying in those jobs to slow down or stall illegitimate actions. Daily refusal to go along with orders coming from an illegitimate executive. Refusal of bureaucrats, tasked with reporting on citizens, to report if it could put their subjects in jeopardy. Refusal of enforcement agencies to enforce. Refusals and resignations in the armed forces. Refusal of those tasked with cooperating with the government to cooperate.

The old rule of thumb for a republic is that all points of view and methods of politics can be endured except the one that denies rule of law in the republic. This alone can and should be treated as a threat, as if coming from outside. During the presidential campaign, Trump went on record, repeatedly, steadily, and memorably in front of us all—in the debates, in the press, in his campaign communications—to register that he would not obey the norms of the republic. He would not submit to the rule of law, and he would not act in the interests of the republic as a citizen. He would not submit to the result of the election, or a smooth succession, if he lost the vote. He did not acknowledge the independence of the judiciary. He had not paid his share of taxes to the state. He would not separate his policies from personal enrichment. In this sense, he was like many of his class. Trump served a salutary function as long as he was not elected, in showing the compromises and corruptions of American society in his own person. He could say, and show, that the "system was rigged" and corrupt because he had done his best to make it so.

"I alone can fix our nation because I have contributed at the highest level to its destruction and corruption" is not an admission that can command loyalty or legitimacy. It is a whistle-blowing admission that forfeits standing. Trump can only be understood, paradoxically, as an enemy of the republic, who, through a series of adventures and surprises, has been awarded its highest office. His insinuation during the campaign that critics and genuine whistleblowers would be subject to retribution once he was elected makes this recognition urgent. His selection of the fascist Stephen Bannon as chief strategist further underscores his seriousness about these issues. This is what differentiates Trump, an illegitimate individual gaining the coercive powers of the chief executive. He is not an ordinary, merely "Republican" President.

The thing before our eyes, in other words, is the installation of an extralegal and extrajudicial personality into the presidency—an office that has been expanded, through Republican and Democratic administrations, decade after decade, to dangerous excesses of power. This includes the proliferation of executive orders that have the force of law. Executive orders make the President not merely someone presiding over a tripartite government but a premodern monarch or führer. But it is the more ordinary coercive powers of the executive that add urgency to the situation: The Department of Justice. The Attorney General. Federal prosecutors and the FBI. The Department of Homeland Security. Citizenship and Immigration Services, and the TSA. The Department of the Treasury and the IRS. The Department of Defense and the military. Having witnessed the Republican Party fail to eject Trump as a candidate and nearly half of the voting citizenry elect him through the Electoral College, does the system itself have any capacity to restrain such an extralegal personality from reaching the inauguration?

THE BEST WAY TO PREVENT a tyrant's rule is not to seat him at all—even at the risk of unfairness to an individual who might have become better than his word. We've seen the slogan and heard the chant "Not my President," but the slogan should instead be "No President." Trump is no President in his attitudes and beliefs, but we should decide we do not have a President, through the paradox of the legitimate election of an illegitimate officeholder. The most valuable lesson the United States could learn in 2016 is that it can get along without a President. It would throw weight back onto Congress—the place where political power should lie in a democracy. This is close to how the country ran during the years of Radical (or "Congressional") Reconstruction, when Congress all but seized power for the last two years of President Andrew Johnson's reign.

The instinct of "respectable" politicians and the mass media is to regularize and contain, to cooperate and appease—wrongly, and dangerously. This moment places a pressure on individual conscience and judgment, as each isolated person is reminded to join others in a collective will to refusal. It also leaves many of us twiddling our thumbs much of the time, hoping that those individuals who must take orders will refuse or resign. The task for "good people" is noncooperation. This is how to communicate what the republic can and cannot allow.

Along with this must come greater cooperation among ourselves, a commitment to building democratic institutions inside and outside the existing parties. It should not have come as a surprise how little civil society exists among the left, how little prepared we were to pursue projects of social justice against a revanchist administration. We enter this reactionary era more atomized and isolated than we should be.

But there are signs of response. The wave of "joining" that has already taken place in the wake of Trump's victory—the proliferation of meetings and organizational sign-ups, the sudden jump in members of the Democratic Socialists of America, the frenzied petitions and Facebook posts urging us to call our representatives and make demands—is the first step toward creating a denser, less pliant movement. Organizations should grow large enough to command assemblies on the level of a neighborhood in addition to that of a city. (There is a virtue, as Wordsworth held long ago, in "the talk / Man holds with week-day man in the hourly walk / Of the mind's business.") The move to transform the Democratic Party and to build organizations outside it in the hope, forever deferred, of a true party of the left, ought to turn political parties from more than volunteer door-knockers who come around every four years to ask for votes in swing states. This would have been the project no matter who the President. It has only acquired new salience and urgency. +

DAN BAYLES, *GIORNATA*, 2015. FLASHE ON CANVAS. 39.25" × 42.5".
COURTESY THE ARTIST AND GHEBALY GALLERY, LOS ANGELES.

POLITICS

Memoranda

GEORGE BLAUSTEIN

The Obama Speeches

REMEMBER THE "YES WE CAN" SONG? IT WAS 2008, and Barack Obama had just lost the New Hampshire Democratic primary to Hillary Clinton. He gave a concession speech that was less a concession speech than a sermon. Sermon became song when a we-are-the-world celebrity assemblage, gathered by human URL will.i.am, sang "Yes we can" to a camera in unctuous, earnest unison over simple chords. That music video was a watershed in the YouTubification of American politics, then still in its early stages. I found it embarrassing at the time, even with Kareem Abdul-Jabbar and Herbie Hancock in the mix. Revisiting that video now is a harrowing experience. It is electrically unwatchable.

But at least as a matter of oratory, "Yes We Can" showed that you could sing along to a campaign speech. Obama breathed new life into the form. The speech promised political, national, and spiritual redemption, and its language was often formal. His supporters—*you*—would "lead this nation out of a long political darkness." A "chorus of cynics" may tell us we cannot succeed, and that chorus will "only grow louder and more dissonant in the weeks and months to come." But listen—for beneath that loudness and dissonance, you'll hear the whispers of that truer American story: "Yes we can." It was "whispered by slaves and abolitionists as they blazed a trail toward freedom through the darkest of nights." It became a song for "pioneers who pushed westward against an unforgiving wilderness." *Wait—did some of those yes-we-can pioneers own slaves and kill Indians? Probably!* But in the "unlikely story that is America," darkness gives way to light.

To take stock of Obama's speeches is to be overwhelmed by the prosaic demands of presidential oratory. A modern President makes thousands of speeches, and the text of every one of them is posted to the White House website. Some occasions are monumental, and the juxtaposition of monumental occasions can be dizzying: one day you're in Cairo announcing a new era of American relations with the Islamic world, the next you're speaking in front of Buchenwald alongside Angela Merkel and Elie Wiesel. Many more occasions are obligatory, redundant, or ridiculous ("Remarks by the President at 'An Evening of Country Music'"). State of the Union slogs, speeches to troops on surprise visits to Afghanistan, hollow exhortations to labor unions, self-deprecations and amateur stand-up at White House Correspondents' dinners, toasts, eulogies, Weekly Addresses. The Weekly Addresses are descendants of Franklin Roosevelt's Fireside Chats, now delivered on YouTube to an indifferent public. It is an immense corpus of grandeur and fluff.

Warren G. Harding inaugurated the profession of presidential speechwriter in 1921, paying a newspaperman named Judson C.

Welliver for words like *normalcy*. I imagine today's speechwriters before a diplomatic occasion, Googling inspirational quotes from the major writer of whatever country the President has to address. (Ibsen? Ibsen!) Then they pump the remarks through a teleprompter. This marvelous invention from the 1950s creates a veneer of casualness and intimacy with the audience. It lets you pretend you aren't reading. But it's imperfect: in teleprompted speeches delivered straight to a camera, the viewer can still see the speaker's eyes moving across the text. The effect is slight but creepy.

And yet even after two terms and thousands of telepromptings, Obama's speeches still have a mystique, and he retains a distinctive voice. Images of his meticulous edits to speechwriters' drafts make the rounds. Some speeches are too important to be delegated: he *has to write them himself*. This is what he told Michael Lewis in an interview, and his speechwriters say the same thing. The *New York Times* reports that Obama prefers to write these speeches at night, with a lonely legal pad and an austere snack of seven lightly salted almonds. These orations come to us as the lucubrations of a solitary wise man, grappling with American history, with race, with fate and freedom. They suggest writerliness.

The Bridge

CONSIDER A CLASSIC OBAMA SPEECH STRUCTURE. *There are those who think X, and there are those who think Y. Both X and Y have rich histories and sympathetic spokesmen. But the acrimonies of the past have calcified the X and Y perspectives. No wonder some have sunk into cynicism or despair. We could keep spinning those same wheels. [*Pause.*] Or we could see that now is the moment to reach toward Z, because our story—my story—shows the possibility of change. To embrace Z is not to betray X or Y, but rather to fulfill and pay homage to X and Y even as we transcend them. At our best, we have risen to such heights before. Let me close with an anecdote, small in scale but deep in import, of people reaching across a divide to affirm their common humanity.*

The most celebrated speech of this type is "A More Perfect Union," the so-called speech on race from March 2008. For a while, it was known simply as The Speech. During the Democratic primary, all eyes turned to Obama's pastor in Chicago, the Reverend Jeremiah Wright, whose fiery sermons had flayed America for its sins. "God damn America!" Wright had shouted from the pulpit, and all of Obama's opponents—from Hillary Clinton to Dick Cheney—pretended to be deeply offended, even though Wright was doing what great American ministers have done since Cotton Mather. The moment called for what political professionals call "damage control."

X was Wright. Y was Obama's white, good-hearted, but sometimes racist grandmother. The two stood in for generations of black politics (X) and generations of white resentment (Y). The closing anecdote was about a white woman named Ashley. She had faced hard times but worked to improve the lives of others, and that's what brought her to Obama's campaign. Her story struck a chord with an elderly black man also working for Obama's campaign, who said, when asked why he was there, "I'm here because of Ashley." Ashley and the unnamed black man were Z.

The speech gives voice to all these perspectives. It sits with us "in the barbershop or around the kitchen table," where we vent our bigotries. Obama acknowledges our frustrations and forgives us our foibles:

> I can no more disown [Wright] than I can disown the black community. I can no more disown him than I can my white grandmother—a woman who helped raise me, a woman who sacrificed again and again for me, a woman who loves me as much as she loves anything in this world, but a woman who once confessed her fear of black men who passed by her on the street, and who on more than one occasion has uttered racial or ethnic stereotypes that made me cringe.

Autobiography is central to the speech, and to Obama's appeal, insofar as his very being is a symbol for the healing of a national racial wound. He was "the bridge," as David Remnick called his 2010 biography. The speech juxtaposed the Constitution's promise of a "more perfect union" with Obama's "own American story":

> I am the son of a black man from Kenya and a white woman from Kansas. . . . I've gone to some of the best schools in America and lived in one of the world's poorest nations. I am married to a black American who carries within her the blood of slaves and slave owners. . . . I have brothers, sisters, nieces, nephews, uncles and cousins, of every race and every hue, scattered across three continents, and for as long as I live, I will never forget that in no other country on Earth is my story even possible.

He's a one-man *Aufhebung*! This, as much as his politics, is what has drawn writers to him.

The speech on race is justly celebrated; it is as honest as a political speech can be. It assumes the listener is intelligent enough to follow an argument that unfolds over five thousand words, and open-minded enough to hold contradictory ideas in suspension. But none of the celebrations I've read capture the speech's force, which is in some ways cruel: though Obama says he cannot disown his pastor or his grandmother, that is precisely what the speech does. Wright's "profound mistake," Obama says at the pivotal moment, "is not that he spoke about racism in our society. It's that he spoke as if our society was static; as if no progress has been made." Wright spoke "as if this country—a country that has made it possible for one of his own members to run for the highest office in the land and build a coalition of white and black, Latino and Asian, rich and poor, young and old—is still irrevocably bound to a tragic past." Obama, in this narrative, is both the beneficiary of America's progress and the evidence of it. It is *progress* and the *country* that have "made it possible" for Obama, one of Wright's own congregation, to run for President. Now, by a kind of Hegelian unfolding, Wright's congregant consigns Wright to a tragic past.

This narrative logic is not specific to the speech on race. It is central to Obama's voice. His early memoir, *Dreams from My Father: A Story of Race and Inheritance* (1995), has the same empathy for its characters and the same respect for its reader. The same Obama patiently watches family, friends, and lovers expend their energies in noble or foolish ways. The book is an account of Obama calibrating an identity separate from them. He renders their voices with generosity and care, but writes with the knowledge that in the end, no voice will be as complete, balanced, or wise as his own.

Throughout his Presidency, Obama has often been criticized in two ways: either he is sentimental and naive or he is professorial and aloof. He can capture with remarkable empathy the experiences of others and fashion them into a story representing some larger truth. He's so good at it, in fact, that it comes across as too *trusting*, as not cunning enough for real politics. On the other hand, he seems distant, prone to haughty abstraction, too airy and erudite for real politics. These are contradictory criticisms. How can he be too empathetic *and* too aloof?

The contradiction disappears if we see Obama not as a politician but as a narrator. Narrators in novels have a similar command over intimacy and distance. A third-person omniscient narrator can bring us close to a character and engender empathy for that character, flaws and all. But at key moments, the narrator pulls away. It can read as cold or cruel. Forgiveness is granted only in the unforgiving past tense. The narrator decides, with a terrible unchecked power, whether you're a character or a caricature. Obama's speech on race is a masterpiece of narration, which is to say that it is a masterpiece of empathy and a masterpiece of aloofness.

Narrator in Chief

OBAMA CAME INTO office with three significant advantages. The first was that he was not George W. Bush. The second was that he sounded nothing like George W. Bush. Whatever his private intelligence, Bush was a pitiable speaker, blank and blinking, and seemed not to know what he was saying whenever there was a text in front of him. His best moment of oratory was an improvisation atop a heap of rubble on September 14, 2001, when someone yelled, "We can't hear you!" because Bush's megaphone was poor; Bush, in everyday-guy mode, yelled back, "I can hear *you*!" The crowd chuckled. Obama, on the other hand, was commanding an adoring crowd of 100,000 in Berlin even before the election. Bush was so loathed that Berliners, only a few years earlier, had stuck tiny toothpick-flags of his face into dog shit on the street; now here was Obama, an American President-to-be, cheered in the heart of Europe, putting words together without embarrassing himself or his country. When Ronald Reagan went to Berlin in 1987, he said, "Mr. Gorbachev, tear down this wall." Obama in 2008 proclaimed in the same city that "the walls between races and tribes, natives and immigrants, Christian and Muslim and Jew, cannot stand. These now are the walls we must tear down." He spoke to the Mr. Gorbachev in our hearts.

Obama's third advantage was that he had the story of his own election to tell. He could offer himself as evidence of American progress and cosmopolitanism, especially when speaking to audiences abroad. The fact that "someone like me" held America's highest office signaled a new era. In Istanbul in April 2009, he put it this way: "We are still a place where anybody has a chance to make it if they try. If that wasn't true, then somebody named Barack Hussein Obama would not be elected President of the United States of America." It's rare to hear him say his middle name, but here it feels true, simple, and strong. "Someone like me" is also handy before any audience with a legitimate grievance against American hegemony—at any Summit of the Americas, for instance. It became a good joke in front of a 2009 Tribal Nations Conference. As a Senator, he was ceremonially adopted into Montana's Crow Nation; he imagined his adoptive parents thinking, "Only in America could the adoptive son of Crow Indians grow up to become President of the United States."

The most important of these global speeches was delivered in Egypt in June 2009, where Obama announced "A New Beginning" for American relations with the Muslim world. The crowd at Cairo University cheered even the most basic greeting—*Assalaamu alaykum*—because it was noteworthy for an American President to utter it. Obama acknowledged that the war in Iraq was "a war of choice," and he gently put away the doctrine of preemptive war the way you put away childish things ("It's easier to start wars than to end them"). He consigned earlier administrations to the tragic past.

This speech makes for poignant viewing in 2016. The atmosphere is different now. But it is a good speech, well constructed around the motifs of time and timelessness. "I am honored to be in the timeless city of Cairo," he began, and he invoked the "timeless poetry" of the Islamic world. "In ancient times and in *our* times," he affirmed, "Muslim communities have been at the forefront of innovation and education." Time returns in the peroration, but in a different way: as an expression, Lincoln-like, of humility.

> All of us share this world for but a brief moment in time. The question is whether we spend that time focused on what pushes us apart, or whether we commit ourselves to an effort . . . to find common ground, to focus on the future we seek for our children, and to respect the dignity of all human beings.

X and Y in this speech were those who are "eager to stoke the flames of division" (X) and those who think "civilizations are doomed to clash," here nodding to Samuel Huntington (Y). Z is the "one rule that lies at the heart of every religion—that we do unto others as we would have them do unto us." Obama closed with quotations from the Koran, the Talmud, and the Bible.

For speeches like these, and for not being George W. Bush, Obama received the Nobel Peace Prize in October 2009. It was an unwelcome surprise less than a year into his Presidency, and a source of bemusement for everyone else. Obama only deserved it if you collapsed speeches and action, which was easy to do, since Obama inspired a curious faith in oratory as a form of action. It is fitting, somehow, that his Nobel speech was a poor effort. It suffers from a high school history paper's grand and empty generalizations ("War, in one form or another, appeared with the first man") and then offers—awkwardly for the occasion—a critique of pure pacifism. The speech is strong only when it acknowledges the inadequacy of speeches.

Story Time

ONE CONSTANT ACROSS OBAMA'S THOUSands of speeches is the trope of the "story." My story, our story, the American story. Sometimes the story has chapters: "the story of our nation is not without its difficult chapters." Story links the individual to the nation, as in Obama's refrain: *in no other country on Earth is my story even possible.*

What I'm describing is not the goofy, hackneyed ritual of plopping some hitherto-unknown prop person next to the First Lady at the State of the Union address and describing his or her life (a move pioneered by Ronald Reagan in 1982 with a good fellow named Lenny Skutnik), though Obama does that, too. Nor is it the ploy of introducing a relatable common man—Joe the Plumber—into a presidential debate to make a point. I'm talking about a narrative tic that suggests a deeper logic. Examples abound. In Cairo: "Islam has always been a part of America's story." In a eulogy for Walter Cronkite: "Our American story continues. It needs to be told." Announcing the Lilly Ledbetter Fair Pay Act in 2009: "While this bill bears her name, Lilly knows this story isn't just about her. It's the story of women across this country still earning just seventy-eight cents for every dollar men earn." About Gloria Estefan in 2015: "A humanitarian and a devoted family leader, Gloria Estefan embodies the story of America."

The American story is the immigrant's story. "Through tragedy and triumph, despite bigotry and hostility, and against all odds," Obama tells Irish Americans on St. Patrick's Day, "the Irish created a place for themselves in the American story." The American story is the veteran's story, too: "Each American who has served in Iraq has their own story. Each of you has your own story. And that story is now a part of the history of the United States of America." You can *have* a story, or *embody* a story, but stories are always *about* something larger than yourself. You can *contribute* to the "American story," because America also has a story, and that story is *about* something. It might be about democracy, or diversity, or it might just be about its own aboutness: meaning depends on seeing America itself in allegorical terms.

There's a folksy country-music logic to all this storytelling. "After all, that's what country music is all about—storytelling," Obama told a group of country musicians at "An Evening of Country Music" at the White House, in remarks that were charming precisely because he does not listen to country music. "It's about folks telling their life story the best way they know how—stories of love and longing, hope and heartbreak, pride and pain. Stories that help us celebrate the good times and get over the bad times. Stories that are quintessentially American." Like country music, all this storytelling starts to feel false if you listen to a lot of it back to back.

Even as cliché, "story" reveals something about Obama's understanding of the self. Story is the key to selfhood, whether it's an individual story, the group story, or the national story. Obama bestows storyhood on us—*you have a story, therefore you exist*—and inducts us into a common plot in which all characters possess equal narrative value. Obama's ascendancy is concurrent with the ascendancy of critical theory, and with the theories of selfhood and subjectivity that took hold in the multicultural academy in the 1980s, when he came of age intellectually. Everything is a text, Derrida insisted, but Obama turns text into story and offers a calm of reconstructionism after the storm of deconstructionism. To have your story told—to be included in the canon—is to be.

Before it was the American national motto, *e pluribus unum* referred to the gathering of different texts into a magazine or a single volume; before the American Revolution, *e pluribus unum* was the slogan of the *Gentleman's Magazine,* and it appears in 18th-century poetry collections. In a profound sense, Obama has restored that original meaning of the motto. Pushed to its idealistic extreme, "story" would suggest that politics is not a matter of negotiation, nor even, ultimately, of power. It is a matter of anthology-building.

History

BUT STORIES ARE NOT HISTORY. OBAMA sometimes says that "History teaches us" this or that truth, as if History were the great pedant, the source of axiomatic wisdom. But more often, history is the thing you grapple with. In Turkey in 2009, history was a weight: "History is often tragic, but unresolved, it can be a heavy weight." In Cuba in 2016, history was a barrier: "Havana is only ninety miles from Florida, but to get here we had to travel a great distance—over barriers of history and ideology; barriers of pain and separation." History is the ocean in which we float or drown. "The blue waters beneath Air

Force One once carried American battleships to this island." The same waters "carried generations of Cuban revolutionaries to the United States," and the "tides of history" brought conflict, exile, and poverty in the cold war. "I know the history, but I refuse to be trapped by it," he pivots, consigning the cold war to the tragic past. The speech can then cross that distance: "And I've come here—I've traveled this distance—on a bridge that was built by Cubans on both sides of the Florida Straits."

History wounds. Story heals and transcends. A repetition of history signals a failure of politics. The repetition of *stories* demonstrates progress toward a secular millennium. History is tragic. Story is romantic or comic.

Theories of history are always theories of the future, and Presidents' theories of history often involve occult, oracular communications with the future. George W. Bush, as the disaster of his presidency wore on, became a desperate reader of biographies. When Bush said "history will judge," *history* was a kindly future biographer who would rescue him from the condemnation of every historian of the present. As time wore on, his speeches amounted to little more than clumsy, frantic prayers to that future pardoner. When Bush called himself "the decider" and called his memoir *Decision Points*, he was not just arrogating power to himself or speaking businessmanese; he was suggesting that history consists of individual decisions, a leader alone in a room with limited options, a red pill and a blue pill, time marching mechanically on. With such a narrow view of history, and such a record of terrible decisions, it's not surprising that decisiveness was his only remaining virtue.

Obama dramatizes not the individual decision but the generational one: the *we* of "yes we can" is a generational *we*. Rhetorically at least, he is not the one making the decision; he summons a generation and narrates that generation's decision. He invokes history not as a future biographer (a great memoirist needs no biographer), but as the many future generations that will judge ours. His theory of history posits not a mechanical series of decision points, but a mystical series of generational moments.

In Obama's speeches, every historical achievement is framed as a generational achievement, even if the demographics are vague: the American Revolution, the abolition of slavery, the civil rights movement. Early on, abolition was the generational achievement he called on most often to inspire the present. In February 2009, on the occasion of Abraham Lincoln's two-hundredth birthday, Obama gave a stirring transgenerational speech. It is one of his best. "When posterity looks back on our time, as we are looking back on Lincoln's," he said,

> I don't want it said that we saw an economic crisis but did not stem it; that we saw our schools decline and our bridges crumble but we did not rebuild them; that the world changed in the 21st century but America did not lead it; that we were consumed with small things when we were called to do great things. Instead, let them say that this generation—our generation—of Americans rose to the moment and gave America a new birth of freedom and opportunity in our time.

Generation occurs in Obama's speeches almost as often as *story*, and it might be the quintessential Obama term. It has both a biblical and a marketing resonance: it calls to mind both Ecclesiastes and *Adweek*. Consider a paragraph from Obama's Second Inaugural Address:

> This generation of Americans has been tested by crises that steeled our resolve and proved our resilience. A decade of war is now ending. An economic recovery has begun. America's possibilities are limitless, for we possess all the qualities that this world without boundaries demands: youth and drive; diversity and openness; an endless capacity for risk and a gift for reinvention. My fellow Americans, we are made for this moment, and we will seize it—so long as we seize it together.

The "generation" at work here has no demographic coherence or specificity (although I suspect he had in mind every demographic except the boomers), but it does have an essential narrative logic. It exists tautologically: *We are made for this moment.* A generation can be defined as the thing that exists in the *now* of the narrative.

In the narrative world of an Obama speech, the protagonist of every story is in some sense a generation, and the climax of every story is a moment. For Bush, time was always running out, like Jack Bauer's clock in *24*. The decision point was that instant when one billiard ball hits the next, and God willing, your aim was true. But in the greatest Obama speeches, because of their eloquence and ceremonial grandeur, time itself slows. The *moment* is a sacred, baptismal pause. Christened as part of a generation, you, American citizen, are given a glimpse of the eternal. When Obama says, "This is our moment," he means both the moment in the story and the moment in the speech—that dilated, mysterious, oratorical *now.* "This is our moment" is an incantation, powerful because it collapses speech, story, and action into a single, salvific, visionary event. The speech announces the moment, and it *is* the moment.

The particular mood of the late Obama years—that inevitable feeling of loss or coming down among liberals, Democrats, and the center-left—is hard to name. *Disappointment* is too parental; *disillusionment* not right, either, because the heights of Obama rhetoric and inspiration were not necessarily illusions. The mood is not simply a product of paralyzed government, of the crimes and tragedies of foreign policy, of the Nobel Peace Prizes that brought no peace; it isn't really about Obama's failures or his successes, which are not my concern here. The feeling needs one of those compound German words, like *Bedeutsamkeitserschöpfung*: momentousness fatigue. It's a curious ambivalence to want salvation while you're weary of being saved.

That mood was itself a luxury.

War

SO FAR I HAVE SAID LITTLE ABOUT WAR. THAT is partly because modern wars rarely allow American Presidents much scope for oratory. Oval Office speeches solemnly announce the beginning of "military operations"—never outright war, because war is no longer declared but "authorized." These speeches are pale impressions of Winston Churchill. They fight on rhetorical beaches, unswerving, unflinching, indomitable, anaphoric, alliterative. Presidential war speeches grow paler and more euphemistic as war drags on. It proves impossible to orate a war's end if that war has no end. George W. Bush's attempt—the "mission accomplished" speech aboard an aircraft carrier—was an embarrassment and a moral crime.

Oratorically at least, "Commander in Chief" is the worst of all presidential personae. The title is drawn from a neutral and bureaucratic phrase in the Constitution (Article II, Section 2), but with the rise of the national security state in the 20th century, the term has taken on the weight and sanctimony of empire. "Commander in Chief" is our imperial cant, a robe and scepter in verbal form. Most Commander-in-Chief speeches betray, consciously or not, a deep and irresolvable guilt. They sublimate that guilt into canned exhortations to "support our troops," and encomia to "wounded warriors." They deploy the falsest national "we."

In general, Obama has avoided blustery war speeches. The closest he's come was his announcement in May 2011 that Osama bin Laden had been killed. It was delivered in the White House's East Room, with the podium placed in the open doorway of a pillared hall for added pomp. It was one of the rare Obama speeches delivered live to TV stations as an Important Interruption, and was spoken to a camera with that awkward teleprompter effect. As a speech, it is almost as hollow and stilted as Bush's "Mission Accomplished," minus the banner and the aircraft carrier. It is heavy on justification, insisting that "Americans understand the costs of war" even though most Americans do not. It rests on clichés about values: "We will be relentless in defense of our citizens and our friends and allies. We will be true to the values that make us who we are." The peroration boasts that "America can do whatever we set our mind to" and then clumsily states that "that is the story of our history." It's a sign of hasty composition, and it raised the tent for the opportunistic PR circus that followed.

Obama tried to convey the sense of an ending, but nothing of substance had ended. He presided over war that doesn't feel like war, so why should we expect great war oratory? Drones need no Churchills and deserve no Lincolns.

Who We Are

OR PERHAPS I SHOULD PUT IT THIS WAY: Obama has given great war speeches, only not about war. Obama's great war speeches have been about domestic shootings. The saddest irony in the Obama corpus is that these moments bring him closest to Lincoln.

The first was in November 2009, after the shooting at Fort Hood in Texas. Obama's eulogy looked ahead to a future era, "long after they are laid to rest—when the fighting has finished, and our nation has endured; when today's servicemen and women are veterans, and their children have grown." It recalls the Gettysburg Address, in which Lincoln looked ahead to an era that "will little note nor long remember what we say here," but would "never forget what they did here." Lincoln's Second Inaugural likewise deploys a poignant future-perfect tense, imploring us "to care for him *who shall have borne* the battle and for his widow and his orphan."

Because the victims of the Fort Hood shooting were servicemen and women, it was possible to see them as martyrs and to state with alliterative confidence that "we press ahead in pursuit of the peace that guided their service." An archaic style is appropriate when the setting is military, as it was at the Washington Navy Yard in 2013: "May God hold close the souls taken from us and grant them eternal peace," Obama said in closing. "And may God grant us the strength and the wisdom to *keep safe our United States of America*." Note the pointedly formal word order: *hold close the souls* and keep safe our United States.

After the 2011 shooting of Gabrielle Giffords and eighteen others in Tucson, Arizona, Obama gave another war speech, though the setting was not military. He spoke of the men and women who had tackled the shooter and aided the wounded. They "remind us that heroism is found not only on the fields of battle. . . . Heroism is here, in the hearts of so many of our fellow citizens, all around us, just waiting to be summoned." The speech refines grief into patriotism. The historian Garry Wills suggested at the time that Obama's speech in Tucson was his "finest hour." Obama echoed Lincoln's mourning at Gettysburg ("from these honored dead we take increased devotion to that cause for which they gave the last full measure of devotion"), but moved beyond mourning toward the inspirational rhetoric of Henry V at Agincourt ("For he to-day that sheds his blood with me / Shall be my brother"). There was even a touch of the miraculous, when Obama reported that Giffords "opened her eyes for the first time" while he was in the hospital with her.

The devices of traditional war oratory give order to chaotic events. At Fort Hood, Obama reflected on *who we are*: "We are a nation that endures because of the courage of those who defend it." "We are a nation of laws." "We're a nation that is dedicated to the proposition that all men and women are created equal." "That's who we are as a people." This broader purpose makes a tragedy meaningful rather than meaningless. But over time, the randomness of shootings becomes a challenge to oratory, because randomness defies any national purpose or story. And the affirmations of war oratory erode. "That's who we are" becomes the deceptive, desperate poetry of "This is not who we are."

Obama first stepped beyond the templates of traditional war oratory in 2012, after the school shooting in Newtown, Connecticut. The speech begins with the standard national "we" and the formal language of eulogy ("I am very mindful that mere words cannot match the depths of your sorrow, nor can they heal your wounded hearts"). But then the language turns normal, and the national "we" turns inward: "This is our first task: caring for our children. It's our first job. If we don't get that right, we don't get anything right. That's how, as a society, we will be judged." There follows a set of questions:

> And by that measure, can we truly say, as a nation, that we are meeting our obligations? Can we honestly say that we're doing enough to keep our children—all of them—safe from harm? Can we claim, as a nation, that we're all together there, letting them know that they are loved, and teaching them to love in return? Can we say that we're truly doing enough to give all the children of this country the chance they deserve to live out their lives in happiness and with purpose?

Lincoln's Second Inaugural posed a knotty theological question about what the "mighty scourge of war" revealed about the Almighty's judgments upon us. Obama's straightforward questions in Newtown dispense with reflections on the Almighty's mysterious purpose: "I've been reflecting on this the last few days, and if we're honest with ourselves, the answer is no. We're not doing enough. And we will have to change."

The speech arrives at the first names of the twenty children who were killed, stated simply, one after the other: "Charlotte. Daniel. Olivia. Josephine. Ana. Dylan. Madeleine. Catherine. Chase. Jesse. James. Grace. Emilie. Jack. Noah. Caroline. Jessica. Benjamin. Avielle. Allison." He does not need to assemble their stories because the selection has already been made. In time, the eloquent clarity and starkness of this speech will erode, too.

His second departure from the template of war oratory was in June 2015, after nine people were killed in the oldest African Methodist Episcopal Church in the South. Obama delivered the eulogy for one of the victims, South Carolina State Senator and Reverend Clementa Pinckney. The first line—"Giving all praise and honor to God," without any presidential pleasantries—tells us right away that this is not a speech but an actual sermon. Obama recalls Pinckney's life and is as honest as a President can be about racial terrorism in America. The shooter, he said, "drew on a long history of bombs and arson and shots fired at churches, not random, but as a means of control, a way to terrorize and oppress." Against that terrorism stands the black church and its heroic history. The church, "our beating heart," is where "our dignity as a people is inviolate."

The pivot of the sermon is not the pregnant pause that usually comes before Obama reaches toward that transcendent Z and consigns X and Y to the past. (There is no X, Y, or Z in this speech, nor was there a teleprompter in the church where he gave it.) The pivot is a preacher's pivot: "*Ohhh,*" he says with a gentle laugh, about halfway through, "but God works in mysterious ways," and the congregation erupts in knowing cheers. The killer, Obama says, "didn't know he was being *used* by God." This is a new interpretation, untried in any other speech. To suggest that the shooter was, unbeknownst to himself, an agent of God's will, that he was sent not as a punishment for our sins (for Pinckney was no sinner) but as the divine mechanism that allows us to receive and express God's grace—such an argument could fly only in a sermon. It needs the rhythm of a sermon, it needs the delivery of a sermon, and it needs the affirmations and amens of the congregation.

The congregation, after all, has to follow the preacher into a paradox: that we are saved by tragedy, that while the shooter was "blinded by hatred," his blindness makes us see love. The shooter visited terror upon a church, but in the same moment, "*God* has visited *grace* upon us, for he has allowed us to see where we've been blind." Lincoln could not have made this argument. Nor could Obama have made this argument before. All the other models of oratory were exhausted.

The sermon soars. The band bursts in occasionally, punctuating Obama's catalog of ways we can "express God's grace": by taking down the Confederate flag, as South Carolina's governor had finally done soon after the shooting; "by recognizing our common humanity by treating every child as important, regardless of the color of their skin or the station into which they were born." If we were to change our gun laws, we would "express God's grace." Near the sermon's end, after a long pause, Obama sings the first verse of "Amazing Grace." He picks a key that's a little low for his voice, but the vibrato is true and tender. The band finds the key and the congregation joins him. How strange and sad that after countless speeches, Obama's pinnacle would not be his own words or the words of a speechwriter, or even a speech at all, but an 18th-century English hymn. It is beautiful, and also a last resort.

After that the speeches grow bitter. In October 2015, after a shooting at a community college in Oregon, Obama's speech acknowledged its own redundancy: "Somehow this has become routine. The reporting is routine. My response here at this podium ends up being routine." We're left with a basic civics lesson recited to a listless classroom: "This is a political choice that we make to allow this to happen every few months in America. We collectively are answerable to those families who lose their loved ones because of our inaction." In June 2016, after the shooting at the Pulse nightclub in Orlando, we are left with a grim, graceless prediction: "If we don't act, we will keep seeing more massacres like this—because we'll be choosing to allow them to happen. We will have said, we don't care enough to do something about it."

We will have said. It is a rare instance in the Obama corpus of the future-perfect tense. Lincoln said at Gettysburg that "we cannot dedicate, we cannot consecrate, we cannot hallow this ground." That refrain has become, in Obama's late speeches, the pained possibility that our dedications, consecrations, and hallowings are themselves acts of bad faith. It turns out this is who we are. +

AZIZ RANA

Decolonizing Obama

ON ELECTION NIGHT IN 2008, BARACK Obama declared to a crowd of nearly a quarter million people in Chicago, "This is your victory." That was how countless Americans experienced his election. For those who were old enough to recall the era of Jim Crow, the elevation of a black man to the Presidency appeared to be the culmination of generations of arduous organizing and struggle. For students and young people newly activated by his campaign, it was an ecstatic entrance into political adulthood. The campaign itself had produced the feeling of a mass movement. At the time, Obama represented the cutting edge of American progressive politics—the very horizon of what seemed thinkable after three decades of triangulation, hawkishness, and conservative political dominance.

Now, as Obama prepares for the "peaceful transfer of power" to a white nationalist who came to prominence by questioning the legitimacy of Obama's birth certificate, that night seems to belong to an alternate universe. Obama remains perhaps the most popular and respected politician in the country—certainly far more respected than those poised to control virtually every level and branch of government. But the failure of the Obama coalition to produce a durable Democratic majority suggests that night in 2008 was something of a mirage. Rather than a decisive victory for new progressive ideas, the Obama era feels increasingly like the last days of a now moribund centrism.

Even before Trump's ascendancy, esteem for Obama existed alongside real uncertainties about his ideology. A key warning sign came from the left, where a gulf emerged between him and many of the very people he'd mobilized. While Obama extolled the "free-enterprise system" but called for "corporate responsibility," young activists began to decry neoliberalism and to demand full employment, a guaranteed income, and the dismantling of the banks. Obama expressed outrage at police violence and proposed criminal-justice reform; insurgent social movements called for the end of the prison system itself. The fact that Obama criticized the invasion of Iraq but went on to expand the war on terror, traveling the world to champion the goodness of American hegemony, was not lost on this younger generation. For them, the national-security apparatus created instability and fostered authoritarianism in the Global South. *Imperialism* became a word with renewed meaning.

This divide between the President and everything from Occupy and the Fight for $15 to the Bernie Sanders campaign and the Movement for Black Lives was more than a matter of pragmatism, the difference between what one could demand in the streets and what could be passed in a Republican-controlled Congress. It marked a fundamental disagreement over what the United States was and what it ought to be. One can see the stakes in the rhetorical moves that made Obama such a charismatic political figure a decade ago: the way he wove together his biography with the story of the nation. In speech after speech, Obama reminded us that to witness his rise—that of an interracial child of a single mother from a middle-class background—was to know something profound about the United States, that "in no other country on earth is [this] story even possible." He tapped deeply into what the Swedish sociologist Gunnar Myrdal famously called the "American Creed": the belief that from its founding the United States has been committed to equal opportunity for all, and that the collective project of the nation has been the steady fulfillment of this promise. Obama's skill as a politician was bound to how perfectly he embodied that creed, even as more Americans grew suspicious of the story—from its presumptions about class mobility and inevitable racial accord to those concerning the basic justness of existing institutions.

As I listened to Obama retell this narrative over the years, I found myself struck by the singularity of the tale, its growing disconnect from the experiences of many. I also kept returning to what he seemed to leave out. In part, this was because I, too, am half-Kenyan, and it was hard not to hear the story of Obama and his parents without thinking of my own. The comparison underscored the variety of meanings in the experiences that shaped Obama; it also revealed how the most archetypal version of his story served specific political ends. Obama, we knew—because he told us so many times—was at once the promise of the immigrant nation (open even to the son of an African goatherd), the black fulfillment of Martin Luther King Jr.'s "dream," and the success story of the hardworking white middle class. He was the living proof of American exceptionalism, an embodiment of self-advancement through meritocracy.

I have no doubt that affirming these narratives was the only way for a person of color, in the period Obama arrived on the national stage, to achieve leadership in this majority-white country. In the Clinton and Bush years, for someone like Obama to cast his or her life story in more radical terms—in the anticolonial framing, for instance, that I grew up with—would have meant abandoning mass electoral success within the two-party system. But once in office, this affirmation came at the price of rejecting a broader left imagination that had long overflowed the bounds of a staid Americanism. And it had profound costs at a time of national reckoning. At a moment when the country faced convulsive social crises, and more and more of his supporters called for a fundamental reconstruction of American institutions, Obama marshaled his personal story and oratorical gifts to defend hollow tenets: the righteousness of American primacy, the legitimacy of global market liberalism, the need for incremental reform, the danger of large-scale structural overhaul. The consequence—intensified by a virulent right—was that fundamental problems continued to fester and became harder to ignore: mass incarceration and structural racism, dramatic class disparities in power and opportunity, interventionism abroad, and national-security abuses at home. Obama was, in a sense, the most that was possible in 2008. But his limitations, which were really the limitations of a broad generation of center-left politicians shaped by the fallout of the 1960s, point to what is now needed for radical liberation movements to reach the political center and defeat the forces of reaction.

OBAMA'S INVOCATION of the Creed was the most persistent feature of his rhetoric. In the conclusion to *Dreams from My Father*, Obama implied that his individual journey had taught him the truth behind the Declaration of Independence's claim that "all men are created equal." The principle may have been compromised from the outset by the violent expropriation of indigenous people and the existence of slavery, to say nothing of the countless forms of targeting, exclusion, and prejudice to come, but the project of America had been the steady effort to overcome these sins. "*We hold these truths to be self-evident*," Obama wrote. "In those words I hear the spirit of Douglass and Delaney, as well as Jefferson and Lincoln; the struggles of Martin and Malcolm and unheralded marchers to bring these words to life." He saw himself following in the same tradition: the Declaration was not a past accomplishment that had to be honored but a spur to greater efforts. The goal of his career—as a lawyer, a constitutional scholar, and a political activist—became to help Americans "choose our better history."

This creedal nationalism, a central ideological legacy of the cold war, has always had a dual quality. When used by Reaganite conservatives to laud America as "the greatest nation in the history of the earth"—Mitt Romney's phrase of choice—it became a language of self-congratulation, a way to excuse ongoing injustice. When claimed by King to describe America as "a dream as yet unfulfilled," it meant a reformist mission to overcome legal barriers to full citizenship, to finally make that dream real. Obama's accomplishment was to fuse these two sides of the Creed. The fact that he could become President reminded us of both the persistence of racism *and* the perfectibility of the American project. Nothing about this political vision was new. It was the power of Obama's biography that gave the rhetoric new appeal.

But this story is not the only conclusion one can draw from Obama's life experience, and it is not the conclusion I draw when I think about the parallels between my family background and his. My father, too, is a black man—half African, half Indian—who was raised in a small town in western Kenya. He also came to the United States as a foreign student, and in the mid-1970s met my mother, the daughter of an assimilated Lebanese family that was coded as "white" and lived through the Depression and World War II. The echoes don't end there. One of the main speakers at Obama's first act of political engagement, when he helped organize an antiapartheid divestment protest at Occidental College, was my godfather, a South African activist and one of my parents' closest friends.

In my own life, these elements formed a very particular identity, one I shared with many other children of color born in the '60s and '70s. I was a "third world" American. I grew up in a household that did not see the history of the United States as a long, exceptional national drama about the fulfillment of founding ideals. Instead, I was raised to view the US through the struggles against colonialism that were engulfing Asia and Africa. The United States was divided between racially privileged insiders and nonwhite peoples, whose land and labor served as the basis for elite wealth and power. As in apartheid South Africa, the fact that American society was founded on oppression meant that liberation would require more than inclusion in the existing social order. It would require a full-scale transformation of the country, on terms of real material equality for those subordinated. The goal was not civil rights but *decolonization*. I was thoroughly American, but of a specific kind: in my family, Malcolm and Martin were linked not to Jefferson and Washington but to Lumumba and Cabral.

The stakes of this difference are evident when Obama's creedal narrative is juxtaposed with that of the third world left. Obama often spoke of his father's coming to the United States ("a magical place" of "freedom and opportunity"). He said much less about why his father did not stay. For my father and his independence heroes, the point of getting an education in the West was gaining the technical tools to contest empire at home. He planned to go back to Kenya, to take what he had learned to help shape a postcolonial Africa on independent terms. He thought of himself as more a sojourner than an immigrant.

When Obama described his mother, it was as a single white parent who instilled in him durable all-American values. He played down just how unconventional her life decisions were. For my own mother, there were reasons why she married an African man, chose to move back with him to Kenya, and devoted herself to the problems of public health in the rural countryside. In the '70s, she identified with the self-determination movements in Asia and Africa and chose to cast her lot with those communities and their struggles. As a woman who had been fully assimilated into American culture as a child, her decisions were incomprehensible to family and friends. Her politics and her self-conception as an Arab person broke with the conformity that shaped towns like Whittier, California (her birthplace, where Richard Nixon spent his childhood)—towns where, in the postwar years, having a parent who spoke another language at home was something to hide.

My parents met through the antiapartheid and anticolonial protests that swept American campuses in the '70s and early '80s. This was how they came to know my godfather. When Obama wrote about those protests in *Dreams from My Father*, he focused on his discomfort with the theatrics and playacting of student activism ("The whole thing was a farce") and more or less avoided discussing the actual politics. What the reader might conclude is that the antiapartheid struggle was a rather straightforward extension of the traditional civil rights movement, with its focus on legal equality (a matter of "dignity" and "fairness," as Obama remembered declaring to a crowd). My parents and godfather, with their commitment to black internationalism, instead saw university campuses as a significant battleground over not only formal rights but the fate of capitalism and empire. Whatever the occasional youthful theatrics of campus politics, when the University of California divested $1.7 billion from South Africa in the mid-1980s, it was experienced by the apartheid state's white rulers as a profound challenge.

Even my parents' decision to give me an "ethnic" name expressed their commitments. Obama described his own name as the product of a belief that "in a tolerant America your name is no barrier to success." For Obama, it was a multicultural marker that exemplified the country's pluralism, in which one could as easily be Kenyan American as Irish American. For my parents, the Arabic name Aziz was not a mark of ethnic or religious pride, a way to affirm the American mythos. The name was a statement of affinity—an effort to locate their child culturally in the world of the Global South—and so an act of solidarity with liberation movements abroad.

THERE ARE REASONS why Obama may never have seen himself in these terms, whether the early separation from his African father or the centrality of his white grandparents to his upbringing. More interesting to me is how Obama's ideological turn became the only one a person of color interested in national office could take. This may seem obvious today, given how the right has built a cottage industry around accusing Obama of being a third worldist. Even though his entire political identity was premised on embracing American exceptionalism, he was still to them a Kenyan-born Manchurian candidate, as if to be anticolonial were somehow a crime. The conspiracy talk nonetheless recalls a moment when, in the 1970s, third worldism wasn't simply a racist accusation or a demeaning put-down of nonwhite societies.

When Obama came of age politically, a vibrant American left still existed. Arriving in the United States in 1973, my father found himself surrounded by people like my mother: students, white and nonwhite, radicalized by growing economic uncertainty, the failures of civil rights liberalism to transform the everyday experience of poor minorities, and the ongoing abuses of the national-security state, which spied on citizens, infiltrated and violently suppressed social movements, and prosecuted illegal wars abroad. Despite the factionalism on the left, virtually every constituency my father interacted with—from Panther offshoots to antiwar activists to more traditional democratic socialists—shared a basic critique of American capitalism and global power.

This critique identified capitalism, white supremacy, and the national-security state as the three pillars that sustained economic and racial hierarchy in the United States. At home, it required imagining the black freedom struggle as a poor people's campaign for all who were excluded: African Americans, immigrants, indigenous peoples, and the white working class. The goal was to replace capitalism with a more equitable economic order, one in which wealth would be redistributed to abolish poverty and increase the actual social power of ordinary individuals. The overarching demand from the left was for *self-determination*.

As for foreign affairs, the problem was not simply the Vietnam War—which anyway had formally come to an end in 1973—but the cold-war mentality and national-security infrastructure that enabled continuous intervention abroad and the sabotage of dissidents at home. Left activists called for a new internationalism built on the self-determination of communities in the Global South. With these twin demands—self-determination at home and abroad—activists rejected the liberal assumption that had come to define cold-war politics: that an easy transition to racial and class harmony in the US was possible, and could be accomplished alongside the establishment of a global *Pax Americana*.

The problem for the left was how exactly to bring political efforts against foreign injustice together with a broad-based poor people's movement. The central enigma was the growing conservatism of the white working class, who given their sheer numbers would be necessary for any successful mass mobilization. Falling union density created an unorganized white constituency increasingly susceptible to right-wing rhetoric, while even the unions themselves—now part of a postwar compromise between labor and management—bore less and less resemblance to the creative and insurgent labor-movement radicalism of the 1930s and '40s. Leftists tended to take separate approaches to these developments. The first was to argue for the need to take over and reconstruct the classic New Deal institutions. Some veterans of the student and civil rights movements hoped to build an interracial class-based identity organized around work. This required reshaping unions like the AFL-CIO from within—eliminating the final internal vestiges of discrimination—and pushing for the Democratic Party to use the levers of the state to transform the economy.

The competing approach remained skeptical of the New Deal establishment. It focused instead on building alternatives at the local level, from the Dodge Revolutionary Union Movements in auto manufacturing to the Black Panthers in political life. The idea was to generate a comprehensive and parallel institutional apparatus, a government outside the government. It could educate its members, provide basic services, and embody a continuous source of dissent from structures of corporate and state power.

The third-world left in the United States generally embraced the second approach. They highlighted the costs of working within both the Democratic Party and traditional unions. For them, the AFL-CIO often colluded with employers to undermine worker safety, preserve institutional racism, and defeat shop-level radicalism. The Democratic Party establishment—especially after George McGovern's massive defeat—remained deeply invested in anticommunist interventions. To ally with the existing state would require cleaving the domestic and the foreign, making common cause with a security apparatus that fought independence movements abroad and repressed social movements at home. Third worldists envisioned new political communities and institutions that cut across national lines and that linked autonomous, often black-led political efforts at the local level with anticolonial movements internationally. For my parents, the consequence was participation not just in protests but also in the plethora of grassroots institutions that emerged at the time—in particular, the new liberation schools and alternative educational projects aimed at both adults and children.

This third-world alternative faced its own weaknesses. Black militant organizing failed to win union elections, often alienating older and more moderate African American workers and working-class whites. By focusing on community development and cultural pride, third-world localism could at times devolve into a new brand of ethnic politics, at its worst deemphasizing class radicalism and appearing to mirror elements of the white localism it opposed. Toward the end of the '70s, both left approaches had proved incapable of creating a durable progressive base and had failed to stem the tide of working-class white backlash.

In attempting to explain this backlash, Democratic Party elites and some past movement activists obsessed over the alienating effects of black militancy, as well as its embrace by white radicals ("radical chic"). Third worldism was singled out for blame. Its revolutionary rhetoric scared off white allies, so the story went, and in the process fatally compromised interracial solidarity. As Richard Rorty later argued, the only way to "mobiliz[e] Americans as political agents" was to mimic cold-war patriotism and its creedal myths, to "share in a national hope" of exceptionalism. To fight against the deeply ingrained cultural identity of most white citizens was to be marginalized and veer between "self-disgust" and "self-mockery." The center-left needed to connect Nixon's rhetoric of individual opportunity and national greatness to the social-welfare achievements of the New Deal, as well as to the civil rights advances of the Warren Court and the Johnson Administration. These arguments began as critique of the left's messaging: doubts that white Americans—with their presumed faith in the Constitution and the Creed—could be organized through either socialist strategies of class "warfare" or black radical arguments about colonialism and white supremacy. But increasingly, messaging and substance merged. For some post-Sixties Democrats, avoiding class and race came to mean defending market ethics and turning the page on racial reconstruction. It required rejecting the left's diagnosis of American society as well its agenda for liberation.

This was the fight between the center and the left when Obama arrived at a college campus in 1979. As much as any politician of the past thirty years, Obama internalized the centrist narrative of the good 1960s versus the bad 1960s. It recurs in his speechmaking and throughout the early pages of *Dreams from My Father*. In the latter, he charts the disintegration of the left through the political trajectory of his white grandparents. He tells how their love of their interracial grandchild and deep-seated antiracism had come out of the optimism of the era between Kennedy's inauguration in 1961, the year he was born, and the passage of the Voting Rights Act in 1965. This was the time, he writes, when it seemed "universalism" would "triumph" over "parochialism and narrow-mindedness."

But by 1968, Obama's grandparents had voted for Nixon and fallen prey to "law and order" rhetoric. With left radicalism displacing the traditional civil rights movement and its discourse of national pride and American exceptionalism, Obama witnessed the optimism of his grandparents dissipate. "They saw no more destinations to hope for," he recalled, and settled for "hanging on" rather than social change. His own brushes with the left struck him as a dead end, even dangerous. In the early '80s, he went to see Kwame Ture, formerly Stokely Carmichael, speak at Columbia and thought it was "a bad dream." Ture's movement "had died years ago," Obama wrote. Far "removed from the struggles" he "purported to serve," Ture was also "just plain crazy."

Dreams from My Father begins with youthful anger and collegiate dabbling with radical chic ("We smoked cigarettes and wore leather jackets. At night, in the dorms, we discussed neocolonialism, Frantz Fanon, Eurocentrism, and patriarchy"). It ends with a mature and full embrace of the Constitution and the Creed as the only true paths to collective improvement. The book is an account of how, through disillusionment with the left, Obama learned to see his life history as a quintessential example of the American story.

WHAT DID ALL THIS mean as a matter of policy during these past years of growing social unrest and discontent? Obama's substantive actions as President weren't far removed from the approaches taken in the 1990s: a mix of cold-war foreign policy—marked by a presumptive right to intervene wherever the state deems fit—and post-cold-war domestic incrementalism. By 2008, in the aftermath of the invasion of Iraq and amid the run-up to the financial crisis, this was already a tired tradition, exhausted by a basic inability to come to grips with persistent structural failures on matters of the economy, race, and peace. Obama's most remarkable accomplishment therefore was not the achievement of any specific policy objective—the passage of the Affordable Care Act, the killing of Osama bin Laden—but the way he infused an exhausted American centrism with new energy and attractiveness, coating a familiar brand of American liberalism with the sanctity and power of his own personal biography. There are many tragedies embedded in this success. For one, it meant that Democrats held the reins of power when the Party's leaders had the least to offer the country's most vulnerable members.

This is not to say the Obama Administration made no material improvements. Millions gained health care who did not previously have it, albeit within a convoluted market structure that cut against the basic principle of health as a universal public good and a guaranteed social right. The Consumer Financial Protection Bureau, however hamstrung by the right, provided a mechanism for safeguarding citizens from financial fraud. Obama's executive actions and agencies protected Dreamers and LGBTQ persons from discrimination and added countless regulations to protect the environment, consumers, and employees. These were worthy developments, and many people now find themselves wondering what the future might bring, since they made choices—from what job to take to whether to live out in the open—based on the belief that Obama-era practices marked a real turning point.

But the Obama Administration's reforms all fell within the same philosophy that long informed the "American century": faith in markets and in technocratic and national security experts (despite the repeated and catastrophic failures of all three), and suspicion of politics formed through mass democratic mobilization. We can see the consequences across numerous policy arenas. Obama's signature educational program was the aptly titled Race to the Top. The program encouraged states to give teachers whose students got higher test scores bonuses and to fire those whose students tested poorly. This focus on teacher evaluation and student test-taking deemphasized the central driver of unequal educational achievement: poverty and the structural conditions that reproduced it. Without a sustained attempt to link poverty to the classroom, tests, accountability, and assessments served mostly to create a competitive setting for a small number of individuals to excel and for many to fail. For all the talk of boosting outcomes for all, Race to the Top, in keeping with its name, was an educational vision for the "gifted"—making sure that school was a meritocratic mechanism, tied to market ethics, that functioned to make the cream rise.

As for the economy, Obama more than anyone else was the central force behind the now widely derided Trans-Pacific Partnership. As activists have tirelessly contended,

TPP should not be understood as a trade deal (of its thirty sections, fewer than ten deal with tariffs). It was an attempt to protect transnational corporations' property rights. Stated commitments to union rights and anti-discrimination norms came at the cost of constraining the larger capacity of the state to pursue social-democratic interventions in labor, health, and safety. TPP was premised on open borders for capital, while for labor the default remains a system of limited bargaining power and restricted movement. The agreement was not only a direct repudiation of the left imagination but an unambiguous embrace of the consensus market liberalism that emerged toward the end of the cold war and flourished after it.

We see the same tendency at play in national security. In his Nobel Peace Prize acceptance speech, Obama infamously took the opportunity to defend not simply the idea of just war but the justness of American conduct in the cold war and the nation's post-cold-war dominance. "The United States of America has helped underwrite global security for more than six decades with the blood of our citizens and the strength of our arms," he declared. These dozens of military interventions and proxy wars were a necessary "burden," according to Obama, the product of a national mission and an exceptional embrace of global freedom and democracy, rather than any desire "to impose our will." For Obama, American interests as defined by the national-security state were coterminous with the world's interests. It was hardly a surprise that the administration's foreign-policy practices and domestic counterterrorism actions followed the path laid down by George W. Bush and Dick Cheney.

Regarding race, Obama again seemed unwilling to confront the structural nature of the problem. Obama's central initiatives, grounded in the creedal imagination of color-blind inclusion, focused on police training in a way that amounted to a more professionalized "law and order." So, too, did his turn to programs like My Brother's Keeper, which sought to give, as one White House official put it, "every young man of color who is willing to work hard and lift himself up an opportunity to get ahead and reach his full potential." Even if the American justice system were to become truly race-neutral, the prison and the police officer's gun would still remain the primary way the American state manages and controls the poor. White House initiatives aiming to create pathways out of poor neighborhoods for select black male teenagers not only reproduced a gendered framing of black precarity but also did little to address the fact that growing up in poverty is a losing proposition for the vast majority of those very teenagers. This was why even centrist white liberals—some of Obama's strongest supporters—started to consider it a joke, well before the Republicans' explicit mainstreaming of white nationalism, to say that the United States had entered a postracial stage.

BUT UP UNTIL OUR most recent and fateful Tuesday night in November, it is noteworthy that Obama and the Democratic Party's leadership had not had to face the limitations of their politics. Through a combination of auspicious historical timing and oratorical mastery, Obama's narratives of self and nation managed to repackage old wine in new bottles with real electoral success. While the administration's policies were not up to the country's problems, the Obama years were good for the Democratic Party. Midterm defeats seemed more like an anomaly than the foreshadowing of a future in the electoral wilderness.

Obama benefited from shifting demographics that transformed the white working class from the American majority into a far narrower constituency. When Reagan's victory over Carter put the final nail in the coffin of the left dream of a class-rooted progressive political base, 65 percent of the voting public were whites without a college degree. In 2012 exit polls, that percentage was cut nearly in half, to 36 percent. As long as Obama's repackaged liberalism could hold minority voters, it seemed, a new Democratic majority would not need a majority or near majority of working-class whites at election time. And with the rise of white nationalism and ethnic xenophobia on the right, it was inconceivable that minorities would go anywhere else. The consequence was that Obama's rise appeared to coincide with a defining moment in American political history. For most of the period since the New Deal, the ability to win non-college-educated whites had been the central test of any electoral coalition. But, perhaps for the first time in the modern era, Democratic leaders imagined they could have a permanent electoral majority while losing decisively with such voters. It was hardly a surprise that just as the party's vision of the economy aligned with the interests of global capital, its appeal to non-minorities emphasized meritocratic competence and focused on upper-middle-class and professional whites.

Whether consciously or not, Obama crafted a set of political narratives aimed at this new electoral coalition. His story beautifully embodied the aspirations of the upwardly mobile, white and black, who saw in themselves and their children the dream of educational achievement and professional success. To poor minorities and immigrants, not to mention white working-class union members who stayed true to the Democratic party, there were fewer tangible benefits. Yet Obama the living symbol held real power—and the centrality of Obama the person to that power was, ultimately, the problem. The sheer charisma of his story and personality captured just enough of the white voters to whom the Party no longer catered culturally or economically, and at the same time expanded the vote among minorities whose material conditions had not substantively improved. He succeeded in providing liberalism with a temporary vitality that Party leaders tragically mistook for a permanent one. Remove Obama, and the exhaustion of the old cold-war and creedal American center lay exposed.

Even before election night, when Clinton still seemed likely to win, I couldn't help but see the Obama coalition as a Faustian bargain. I found myself reflecting on the aspirations of the left and of the American third worldists I grew up with. The Obama presidency—and the Clinton one that might have followed—underscored the profound difference between the Democratic electoral majority as envisioned by its architects and a majority that would actually embrace a freedom struggle, reconceive American power, and demand liberation in terms that linked race and gender to political economy. In essence, to give up on the class politics that left activists hoped would bring poor whites and blacks together, as well as on the anti-imperial ideals that connected the "inner city" to the third world, was to abandon the conditions for real social change.

Where Obama once marked the horizon of political possibility, he now exits as the embodiment, albeit an honorable one, of an earlier and antiquated time. We seem to be shedding the last remnants of the cold war—with an ethno-nationalist (repeatedly accused of ties to Russia) and a self-described socialist as the new American personifications of the relevant political sides. With the center in greater disarray than at any point since before World War II, the options feel stark: liberation on anticapitalist and antiracist terms, or the deep entrenchment of racial and economic hierarchy. But as he leaves office, Obama's inadvertent legacy has been to help bring back the very American radicalism he once rejected. Representing the apotheosis of the creedal story, Obama unintentionally encouraged his own youthful supporters to move beyond the terms that essentially marked American politics from the 1970s to the 2000s. These supporters today have much more in common with the left that Obama repudiated than with him. We can see this in the Movement for Black Lives vision statement and policy demands, which call to invest in an authentically democratic economy while divesting from the militarized police and security state—a state at work both in Baltimore and in North Africa. Such demands reclaim everything from the specifics of the Panthers' 1966 Ten-Point Program to the broader language of third worldism, decolonization, and divestment. The larger activist focus today is on capitalism and empire; it is a call for a revolutionary politics and not an incremental one. These activists are now the organized base of the opposition.

We may be witnessing the completion of a political cycle, one that brings us back to the left dilemma of forty years ago: how to create a truly transformative majority, at once cross-racial and class conscious? This majority will need to be built at a moment when the right is as ideologically and institutionally unconstrained as at any point in the postwar era. We are entering a period of real political struggle. How we answer will speak to the legacy not of Obama but of the freedom movements that have emerged in his wake. +

PIERO DEL POLLAIUOLO, *APOLLO AND DAPHNE*, 1470–80, OIL ON WOOD. 29.5 × 20 CM.
COURTESY OF THE NATIONAL GALLERY LONDON.

INVERSION OF MARCIA

Thomas Bolt

"YOU AWAKE?" Alicia asked. No answer.

I opened my eyes: Alicia stood there in the dark, watching my sister sleep. After a minute she leaned over Marcia's bed and whispered, "Hey. It's chilly. I'm getting in with you." Bracelets jingled. The bed squeaked. I heard her kiss my sister's cheek and say a few words in Italian, probably a joke. They began to whisper, too quiet for me to hear.

Great. Now if I made a noise they'd say I'd been *pretending* to be asleep so I could lie in the next bed and listen. I kept so still I wasn't there at all, and thought about building a tiny house in the woods one day out of silvery lumber; about how Dad kept missing the turnoff and driving us through the same ancient arch; about painting my nails, which were disgustingly bitten and chipped and had last been painted in the United States. (I'd happily try some random Italian color, but we were out in the country, sort of, and you couldn't walk on these roads.)

Marcia whispered something and they laughed. Fine: I didn't want to know.

Mom called this place a villa, but really it was a cross between an old hotel and a school. There were sandpapery towels and glass doors with golden coats of arms, but also rows of coat hooks and a library. Anyway, Dad's friend Ian had gotten us a deal, and it was obvious why, since we were the only people here. But you could see the Gulf of Naples from your room (unless it was the Mediterranean). It looked close enough to walk to, though I was the only one who wanted to try.

The whispering went on and on and on, like rain falling so softly you wonder if it's rain at all. I woke from a wild dream about kids with flashlights racing through a construction site: still dark. Marcia's bed was empty. That interested me: where else was there to go?

The big tiles were cool underfoot. You could feel how old they were, uneven and smooth.

At the end of a long hallway, I saw their backs: they were standing out on a balcony, sharing a blanket. I wondered what they were doing till I saw the smoke.

My feet were freezing, so I went back to bed. Anyway . . . we'd only been in Italy a few days and already it felt completely normal, as if *this* was the way things ought to be and it was everything else that was strange. I'd never been out of the US before; never heard of Cuma, where we were staying. My dad said it was where the alphabet came ashore in Italy, but he said things like that. Whatever it had been thousands of years ago—famous religious center, Greek colony, biggest city in Italy—it was off the main highway now.

So was I: I'd been "asked" not to bring my computer, and my phone was the wrong kind, so I couldn't even *text*. Mom and Dad probably thought it was "healthy for Mary to take a break," but they didn't under*stand*: it was like my friendships were these tiny twinkling lights and they'd yanked the plug. I put my earbuds in and skipped from song to song until I realized I didn't want to listen to anything, not even silence: I listened to the wind. Where was it coming from? Probably the whole building was infiltrated by any breeze that really took an interest.

We were going to Pozzuoli and Pompeii—both close by, out there in the dark somewhere; then back to Naples to see more churches and museums, shop, and eat more amazing food; then north for a bit; and back to Connecticut. Simple, but fine with me. I liked it here. Even the villa was interesting, all curves and scrolls, with odd little balconies. Our room looked out onto an orange grove that was just *there*, and the trees—with real fruit you could actually eat—grew on a sloping, stepped hollow that exactly followed the shape of the amphitheater buried underneath. Beyond that some olive trees that got a faint silvery look when the wind blew, something industrial, a stretch of absolute darkness, a few lights, and the black of the sea (unless it was the gulf). Across the water was Naples, a crazy city with traffic worse than New York. The pizza there was completely different from anything we had in Norwalk or even the city, but it happened to be perfect: these people knew *exactly* what they were doing. All you had to do was forget what you already knew and just *go along with it*.

Marcia was really taking her time. Getting high, fine—but Alicia was in *college*; my sister wasn't even 16 until next month, so it was a little weird the way they were hanging out so much. And a bit insulting, since the way Alicia probably saw it, there was no one else to hang out with but *me*. I closed my eyes. I could always sneak down to the library and pick through the beach novels, old board games, random histories ("the emperor's pallor worried his advisers"), guidebooks from before I was born, and rows of serious scholarly thingies bound in red or green, by or about people like Chrysippus, Lucretius, and Philo of Megara. There was even a book called *The Tenth Muse: A Life* (as if muses were real? I loved it). Whole shelves were in Latin or Greek, some with no English at all . . .

They were never coming back.

Actually, Alicia was all right. She had this little philosophy book that proved that whatever you thought (though she had *no* idea what *that* might be) was wrong—as much a part of the past as whatever was in those red and green books. Her blond hair was cut short in a way that made her seem almost tough, but had a cute flip to it. Her lips were big and soft-looking like a wilty flower, one of those huge blossoms with droopy clinging petals, so she'd start to look all pretty and romantic—but then would say something hilarious and sharp and her eyes would squeeze almost shut, and if she laughed she wouldn't make any noise at all. She had a nice body—her breasts were very proud of themselves. Anyway, you have to be careful not to dislike people for no reason.

I turned on my side. When I opened my eyes it was bright out; Marcia hadn't come back.

No sign of Mom and Dad. I followed the smell of coffee down to the kitchen. Alicia and Marcia sat at the end of the long table reading my guidebook. They looked up as if it were *their* kitchen and *their* book and I'd interrupted some secret discussion, and would I please go away? I screamed like the goddess Alala until they turned to stone and cracked and crumbled to dust and sifted away, poured myself a glass of blood-orange juice, and sat twisting my bracelet, the one I loved, with the irregular beads of blue and amber glass. "Good morning?"

Alicia yawned. "I need a shower." She winced, pursed her soft, soft lips, and took about four years to slide her leg off the bench. It was like watching someone do physical therapy—only her disability was laziness. She smiled at me and skipped off up the stairs.

Marcia lifted her tiny cup. She had Alicia's lipstick on, deep red with flecks of blue-black sparkle. "Hey," I said. "Where are Mom and Dad?"

The dark lips formed a smile. "Like it? It's called Glitterjack. She'll let you try it. Just ask."

"Thanks?" I wasn't going to ask. "Hey, are they going north without us or something? Did Mom say anything?" For some reason we were skipping Rome, and Rome was what I really wanted to see—though the way Dad kept getting lost, we might end up there anyway.

"Actually . . . Alicia's going to stay with us for a few days. In Dad's friend's place, in Siena."

While our parents took off for Florence, Ravenna, and Venice: *great*. And my role would be to make my sister, who was barely *nineteen months older than me*, feel sophisticated and adult, just by being myself. She'd done her fingernails, too: she looked Alicia's age.

"We'll have the car. She'll drive us anywhere we want. After all, she's our *babysitter*." Marcia poured herself the last of the coffee. "Oh—sorry. You're welcome to make more." She slid the faceted metal pot my way. "You know how, don't you?"

"I thought you drank coffee with lots of sugar and milk."

"When I was *ten*. I like espresso; it's bitter, like my heart. Oh, by the way, we're going to see the Sibyl of Cumae. Her cave's *still there*—cut into the living rock."

"Thanks for the information you got from my guidebook." I headed back upstairs.

"And we're going out for *cinghiale*," she called after me. "Wild pig! Alicia says it's delicious."

"Alicia should know," I said, but not out loud. You don't have to say everything you think.

Dad was standing in the hallway, jacket on, studying a map. He said to get ready and get in the car: we were going to walk around on a flat volcano! "Bring water," he shouted. Mom put on a floppy straw hat, got her bag, and we walked down. Something kept making her smile.

On the way, Alicia told us about the old brick sauna that looked like an oven, and the place where you could camp (*really?* I could already smell the sulfur). We parked and went up.

PERICOLO · DANGER

said a warped yellow sign. Alicia and I laughed: the *sign itself* was smoldering. Steam drifted by or rushed up from under the dirt. Hot spots kept shifting, leaving safety barriers tilted and twisting, about to be swallowed up, or neatly fencing off some harmless stretch. I stared at a distant pit of bubbling muck and tried to get used to the *smell.* "It's literally on fire."

"What do you expect?" Marcia said. "It's a volcano."

Sky was *so* blue. Alicia stretched out her arms and whirled around. I squinted and smiled. Mom put on her movie-star sunglasses.

"So . . . this is a caldera." Dad studied my guidebook. "And these are . . . fumaroles?"

"Sounds like a fancy dessert," Mom said. "Forget the guidebook, Peter, look around!"

He blinked and smiled, but he did look: I could see he liked it, too.

I picked up a rock and wandered toward the lake of boiling mud. Alicia stood by a repositioned fence, nose in the air, wrists against her hips, hands turned out, neck elongated, like she was posing for a fashion shoot. She wore black jeans and a dark red sleeveless shirt that was actually perfect. On her bicep was a neat, needle-thin tattoo, plain punctuation:

? > !

—whatever that meant. Still, her posture *was* a little odd: like she was a model, but a really clumsy one. I couldn't decide whether she posed like that on purpose or couldn't help it.

Must have been unconscious: I saw her do the *exact* same thing an hour later in the Pozzuoli town square. A soccer ball rolled by—followed by a curly-haired boy (dark blond, tan, blue shirt) who looked my way for a second with bright-dark eyes. Amazing, though, to see the palm trees near the ancient columns: pretty obvious where the whole *idea* for columns had come from, right down to the leafy decorations on top.

The restaurant was big and empty and had a woodburning *forno.* The people who ran it were crazily busy but nice. Dad joked about ordering a dormouse glazed with honey, stuck with poppy petals; Alicia slitted her eyes and murmured, "Petronius." Since the menu was a choice between noodles with a gamy sauce and some kind of local mushroom, I asked for a sandwich. While everyone ate flat pasta with wild-boar sauce, aka *pappardelle al sugo di cinghiale,* and went on about how it was the best meal of their lives, I picked at a huge piece of crusty bread and a hunk of cheese. Dad offered me wine, but I said "No, thanks" before Mom could object.

Marcia sucked a long noodle into her mouth and looked up to see if anyone had seen. It was sad: we used to notice things together—find the *meow* in *homeowner*—and laugh till we couldn't breathe. We'd be having fun together now, but apparently we'd been to the beach with Alicia's family when we were little and had both "adored her." We hadn't even *seen* her in six years, but it made sense to them: Alicia could "help out" in exchange for a free trip to Italy.

We all got tired at once. Sulfur clung to the weave of our clothes, a disgusting smell that might never wash out. There was no escaping it—as if it were somehow *inside* you.

No one spoke on the drive back. Marcia fell asleep. We passed an unlit villa—old, crumbly, streaky, and gorgeous, like lots of things in Italy. Even the darkness seemed ancient. This road had older roads underneath; people had lived here, lied to each other here, cried, prayed, fought, spoke languages no one living even knew, and died, and now *we* were here: just for a second, it was our turn.

Headlights swept over trees. I caught Alicia staring at me, her head a little to one side: she didn't look away. Instead, she got this irritating look of satisfaction, as if she'd let me in on a big secret in perfect safety, because it was something I would never understand.

"Didn't you take the left fork last time?" Mom asked.

Tall, shadowy, with weeds and bushes growing out of it, the ancient arch passed over us.

Dad didn't reply, which meant he was either angry or super frustrated. I'd been chewing so quietly that the last thing Alicia expected to emerge from my lips was a pink bubble the size of a grapefruit. I let it deflate and wrinkle back into my mouth. Even the *gum* tasted sulfury.

Then there we were, back on the ancient pavement, gliding through the arch again, wondering how many more times we'd see it tonight before we could collapse into our beds. (Or whichever bed we planned to sleep in, anyway.)

NO NOTE. I checked the rooms: everyone was gone. Alicia had left a neat little pile on her pillow. The name on her International Driving Permit was Mary Alicia Minnen—we had the same first name? I sat on the edge of her bed and untangled a wonderful charm bracelet: silver telescope, bronze acorn, enameled ham, tiny hourglass with real sand in it—nice. The velvet pouch I guessed was her makeup bag was jammed instead with prescription medicines. Wow. Why so many?

Their names made me think of those late Roman emperors who issued coins, marched around the frontier for a month, and died without visiting Rome: Valpax, Mortorian, Afflexitor, Numerian, Cerulazapam. I picked up her music player and touched the button:

> If you work hard and get counseling
> You can turn your life around, but . . .
> I don't fucking WANT TO!
> I don't fucking WANT TO!

Sleep in and everyone abandons you. I showered and put on jeans, a dark red shirt, and a thin charcoal cardigan with one tiny hole in it. Touched my lips with the Lipdust Matte Stick I'd brought, so my shirt and lips were almost the same red; and that was it. I couldn't *go* anywhere, but at least I was dressed. I couldn't drive, there was no place I could walk to, I didn't speak Italian; but that was just a situation. I felt like I *knew* this place. You don't have to kiss someone to know *exactly* how the kiss would be. When that boy in the soccer shirt walked past, guiding the ball without ever seeming to touch it, I didn't *know* him at all, but I knew what it would be like: his breath hot, his lips a little chapped, his mind on something he couldn't describe. (It's amazing how defenseless people are.)

I slipped through my secret passageway, a cloakroom that joined the LOUNGE to the LIBRARY: narrow hall, long shelves, row of hooks. I liked the stillness, the way the old books smelled. I sank into a chair and tried to follow the mental adventures of Diodorus Cronus.

Alicia and Marcia bubbled into the lounge next door, laughing and talking. I turned the page but didn't read. "No, but his villa was *walking distance* from here. When they put him under house arrest, he threw a suicide party. Just a normal night with friends—except he let himself bleed to death." Alicia, talking about some guy she knew—or some musician or director she only knew *about*. I couldn't hear Marcia's voice. "Anyway, he liked *you*. Did you catch what he said? In English it'd be something like: 'I want pictures of you to decorate my dreams.'"

I read on over their laughter: I didn't really get the Master Argument.

"I'm not a good example," Alicia said. "I was having sex before I knew what sex was. Mostly older men who 'thought' I was 20—and I was your *sister's* age. She's pretty, your sister."

"She's afraid someone'll *think* she's pretty," Marcia said clearly.

My chin touched my chest. I blew air across the pages of my book.

"Oh, come on . . . you two look alike! Big brown eyes, olive skin, brown hair . . . long-waisted—"

"My eyes aren't 'brown' at all. They're hazel, actually. See?"

I was sorry I'd looked in Alicia's pill bag. At Solfatara she'd dragged me over to the old brick sauna and shown me where to stick my hand, into a gap in the brickwork: *hot.* Quite hot, but I could stand it. *OK, now move your hand a tiny fraction higher, and keep it there.* What? It was so hot my hand just jumped away on its own.

My sister squealed in the next room. "You're playing with something dangerous." She was out of breath.

"What am I playing with?"

"Me."

They went quiet. After a minute I got up but didn't leave. I felt ticklish all over, like when someone tells a ghost story late at night and stops at a scary moment and everyone *listens.*

"You lose," Alicia said. "Now you have to do what I say."

A muffled laugh. "All right—this one. Wait: does it actually work?"

"Oh, it works. It's a kiss timer. We'll have until the sand runs out: no more, no less."

"That's not much sand." Silence. "Barely a pinch. Anyway, no. You'll mess up my lipstick."

"I'll mess up your *life.* Did I say you could stop? You lost: pay the price. *Andiamo, amante.*"

Leaves rustled overhead; wind flung my hair around. I hiked past the excavation, sat down on some crumbly steps, and spoke mock Italian to Luca, one of the dogs. Trees creaked. It was already getting dark. What a waste of a day! Where were Mom and Dad? Why bring us to Italy and disappear? One star out. No, that was Venus: slightly blue and very, very bright.

I went in. Whatever had happened was over and they'd slid the wooden doors open. Marcia was telling Alicia that Mom and Dad had lost a lot of money, taken out a loan, and were trying to start a new business. Huh? What money? What business? Was she making it up?

I went down to the kitchen and turned on the tiny TV. Weird ads, then girls in miniskirts and lots of makeup singing jingly love songs and smirking. I trudged back up: now the lounge was empty. I sat and wrote postcards to Kristen Wilbeck and Anita Alvarez, and thought about writing one to Anita's brother, which made me so nervous that

I had to stretch out on the rug and close my eyes for a minute. Even so, I was smiling.

Alimar and Malicia dropped onto the couch and started leafing through magazines. I ignored them. *Whaaaat?* Now Marcia was wearing Alicia's socks, the ones with the helmeted cartoon Martian. I wrote another postcard, got some tiny thing wrong, and had to tear it up.

"Ooh. I *want* that," Marcia said.

"The handbag? The skirt? . . . Or just the model?"

"Very funny, Lee." Every time they laughed, I ruined another card—and they laughed at *everything*, as if they were high. Wait; they were definitely high. I could smell it. Fine . . . Whatever Alicia did, my sister was right behind, like a towed boat.

"Wow . . . the Tetrarchs live on in the old 'marching *K*s' Krispy Kreme logo. That's the Nicomedian Augustus on the left." Alicia sat up. "Hey, Britta Choatelle! I used to work for her."

Marcia leaned over the page. "You *know* her?"

"I don't know anyone. *Britt* knows a lot of people. I was her assistant for three weeks once, while her real assistant was sick. It was pretty crazy: she has this *huge* space in Chelsea—"

I felt like asking them whether celebrities and scenesters were the only people worth knowing, but they'd be all "Of *course* not," whatever they really thought. I copied my words onto a fresh card, and wrote two more before they distracted me again, reading a love letter out loud and laughing. It was apparently from some man Alicia barely knew. Marcia laughed so much I had to leave: it was *not* her normal laugh.

I moved my postcard operation to the MAP ROOM, which no one else had discovered—or so I'd thought. An actual letter lay on the table half-written, next to Alicia's little notebook.

Dear E, hope you just dumped me and aren't ill. Either way, I miss you. I miss the way you used to bring me toast and juice (with a lemon slice) on your old Bakelite tray, the one with the rooster on it. I miss your black kimono and how you never smiled (not before coffee, anyway). I miss the hand-lettered newspaper you wrote out on rice paper that morning, just for me. I miss the complicated board game with the dozen dice and the awful penalties we dreamed up, and I miss your laugh, all soft and papery like a hornet's nest falling in the woods. I miss fucking you. I miss kissing your throat, I miss nuzzling around to find the source of your smell, I miss that old shirt you used to wear, I miss seeing you without your glasses. By the way—

By the way, in the morning, once we got outside, it was almost warm. It had rained, a dirty wash that left a spatter of silt on everything. Dad tested the fine grit between finger and thumb and told us it came straight from the Sahara—picked up in a storm and blown across the sea to coat the hood of our rented Zeus. "A sirocco." And, for a moment, everything seemed fine.

At the museum in Naples, we all stared at Hercules, at the hard curves of his muscles, at his tremendous marble buttocks, and were impressed. "Why does he carry that enormous *pickle*?" Marcia said, and giggled at her own dumb joke, one I guarantee every child makes. (His club *was* exactly like a pickle, but so what?) She had too much mascara on, but looked good—really good. Alicia ignored her for once, absorbed in some lustery glassware from Pompeii.

"What are you thinking?" Mom took my hand. "You're like your father—he could lie on the floor for hours and stare down at the dust. What do you see? Are you having a good time?"

"Yes," I said, and squeezed her hand and let go.

We feasted on *filetti di baccalà* and marinated zucchini and *gnocchi alla sorrentina* at an amazing restaurant near the water. My father raised a glass to the stuffed boar's head on the wall, its neck still draped with last year's Christmas tinsel. On the drive back, Alicia held her philosophy as steady as she could under the trembling clip-light. As a reader she seemed completely different—serious and at ease. She read as if she slowly took things in without rejecting or accepting anything right away. If she could really do that, she was wonderful.

The arch loomed up and passed over. We made the loop ten times, following the same exact route; the eleventh time, the villa was just *there*. We crunched to a stop. A dog barked off in the dark, near the olive grove. This place was nothing like Connecticut.

Mom headed for the villa, walking fast, holding Dad's phone, which was all lit up.

Dad got out and stood petting the dogs. Bracelets jingled as Alicia bent over to adjust the ribbons on her shoes. Her breasts almost came out of her top; I heard the juicy little click of metal as her tongue arched and the steel bead in her piercing touched her teeth, but Dad just went on patting Luca. He hardly noticed her, and I loved him for it: no matter how she dressed or what she did, he ignored her completely, without trying to at all.

Marcia went right to our room, so Alicia and I ended up in the kitchen, drinking supercold mineral water. She swung her feet up onto a chair and cursed. "Left my philosophy in the car."

"Lots more in the library. Try Philo of . . . someplace? Not Parmenides, there are a bunch of loose pages. And, I only read a little bit, but Lucretius is *awesome*. One of the red books."

Alicia slumped down, tilted her head to the side, and gave me a look like: *I wish you were prettier. The way you look really depresses me.* But all she said was, "You seem older than your sister sometimes." *(Thanks?)* "Anyway . . . you can have my book if you find it, Mary. In a way it's the only thing I really own; but I'm pretty much done with it." She kept looking at me, and for a second I could see how tired she was. "I'm only evil part-time," she said. "Aaand, like most people, it's when I'm thinking fairly highly of myself." She went up to her room.

I got out my flat little zip bag and wrote a Vesuvius postcard to Bethany Taylor and one to Maya James, and spent a long time drawing Hercules and his club to send to Todd Chan. It got messy and the club looked too weird and I threw it away. I made another drawing that was sort of worse, but decided to send it anyway, mistakes and all, because *why obsess?* Also, the ribbons on Alicia's shoes were actually *beautiful.* You had to give her that.

Marcia wasn't in our room. The clothes she'd had on were strewn on her bed. The floor was solid—no one could hear a thing—so I popped my earbuds in, put on crazy music, and danced.

I SAID, "MORNING!" but Mom didn't seem to hear. I went back in after my shower: she sat brushing her hair. She stopped with the brush still in; leaned forward little by little; the brush dropped. All I could think of to do was leave: I closed the door as quietly as I could.

It had rained again and was cool. In the kitchen we ate *pizza bianca* and delicious little yogurts in glass jars, and peeled the fat, round oranges a landscaper at one of the villas had given Alicia and Marcia, who'd risked their lives to take a walk along the road. Handsome, Marcia said, but married, with a newborn baby named Eleonora Orfanelli.

Mom came down and sat with a cup of tea. She smiled, like she was trying very hard to be herself. "Mmm," I told her. "*Frutti di bosco* is the best flavor in the world."

"I miss bacon," Marcia said.

"Seriously? Since when do you even eat bacon?"

"I don't. I miss its being *available*." New earrings: rubies like tiny drops of blood.

"They do have bacon here, honey," Mom said. "Pancetta. It's better than our kind, in some ways." Marcia looked at me: *We have pancetta in Connecticut.*

Dad showed us a photo of an octopus relaxing in a bed of seaweed, taken just a five-minute swim from where we sat. Alicia reappeared in an olive-green raw-silk sheath and wooden jewelry. *Where* was she getting her clothes? Midnight shoplifting expeditions? Waking up to find the outfit she'd dreamed about in a neat pile at the foot of her bed? Anyway, she looked sophisticated, completely comfortable. She smiled at me.

We spent an amazing day exploring Pompeii, but got lost coming back: Mom drove us straight through Naples, into the craziest rush-hour traffic I'd ever seen—in and out of tunnels, along the waterfront, and then onto a huge highway . . . heading *away* from the coast. Dad gave up and handed me the map. I got us as far as Cuma, but the villa was *gone*. We glided again and again past old walls, shivery bamboo groves, dark restaurants, palm trees, signposts, tiny trucks, sudden forks in the road—but any choice we made took us back through the arch. No one spoke. Once, I was sure we'd found the way—but there we were, on the Roman road again, the archway rising up ahead. Alicia said it used to carry a new highway laid out by the emperor while Pompeii still smoked under pumice and ash. "We're on the even *older* road it replaced." I didn't think so; couldn't be sure. I rested my forehead on the glass and closed my eyes. We would all dream of gliding through that arch: recurring dreams.

I WOKE AND LAY LISTENING to Marcia breathe in the other bed. Almost dawn: you could *hear* the quiet; nothing moving at all, just still things waiting. Then Alicia's voice, somewhere nearby—on the balcony of an empty room, or stretched out on a couch in the hall. Of course, *her* phone worked. But when did she *sleep*?

Down in the cool, dim kitchen, I sat with a glass of blood-orange juice and watched the sun touch each tomato on the sill, until all five seemed to be lit from inside. I stared at the bulletin board until it blurred, thinking of things that might happen in my life, turning them over like curious stones, bits of surf-smoothed glass, slivers of shell. So many choices I might make; so few I really would. I went back upstairs and slept for three more hours.

There was a note from Mom in the kitchen: she'd taken Marcia out for breakfast. I poured a glass of cold peach tea, went to the library, and grabbed a book about satyrs. They had tails and pointy ears and were incredibly horny. As the book put it, "They bring the wine, provide the music, and misbehave." Ha! I *loved* the vase paintings: in one, a tame and pleasant satyr pushed a lady in a swing, but they had horse-size erections everywhere else. *Hilarious.*

Alicia came in, stretched out on the couch, and swung her feet across my lap. "Is this old place really safe, do you think? I mean, if there were a fire, where would we go?" With a silent finger, I showed her: there were signs on all the walls, everywhere in the building.

"And if there's not a fire?"

I didn't bother to roll my eyes. I wanted to say: "You can take a break, Alicia. There's nobody here but us." Instead I sucked cold, sweet tea through my sparkly straw.

Her eyes moved all around the room. "Can I tell you something?"

"I guess." I turned the page. "Wait. Are you wearing my mom's per*fume*?"

She tilted her head. Of course she was too smooth to say anything, but I knew that smell.

"So, I had this *thought*," Alicia said. "About pornography. That the people who make it aren't trying to imagine or portray actual people, but only a situation. Then I realized: philosophy is pretty much the same. Right? Back in a sec. Then I'm going out again."

"Wait, wait, wait. Isn't being a person a situation, too?" (Also: exactly how much porn did she think I watched?)

Alicia swooped back in and set something down with a *click*, as if she'd put me in check: a lipstick. I said, "Oh . . . thanks!" but she was already gone.

In the bathroom upstairs I screwed the color out, almost touched it to my lips, and stood like that, thinking. Somewhere a wild wind was peeling signs off walls. Somewhere a girl my age was practicing her sport with a serious trainer. Somewhere millions of strangers were doing billions of things I'd never know about. And, in the mirror, a girl who was me and no one else stood waiting for something to happen.

Nothing did. I screwed the color in, capped it, and dropped it in my pocket. (Not today.)

"We had breakfast at Baia Castle!" Marcia called up from the entranceway. She wore a floppy straw hat and a sky-blue shirt, and looked completely happy. "We went window shopping, too! Ugh, dude, those Shroud of Turin beach towels are in poor taste."

Mom looked worn out. She said our dad was waiting to take us to the Sybil's Cave.

"—and of course the Arch," Marcia joked. "Mary, the castle was *amazing.* You *have* to go. Wish I'd brought Rollerblades."

Mom said she would stay behind and have a nap. Her smile was small and tight; you could tell she'd stop smiling as soon as we left.

Dad took a detour to the Birdless Lake to show us the Entrance to Hell, so we got to the Sybil's Cave right before closing. The men at the gate weren't going to let us in, *especially* after Dad told them in his flimsy Italian that it was their *job* and they *had to*, but Alicia stepped forward, pushed her soft lips out, and asked them, *Please, per carità?*

The gate swung open. They didn't even let us pay.

We spread out over the site. It was late, so we were more or less alone. Alicia jogged ahead, sprinted to the end of the cave, and stood there, arms outstretched: her mouth made an *O.* The Sybil's scream went on and on and on: echoed down the rock walls and left everything quiet.

Alicia dropped her arms and laughed.

On the path to the acropolis I ran into Dad; we walked up together. "Having a good time?"

"Yes," I said.

We climbed all the way up to where the temples had been and looked out over the gulf. Far below, three people on horseback galloped along a beach. Sun was about to set: in a few minutes we'd all have one less day (obviously). Dad seemed to want to say something, but didn't. We just watched the horses, and a speeding, bucking motorboat way out on the water that made no sound at all. Maybe he wanted to tell me why he and Mom were so preoccupied, as if they had to remind themselves that they were here with us at all? Or why Mom was so upset?

I didn't ask; he didn't say. It seemed like those were the rules.

We sat down on a slab. "About Marcia," he said. "Hey. I know she must seem a little annoying these days . . . but please don't take it personally."

"Oh—I know." I looked over, but couldn't tell what he was thinking. "I love these long bricks. And the color of the water. I guess the marketplace would have been up here, too?"

"Exactly: the agora. You know, the last king of Rome died here. Julius Caesar spent time in Cumae, too. And, after Hercules finally caught him in the snow and hurled him into the sea—"

"Dad? Sorry. What were you going to say about Marcia?"

"Oh . . . I just don't want you to feel outnumbered. But your sister's at an age where, sometimes, you feel so *ready*. Whether you really are or not."

We looked off at the water: the boat was gone. The horses and riders were specks. *Ready or not, here I come.*

"You'll get your turn, Mary. Soon enough—too soon for me!—but for now, please don't take it to heart. Shall we head back down? I don't think the others are going to make the climb."

And in not so many years, first Marcia's room, then mine, would be as empty as these archaeological sites, and things would be different for all of us. Maybe we would love our parents just as much, or even more, but we wouldn't need them at all. We went down the hill.

MY SISTER GRABBED A SHEET, tripped on it, ran out of the room naked. I stepped back, mouth open. Marcia's bare feet pounded down the hall. A door slammed.

Alicia was naked, too, but she didn't move. "It's OK," she said slowly. "It's all right."

I closed my mouth. (Why was *I* the one blushing?)

Alicia kept giving me the same steady look, but I could hear her breathe. "OK? It's no big deal. We were playing around."

I was *shaking*. I tried not to shake. "I couldn't find Mom or Dad. I was just going to ask if you wanted something to *eat*."

The Italian boy went on getting dressed, taking his time, as if he were in his own house. His skin was smooth and very, very tan. His lips curved like a statue's. He didn't look at me.

Wait—no—he wasn't a boy at all! He was one of the landscapers from down the road, the one who'd given them oranges, the one whose wife had just given birth to a little girl!

Alicia held her bra like a cat's cradle, looped it over her arms, shrugged into it, fastened the strap, adjusted herself. Shaved bare below, she did nothing to cover up. She seemed amused.

He was way older—27, 28. He had a *family*. The door clicked shut and he was gone.

"You OK?" Alicia asked. "Are you OK?" She came closer, her eyes on mine.

My face kept trying to smile on its own, which made me hate myself a little. "Am *I* OK?"

"Oh, Mary, I know you won't say anything, of course, you aren't like that at all, but I want to thank you anyway. So here's your reward." She leaned in like an actor in a film and gave me a long, soft kiss on the lips. The kiss went on and on, as if we weren't both girls, as if—

Oh.

"IT'S THE TYRRHENIAN SEA," Alicia whispered, so only I could hear. "I found a map."

We were squished into the car. Mom was driving, Dad was up in front, and they were talking about some "symposium" they had to go to all of a sudden. They were going to dump us with Alicia, leave us stuck in Siena without a car. Oh, there'd be "plenty to do." I watched the traffic. Alicia's arm was warm against mine, our bare skin touching now and then, as if it were a test to see if I'd pull away. I didn't: I wasn't playing her game, whatever it was. Why should I? The road was actually interesting—what I could see of it. On curves, Alicia leaned into me.

Her lips had tasted like grape jelly. Then there she'd been, back across the room, getting dressed, putting her earbuds in, hunting down a playlist as if nothing real had happened and nothing meant anything and that was that. All night I'd tasted traces of that kiss, felt it all over, and now (I could feel my cheeks go warm) I needed a few minutes or days of the kind of privacy that probably only shipwrecked people get. Not because I was embarrassed—because the whole thing had sprung open at me without warning and folded away before I'd had a chance to know what it was. I could still feel that kiss.

Sun flashed on Alicia's piercing. She liked showing it off—catching the little barbell between her teeth, arching her tongue so the steel bead gleamed—but, honestly? It was a little gross. I closed my eyes. Sometimes there isn't much to do but wait. Maybe things will improve: maybe not. You wait.

Alicia was nudging my sister. "That sign again. You're famous."

Marcia laughed. "Yeah: famous upside down."

OK, and that man's wife? Their newborn baby? Are they part of your stupid private joke?

Long day in Naples; night rushed by. It still felt so *different* here. Even when there was nothing special—a highway, some industrial landscape, cars—I loved it. And that dark blue shadow against the darker sky was Vesuvius, the volcano that destroyed Pompeii.

Wheels on gravel woke me. Dogs barked. I avoided everyone and went straight to bed—so of course I couldn't sleep: I lay in the dark thinking of every single time I'd ever been shallow or mean or afraid, or hadn't paid the attention someone or something or someplace had deserved. Would I even *like* college when the time came? From the little Alicia said, I imagined people socializing chaotically while ideas slid by like roadside scenery. Though maybe a real idea would just insist, like that gap between the bricks at Solfatara, where you can't keep your hand in the serious heat for even a *second* before it shoves you back.

Marcia was in Alicia's room again. I wondered what the octopus from Dad's photo was doing right now, this second, tonight. Undulating out there in the dark, moving exactly like the water at first, then suddenly *not* as it reaches for prey, all of its suckers flared.

I read Lucretius until late—his philosophy was all about *sex!*—and finally got sleepy. When I went to the bathroom, Dad was down the hall, his back to me, talking on the old phone you had to put a token in. "I don't know what else I could have done." He listened. "Soon."

God. I'd overheard a thousand conversations on this trip and actually *had* maybe *two.*

I woke up late. Suitcases stood by the door and the whole place felt different. I ate breakfast alone; sat watching a spider with pale, transparent legs investigate the hinge of Mom's suitcase. Dad came in. With care, he took the spider up on the brim of his hat and flicked it lightly onto the nearest sill. "*Siamo pronti?* Time to pack, Mary, we're going north."

I gave him a hug and he patted me on the head, just like he always had—even when I was a baby, probably. Only this time I was feeling nauseous and hollowed out, so it didn't really stick.

We said good-bye to the dogs and got in the car. Dad tried to drive through the archway one last time, for fun, but we couldn't find it. We passed a CUMA sign with a red slash through it, meaning *no more Cuma—ciao!*—and were on the road.

Alicia's bracelets jingled. I let my forehead rest against trembling glass. I *loved* the umbrella pines: I'd seen them in paintings and always assumed they were cartoony, made-up things—but they were *real.* Italy was real. A cloud passed out of sight and into my mind, where it floated slowly on, dimming a little as I closed my eyes and we rushed up A1, the Highway of the Sun.

When I looked over, Alicia and my sister were holding hands. I couldn't see my mom but I knew she was staring out of the window, seeing the same trouble everywhere we went. I wanted to reach over the seat and pat her, but she would only tell me to put my seatbelt on.

"I CAN'T *BELIEVE* they gave this place *two stars*," Marcia said. I had to agree: the room was disgusting. You couldn't bathe without brushing against the toilet, which was *inside* the shower, and the bathroom ceiling was black with what Mom called "terrifyingly mature" growths of mold. Still, when you stepped outside, there was Siena. Dad and I climbed to the top of the old tower and saw the city spread out like living geometry; Piazza del Campo opened like a fan.

We all met up at a pizzeria on a steep narrow street. Marcia wore a thin white sweater over a wine-red dress that was practically see-through—Alicia's, of course. Mom didn't even notice. "I need a nap before we do the Duomo," she said. In the hotel's tiny lobby, the TV was on. An American actor whirled to face the camera and shouted: *Che cosa fai?*

"*Non lo so, idiota,*" Alicia told the TV, and gave me a quick smile. She wore a perfume that smelled like lemon peel and grass and some spice you couldn't be sure was there or not, but I was honestly getting a little tired of her. Something about her was maybe a little cruel? What I'd thought when she'd kissed me (or a bit after, once I could think again) was mostly, *why?* It was like sitting in someone's car and revving the engine, then not bothering to take them anywhere.

Back in the tiny room I shared with Mom, I lay on my bed reading. Dad came in and said something that made Mom jump up. "No. Absolutely not. I'm not letting you out of my sight!"

I got up and left. I didn't hear what he said back, but it sounded like he was trying to be quiet and patient in a way that wouldn't calm you down at all.

Marcia and I went for a walk. We wandered all over Siena, stopping to look at the yellow pottery or figure out which *contrada* we were in—we loved all the different coats of arms. We didn't really talk, which was nice. After an hour she headed back; I stopped at a newsstand. Some of the magazines had little presents shrink-wrapped onto them—change purse, lotion sample, diary. I flipped through a flimsy gossip magazine: an ad for lingerie. Rings. A baby carrier. A wristwatch encrusted with every color of jewel. Gardening soil. Goofy furniture. Puffed-up, perforated weight-loss pants. Little muffins sealed in bags. Ugly suede wedges. Biscuity cookies that looked like little gears, that you somehow had to buy at the pharmacy? Amazing furniture. A special fitness shoe that would definitely injure you. A crystal ball (though the ad was for something else). Oh, and the articles all seemed to be about old men in bathing suits and topless women with lots of makeup on. The pictures were amazing: an ominous old man gripping a young woman's duffel bag. A woman in plush purple sweatpants talking on a jeweled phone. And I recognized none of the celebrities, which made me feel FREE.

Mom and I both went to bed early. I slept pretty well—until a man screaming for quiet woke everyone up. Down the hall somewhere, an Englishwoman went on shouting at her daughter. "I should *not* be doing this! I should not be cleaning *your vomit* from *my* car keys!"

¡Cállate! ¡Quiet! screamed the Spaniard in the next room, ten times as loud.

Mom put a pillow over her head. I put my earbuds in, set an instrumental track on endless repeat, and went back to sleep with wild jazz in my head.

Alicia and I lived in a big old house in Rye, near the amusement park, playing a game with complicated rules. We had to act like we were married; but, since the whole point of marriage was to get the upper hand, you could never relax or be nice. When the wind blew, the house creaked like a ship. She sang while she loaded the dishwasher: *O, O, they call me Jack-A-Roe.*

I was glad to wake up and leave the moldy hotel forever.

We moved into a neat little *appartamentino* in the newer part of town. Our parents took off right away, saying they'd be back in time for dinner, which no one believed. I put Mom's sunglasses on. Pushed my bottom lip out as far as it would go, just to see how far: pretty far.

"Teach not thy lip such scorn," Alicia said. Silent, unsmiling, like a cop who was half machine and half man, I swiveled and turned my dark lenses on her. She laughed.

Marcia was in the kitchen painting a hunk of bread with Nutella. While I waited for her to offer me some—since that might take forever—I poured two glasses of mineral water and put one in front of her. "When we get back," she said, "I'm getting a labret."

"A lab rat?" I felt my nostrils widen: the gloss on her lips smelled like grape jelly.

"A *piercing.* Right here. A little silver loop over my lip. Alicia says it's good for kissing."

"Alicia would know. God. You're consuming that whole thing? What would Mom say . . ."

Marcia chewed intently. "You really don't get it?" She licked her fingertips. "Our parents are breaking up, Mary: divorcing, separating, ending things, moving on."

"No, they're not."

"They're probably working out the details now."

"Shut *up.* You sound like something on TV."

"Yeah . . . OK . . . My brain weighs as much as an adult's. Yours won't for at least another year." She took a giant bite of the loaded bread and walked away, leaving her mess behind.

I wanted to shout: "I'm not a dumping ground for your MOODS." Instead I rested my cheek on the marble counter and breathed. Anyway, it wasn't true. Nothing was going to change. Was it? I reached for the sparker wand and clicked out sparks. *Spark-lick. Spark-lick.* Bizarre: Why didn't they just have pilot lights? Why didn't we just have wands?

I put the Nutella away: I didn't want to get blamed and have a fattening-foods discussion with Mom. Of course, I'd seen Marcia at her worst—puffy face, matted hair, blotchy skin, so thirsty we'd had to feed her ice from a spoon. This was all because I *knew* her—I really did—and she was trying to become somebody else.

She sat on the living-room couch, her head on Alicia's shoulder. I didn't go in.

The car keys lay in a bowl on a table by the door. Hey, the compass on the key ring was real! I looked out: our car was right there, so Mom and Dad hadn't really gone to Monteriggioni . . . Unless they'd taken a bus?

"I said, 'Don't even ask me,'" Alicia was saying. "I'm no judge of what's normal.'"

So, there was the car. I was tall enough. I understood the signs. It was an automatic.

"Anyway," Marcia said, "*she's* supposedly very nice. We're going to be there for at least one night while my mom and dad do . . . whatever they do when they abandon us."

I slipped my jacket on, stepped into my shoes. Stepped out of them again and looked into the living room: they were reading an old church magazine and giggling.

"Listen to this! 'Dance, which works to arouse the senses, can never be pure.'" They laughed.

I didn't. Because, actually, if you were honest about it, wasn't it kind of a serious thing, to rouse the senses? Just because it's easy to do at first didn't mean it would go on being easy. THE BODY SEEKS THAT WHICH HAS WOUNDED THE MIND WITH LOVE.

I stuck my head in. "Hey. I'm going out to walk around a bit. See you."

Alicia looked up: they went on talking. I snagged her license on the way out. *Ciao, ragazzi!*

It was quiet in the car. I sat gripping the steering wheel. People my age could probably drive here anyway—couldn't we drink wine? Have sex? Be emperor, if all that started up again?

I strapped myself in, adjusted the seat, played with the mirror until I could see behind me. The engine started right up. I let it run for a bit, pressed down on the brake, and shifted: a jolt of power told me I could move. No one was around. *Ready or not . . .*

I pulled out—whoa, too fast. I went easier on the gas, made a turn, and there I was, driving through streets full of cars and people! No one noticed or cared. I went faster, faster, until I had to stop and pressed the brake too hard: a truck in the mirror came suddenly close.

After that I was a little too careful, too slow; cars collected behind me, but somehow no one honked. I got nervous, pulled off onto a side street, and sat breathing. Sky brightened. Trees rushed and went still. A lean, toast-colored cat trotted by, leaped up onto a wall, and picked his way along: a Siamese. The engine ran on. A woman in a window went on brushing the hair of a doll with brief, fierce strokes. The doll was the size of a child, the woman ancient. When the sun caught her eyes I saw she was blind.

No tourist would come here. Maybe *this* was what Italy was really like. (Though I had no idea, of course.)

I turned the car around. It took me an hour to get back, but, just as I pulled in, a tiny truck backed out of our spot. *Whew.* I parked, cut the engine—and remembered to shift into P.

Mom and Dad were back. Alicia and Marcia sat slumped under a blanket, watching TV. I dropped the keys into the bowl. No one even noticed I'd been away.

I PUT EARRINGS IN, little buttons made of gold. Mom and Dad were going to dump us at the country house of some couple we'd never met, so we were dressing up. Why not make it fun?

Alicia, busy pinning up part of her hair, offered to lend me a skirt.

"Don't bother," Marcia said. "She'll never wear it because of her ugly legs."

I just looked at her.

"What? You said so yourself!"

"After I flipped my bike, and was all bruised and scabby? Anyway, I have tights. Thanks, Alicia." The charcoal skirt was wonderful: *lana cotta* lined with silk. It was nice to wear something so adult. Even Marcia said I looked five years older—*"Non è una gag."*

Mom stared at us, but said nothing. She and Dad drove us *way* out into the country, pulled up at a big old farmhouse—part stone, part brick, with pinkish uneven roof tiles—waited for us to get out, and just drove away.

No one answered our knock. No one answered our pounding, either. Was it even the right place? We stood there like idiots.

Around the side we found a door propped open with a chair. Alicia called *Hello!* and led us into a huge kitchen with uneven ceiling beams and an arch at one end. Shrivelly sausages hung next to strings of peppers; big piles of American mail lay on a long pine table in the sun.

"HELLO?" No answer. A pot steamed and rattled on the stove.

We stood waiting like children in a fairy tale.

A man with shoulder-length gray hair came in, smiled, mock-bowed, and welcomed us. He wore sandals and comfortable pants. His loose black polo shirt didn't minimize his belly at all, if that's what he was after, but he was very polite; we sat and had *acqua minerale* with lime slices in little unadorned glasses. We'd expected a whole family, but Milt Melling—he made us call him Milt—was all alone: his wife had just taken off for Milan with their nephew Giorgio, a boy my age (probably perfect for me). Milt asked us what we'd thought of Naples and Pompeii, and we talked about ancient villas, each with its hidden interior open to the sky.

"Wouldn't work in Connecticut," he said, "except as a metaphor."

Alicia smiled. Milt leaned in close and took her hand "to get a better look at your *charms*," as he put it. I'd seen that smile in a fresco. Her red lipstick smiled back.

He inspected Alicia's bracelet and looked up happily. "But this is the real thing!"

His face was red and puffy, as if he spent too much time in the sun. He was older than Dad, but she *definitely* flirted back. It even seemed to give her energy in some weird way.

He released her hand and turned to Marcia. *I* was being ignored, as usual. I stared at a bowl of artichokes, the long stems still on them; reached over to pet his black, silky cat, who got up, stretched, and moved to a sunnier spot with a view of vineyards, hills, distant dirt-colored buildings. The pot rattled away. Milt got up and turned it down.

"We'll need a few things from the village," he said. "Anyone up for a walk?"

Alicia and Marcia volunteered. Milt gave them a map, a bag, a list, and some cash; they went off holding hands. I sipped my mineral water, but, man, I *still* didn't understand Diodorus Cronus. Lots of things are possible. Once something has happened, sure, its having happened stays true. But all the things that have failed (so far) to happen are not untrue, or not untrue *yet*. You have to come to a definite end before you can say: *Well, here's the list of things that never happened; their possibility was always just an illusion.* Ah! Just thinking about it (or trying to) was like swimming underwater, straining to hold your breath till you touch the wall. And what if the things that hadn't happened (yet) but might were *not* for that reason unreal or false, but only balanced in some unknowable state of potential? *The pre-real. The ready.*

Milt uncovered the pot and stuck a long fork in. He quizzed me over his shoulder: Had I known Alicia long? Did she go to school? Where? What was she studying?

"Hats," I wanted to say. I could feel the steam on my face from across the room. He covered the pot, opened the fridge, and put a bottle of pale green wine in front of me.

"A nice, crisp Greco di Tufo. Do you know Greco? One of my favorite whites: medium dry, a little tart." He gave me a slow grin. "I have some prep work to do. Why don't you open it and pour us both a glass."

Wait: he thought I knew how to open a bottle of wine? The corkscrew he put in my hand was dark with age, heavier than it looked. I peeled back the foil, put the tip against the cork, and did what I'd seen my parents do but never tried. I knew you had to get it in deep, so I aimed at the center; it kept slipping off. Then it went in, but at an angle. I leaned over and got a grip. The farther it went in, the more it straightened: a little pressure and the cork came out.

He set two plain glasses down. "You know, Greco may well be ancient. Pompeian graffiti allude to it—and here it is, straight from *Vesuvio* to our table. I have a Lacryma Christi as well, also white, or, as Marlowe calls it, 'liquid gold . . . mingled with coral and with orient pearl.'" He smiled like an old statue. "Nothing to prevent us from sampling both."

"Oh, no, this one's fine," I said. "Thanks!"

I forced my hands steady—I don't know why they seemed to want to tremble—and poured two glasses out, with just an inch in mine. Moisture condensed on them right away.

Before I could even move he claimed *my* glass, filled it all the way, and raised it to toast me.

I'd never been toasted before. As our glasses clicked, I probably even blushed. I took a sip, just to taste: made my nose wrinkle. But it was nice to be treated as a person for once.

Milt sat down with a little cutting board, kitchen scissors, and some herbs. He finished his glass and poured himself another. "Something's up with your sister," he said. "Am I right?"

I definitely blushed. Was it *that* obvious? I took a sip: watery and strong, cool and tart. I had to force myself not to make a face, but I didn't have to talk if my mouth was full.

He snipped at an herb. "Did you notice Alicia's charm bracelet? The hourglass?"

"Oh, the kiss timer?"

"Ahh. Then you've divined the secret." He snuck the bottle's snout into my glass and poured me more wine before I could even say yes, all right, sure, thanks: *glig glug glug.* "It's an old trick, you know. It *looks* like your time would run out right away, but there's a pinch too much sand." A broader smile. "So it *never* runs out."

"Cute." I took a sip. Though I didn't really get how you could kiss while looking at a tiny hourglass on your wrist? And anyway, why would you? When you like someone enough to kiss them, don't you just want to keep on kissing? I would kiss until I caught fire.

He went back to the sink. "How long have those two been an item?"

"Not long," I said—not what I'd meant to say at all.

He turned and gave me a happy look. I took a quick gulp of wine. I wanted to kick myself under the table, but I wanted to laugh, too! Though it really wasn't funny. (Yes, it was!)

Milt put out a red plate with a slumped-over little loaf of goat cheese surrounded by these amazing pieces of bread toasted up in olive oil, and started asking me all about myself—which was weird because he always seemed to be *insinuating* something, and I didn't even know what he was getting at? So I just kept swallowing little mouthfuls of wine while he chopped and stirred and whisked and told me funny things about his neighbors and the local towns and the history of the region, and something about Renaissance philosophers and the local wine, and someone called Gallino Nero (another emperor?). I was about to mention Diodorus Cronus when he topped up my glass again, *exactly* to the brim. It was like a test: could I avoid spilling it? I had to lean over the table and take a long, slurpy sip before I could even *lift* the glass.

He watched me, smiling. I got very quiet, which seemed to amuse him even more. He kept asking questions; I kept taking long, slow sips. It was actually kind of fun. I drank the last of my wine and tried to smear goat cheese on a piece of toast but it was cakey and crumbly and wouldn't smooth out so I made a mess of it and ate it in one bite: delicious!—but of course I'd left my glass unattended: it was full again. He *had* to know I wouldn't drink a *third* glass of wine (fourth? fifth?), but maybe he was just being ceremonious. Or wanted me drunk so he could drag me off somewhere. I made a note of where they kept the knives, because *fuck* that.

Anyway, how had he even poured it so full without spilling? You could see the surface tension making a dome. Plus, I couldn't *reach*. I had to climb halfway onto the table to bring my lips to the glass—slipped; caught myself and laughed. He laughed, too, but I hadn't spilled!

The glass sweated. I could smell the wine. I bent over, kissed the rim, and slurped.

He stopped stirring to stare. He didn't deserve those blue, blue eyes. Of course, if everyone only had what they de*served*, the world wouldn't be so easy to recognize. I sat back in my seat and drank the rest. "Funny," I said, a little out of breath, "how people with good luck can usually manage to—I don't know. Muster up a feeling that they deserve it?"

Milt made a grave tilt of his head. He poured more wine, but I *liked* it now—I mean, I was *totally* used to it. He started to ask another question, but it was my turn: "So . . . Milt. What do you actually *do*?" Because

I was finding his whole existence a little hard to understand. Was he on vacation? Like, all the time? I mean, he mostly cooked and drank wine?

Once again there was that little smile. "I suppose you could say, having failed at the things I wanted to do most—and having succeeded at something I did not want to do at all—I'm taking time out to rethink my life. For the moment, that means I cook, shop, tidy up, run errands, open and close the blinds, and find my days quite busy enough. I travel a little. I read. Friends come to visit, or we visit them. Do you mind if I put on music?"

I shook my head. He went down a hall and up some stairs, leaving his little smile in midair.

I lolled back in my chair, chuckling to myself without making a sound. Whatever he was cooking smelled good, but it was *hot* in here. I got up, unbuttoned my cardigan, and snooped around a little—sloppily, not caring at all what kind of mess I made. I almost tripped—over nothing. Found a hand-carved walking stick topped with a sort of pine cone; traced the vines that wrapped around its shaft. *Ha!* I loved *D'Aulaires' Book of Greek Myths.* Lots of mail from investment funds. Fancy invitations. But where was the *bathroom*?

Leaning, laughing, I swayed down a dim hallway that was all books, touching spines with my fingertips. In the bathroom, framed pictures showed Milt's wife (amazing cheekbones, ponytail) and Milt himself from years and years ago; he'd been handsome, which explained a lot.

I sat on the toilet and let my head drop back, mouth open, not needing to move. Actually, I felt pretty good. With a loud, scratchy sound, a needle touched vinyl and fast old asymmetrical jazz came on—wind instruments going wild, drums all feathery except for an occasional punch.

As I flushed I saw I'd forgotten to close the door. Whoops! I grabbed the doorframe: the hall tilted away. I *liked* this place. I wanted to explore. Was it really a farmhouse, like Mom had said, or random buildings, yoked together at various times . . . ?

Milt stood at the stove, stripped to the waist. His potbelly glistened with oil and sweat. It was *huge*—bigger than I'd thought—and very tan.

"Mary. Would you care to see what we're having for dinner?" I swayed there for a second, but had no choice: tucked my hair behind my ears and came up just out of reach of the rattling steam, willing myself not to wobble. I was a brim-full glass, trying not to spill my *self.*

Milt's face shone. He poked his fork into the pot, speared something enormous, raised it, and held it dripping for me to see. The huge lump of flesh—a disgusting pinkish gray, pores everywhere—flattened down to a rounded tip.

Oh—gross. It was a tongue. *An enormous tongue.*

"You've had tongue before, of course." He cut a slice from the tip and held the steaming bit of meat, pierced with the point of his knife, right up to my lips.

Actually, it smelled all right: like corned beef. I took it in, worked it over slowly, and swallowed. It was OK, once you got over what it *was* (if you ever did).

I floated to my chair and sat down with a thump. The glass I'd left empty was full to the top. I stared at the sweating green wine and wondered what would happen if I had even *one more* taste. I was going to throw up anyway. Were Marcia and what's-her-name *ever* coming back?

People keep offering me tongues.

I snorted, almost spilling; leaned over and took a long, slow sip.

"Delicious with a little Dijon," he said. "Or the local *senape,* when you can find one sharp enough." He dabbed his face with a cloth. "Hot work, this." His eyes were incredibly blue. "You don't like Alicia much, do you?"

"No, no, no, sometimes I do!" I said loudly. "I don't *know.* I think . . ." (I forgot to talk for a minute.) "She steeps herself in her own psychology."

He laughed so hard he had to wipe his cheeks. "The shape of your lips," he said, "is really quite something. You have an audacious little mouth, Mary. But you know that, of course."

I rolled my eyes, picked up my glass, held it in front of my face, and looked at him through it: he was fatter, greener, smaller. I liked the Wine Milt better. I peeped over the rim.

"No. It isn't even Alicia—not as herself. It's just . . . she's having this effect on my sister." I swallowed more than I'd meant to and coughed. "We went to Solfatara," I explained.

My glass was empty. A chilly new bottle stood in front of me, unopened, complete. Milt came up behind me and leaned in to whisper something secret, but didn't whisper; didn't move away. Just *stayed* there, close enough to smell. Before I could think I felt his hand slip down to my waist, his lips brush my ear, his tickly fingers reach in under my hair—

I ducked under the table and *ran*. Books, bathroom—I slammed into a cabinet and set it rocking. In a side room with dark furniture, a woman sat in the glow of a computer screen—sparse white hair, an ancient face, a profile like the Duke of Urbino, but with headphones on. I scrambled up more steps, turned again, and raced down a second hallway, lined with vinyl records. The hall went on, narrowing as it went, until there were no more records, no more shelves, only plain white walls spotty with dirt or mold. An empty jar rolled after me. Would the hall NEVER come to an end?

A narrow arch led down to a rough-walled room where, past brown quilted jackets, through a glass-paned door, there were hills and sky. I dodged a sink, jumbled a lineup of rubber boots, twisted an old iron key back and forth, and kicked and kicked and kicked the dried-out door until I forced it wide enough to squeeze through: free.

I half-waded, half-limped across a freshly planted field to a country lane, which I trudged along till I could breathe again. It was getting dark. Burrs stuck to my clothes. A dog barked somewhere. I pulled a leaf from my hair, tucked my chin down, and kept walking.

They left me alone with him? Really?

Milt didn't follow: he probably just smiled, topped up his glass, grabbed the big fork—

I vomited into a ditch. Vomited again. Remembered, too late, to pull back my hair.

MOM AND DAD were in their room with the door closed, but we could hear everything: Dad insisting he had "business" in Rome, Mom saying, "Fine! Then I'm going with you. Leave Alicia the car. She can drive the girls down to Terracina. We'll meet them in a few days."

Dad said something very quietly, and that was it: they came out of the room with their bags.

"Dad," Marcia said. She was reading a gossip magazine. "Who's Vittorio Bazzini?"

"Why, dear?"

"He's gross and old and has a saggy potbelly, but the woman he's been seeing (not his wife, though she's nice, too, apparently) is incredibly pretty."

I sat on the couch and watched my parents move around, their eyes never meeting. *The emperor's pallor worried his advisers.* Alicia, in a rust-brown silk wrap, turned cushions over, looking for a lost bracelet. "Can I speak with you?" Mom asked. They went off.

I unzipped my bag and took out the rock I'd picked up at Solfatara: it still smelled exactly like that day, like sulfur and sun, already memory. The emperor carried the bags out to the taxi, Mom kissed us good-bye, and they were gone.

Alicia threw her wrap at Marcia, spread her arms, whirled around, and sang: "WE'RE FREE!"

I'd seen her naked before, so no big deal.

I SAT ON THE CEMETERY WALL, hugged myself, and turned toward the sunrise: didn't help at all. Edges were brightening, making it *seem* a little warmer, but we were freezing. We were lost. We hadn't slept. Alicia and Marcia had gone off to have a smoke and maybe make some kind of plan, but Alicia just kept kicking the side of someone's mausoleum. She wore dark lipstick and more eye makeup than I'd ever seen her use. She looked fantastic. It seemed to amuse her that so many things had gone wrong: the worse things got, the funnier she thought it was—and she was the one in charge. She went on kicking, *scuff, scuff, scuff,* her short skirt flipping up. The weathered marble sparkled like sugar cubes. (I used to sneak those cubes home from restaurants and lie very still while a temptingly crisp shape dissolved in my mouth, uncrunched.)

First Alicia had driven us all over Italy. We saw some amazing things, but our theories about where we were stopped making sense. We circled and circled an enormous crater lake and then got lost in some dusty industrial countryside. We stopped in a random hill town to pee and finally got to eat, in a long, fluorescent basement filled with local soccer players in uniform. After dinner we explored the town on foot, down to its narrowest, most dead-end street, until we were ready to lie down on the cobblestones and sleep; Alicia couldn't find the car keys. We spent hours searching everywhere in the dark, getting lost, arguing, circling back, and found the keys hanging on a nail outside the locked restaurant. The car wasn't where we were pretty sure we'd parked, so we hiked all the way to the *other* edge of town, ran from a barking dog we never actually saw into someone's vineyard (a bad place to run in the dark), and ended up watching the sun come up from inside a little shop that hadn't technically opened, drinking espresso and staring at a mortadella the size of a man. Alicia thought we might be able to see the car from higher up, so we climbed all the way up here, but no. Of course not.

I popped the last mint into my sour mouth. My skin felt sticky and I needed to pee. Were we *ever* going to sleep? I yawned. A humpbacked dog trotted by, nose to the ground: wiry fur, big teeth, spindly legs . . . I had to laugh. Maybe being amused when things go wrong was a good approach. Strange how the wild boar either had *no* neck or was nothing *but* neck: just a massive head with legs and a tail. It was *definitely* a boar: certain animals have that medieval look. Pelicans don't seem modern either; the ones on coats of arms seem as real as any photograph. What did wild boars eat? Acorns? Mushrooms? Girls from Connecticut? I closed my eyes and tried to will myself warm. Alicia had not only lost the *car,* she'd lost the keys *again,* in a stream we were crossing. We'd ended up groping about in freezing shallows for quite a while before Marcia held the key ring up on a wrinkly thumb. They were going to lose me next.

I took a walk to get warm. Some of the tombs were actual little houses where you could visit your dead relatives. It seemed like make-believe to me, a child's tea party with bodies instead of dolls, but the Romans had done it, too; they'd even poured wine into a special hole in the grave.

Wine. Had Milt thought I *liked* him? Oh God. That couldn't be it. More likely he'd been too lazy and self-amused to care who I was at all.

I wandered past slabs, headstones, a pedestal with a sort of stone bathtub on it, and more little houses: NANONE. BIZZARO. CARBONE. STELLACCIO. Old marble, slightly rough to the touch; stone vases empty, or full of dirty plastic flowers, or dried-out husks of real flowers, or fresh flowers just beginning to droop. It was quiet, except for my steps and the wind. I didn't even feel tired anymore—though I *really* needed to pee. Just not enough to risk it in the open, with wild boars running around. D'ELIA. VECCHIONE. PARADISO. MAROTTA. Surprising breezes would sweep past, fade suddenly. I tried but couldn't really picture the lives these people had lived, whoever they were: COLLOMOSSE. CRISCI. DELLE DONNE. I didn't know enough: about the past, about this place, about these people. I could hardly imagine my *own* life, much less theirs. PAVORONE. ACQUAVELLA. DOCILE. One slab looked comfortable enough to stretch out on, close my eyes, and rest like a marble angel in the sun . . .

I heard them both—their voices suddenly *there,* my sister sucking in smoke in a dramatic way, letting it out endlessly. I could tell by the harsh way she breathed and gave dull, one-word replies that she'd been crying and was miserable. *Why?*

Alicia was saying, "That's silly. You're beautiful. You're intelligent. You'll find someone."

"I already did."

Wind rushed the trees. Marcia tried to laugh bitterly but only coughed. Alicia murmured something, but it was none of my business: really. I tiptoed away, turned a corner, and went on. Old slabs blanked with shadow, blanked with sun. A row of tombstones sparkled: DETUCCIO. FICINO. VERDONE. CHIAROLANZA. Maybe I could loop around from the other side, so they'd at least see me coming. Or just take off, head for Venice or Sicily. Why not? They wouldn't notice for days. AGITI. SICONDOLFI. AUTULLO. LA LANCIA. This adventure wasn't going to turn out well. But how do most things turn out? They all end here: grandparents, parents, kids, whole families, nothing left but old buttons and bones. Skeletons in boxes, dressed in rotten clothing long out of style. Atoms and the void.

I turned, walked for a bit, turned again. A cigarette burned on the edge of a slab.

They sat on the front step of a mausoleum, backs to the bronze-barred door. They leaned into each other and seemed to be whispering. No, they were kissing. *Really* kissing.

"Nothing I haven't seen in a movie," I said in a flat voice that didn't sound like me.

Dogs were barking: two, three, maybe more; faint but getting louder, coming this way.

Alicia and Marcia didn't look up. Alicia's hand moved under my sister's shirt.

I chose a big white tomb (DA PORTO), grabbed the window bars, and hoisted myself up to the roof. The barking got louder. A man shouted nearby. Marcia and Alicia stopped, stared into each other's eyes from an inch away, and went on kissing.

Bristling, its jaws wet with foam, the wild boar ran right past them. Gravel chips flew.

Alicia shrieked. I saw Marcia's open mouth, heard only squealing barks.

Dogs formed a ring, but the wild boar whipped around, its snout glistening with snot and grit—and went for one of the dogs. Like an explosion, they all spun away—but circled back right away to face the boar. Dense and muscular, it broke through the line and took off fast. The rush knocked Alicia down. In a second the animals were out of sight.

She leaned over and spat. A spittle thread hung from her lips and disappeared.

"Alicia? Allie, are you OK?" Marcia crept out from behind a tomb. "I think they're gone."

"Um," I said from above, "I wouldn't be too sure—"

More loud barks; an awful yelp. The boar made a strange cry, sharp with agitation and rage.

Marcia was gone. Alicia crouched down, her back to a tomb, and looked around rapidly.

More dogs rushed by. The boar screamed again, sounding almost like a monkey or a man.

A worker in a blue jumpsuit jogged past; a tall man followed, taking his time. His stiff gray hair looked oddly like the boar's; a rifle hung from his shoulder by a strap. He was eating an apple. The sounds moved off with them.

Alicia sat on the gravel, knees to her chest. She raised her head—as *another* boar swept past.

"Alicia!" I called. "Up here!"

She ran to my tomb, jumped up, grabbed at the roof, and tried to claw her way up.

"No, look, it's really easy—use the window. Put your foot—grab my hand!" She almost made it; fell back. "Come on, you can do it. Take a breath."

With a stunned, angry look, she made a running leap, gripped the roof, got a leg up, and slid off before I could catch her. Her lip was bleeding. Bits of gravel stuck to her cheek.

"Use the bars. Put your knee on the window," I advised. My knuckle was raw; Alicia was shaking. Twenty dogs poured in, shouts and barks came from all directions, and the sky was so wonderfully blue! Italy was *by far* the best place I'd ever been.

Another boar rounded the corner, leaning hard, going nearly sideways. Alicia ran, tripped on a step, and crawled off rapidly on her hands and knees.

My mouth was open and I was making noise. I didn't know *what* noise at first: I might have been screaming for help or crying, but I was *laughing*—laughing so hard it hurt. From the roof I saw more men in coveralls, an old farmer limping along, dogs rounding corners only to run into other dogs, and—appearing and disappearing here and there—a blur of brown bristle with live little eyes, enraged or frightened or both.

"*What* are you laughing about!" Marcia screamed. "She could have been trampled or bitten or gored! They could be taking her to the hospital *right now*! We all could have *died*!"

I couldn't help it. I was aching. *Aching!* Face wet, nose running, hardly able to breathe, I *couldn't* stop laughing: just *couldn't*. My face must have had the shape of the empty mask they hang over theater doors. At the edge of the roof, stooped over, shaking, I laughed.

Marcia yelled, "He's back. He's coming! RUN!" but I couldn't even *see*, which made me laugh harder, though I was *so* tired of laughing and *so* needed to breathe . . .

With a quick scrape like a match being lit, the cemetery reeled away: I hit gravel, hard. Lay on my back looking up at blue, blue sky. Carefully, bruise by bruise, bone by bone, I sat up.

After a minute Marcia came up and leaned over me, breathing heavily. Her face was wet: she'd been laughing too. When we looked at each other we started to laugh again; tried not to, but only started laughing harder, though every laugh was its own stab of pain. And of course Marcia was my sister and I was hers; it didn't matter if we liked each other or not. So, that was that—except for the sound of gunshots, far away. I'd been hoping the wild boars would escape somehow, and get on with their lives; and who knows, maybe they did. But probably not.

I WONDERED WHAT it was like to think in Latin. My suitcase having been packed, I sat out on the cozy modern balcony, leaned back in my chair, and picked cloudflowers. Traffic passed below, or didn't pass; I heard its sounds but saw only sky. I felt *good*: though I was going to miss all this. I even missed driving through the arch, which Alicia had been wrong about—I'd checked.

Harsh lipstick. Wouldn't look at me. Even the way Marcia *stood* now was weird. Her slipdress was on backward and she wore Alicia's socks, the ones with the maps of Portugal. She picked up a terra-cotta Buddha and put it back on the shelf; headed off to the kitchen, walking slowly, tilting to one side, the way our grandmother had the year she died. It made me feel like being nice to her, though she hadn't been nice to me. Anyway Marcia had to be feeling what I felt, that Alicia's power or glamour or charm was just *gone*: as if she'd been disproven.

I went inside. My jaw felt heavy, delicate as glass. It rested on my chest as if on a velveted display in some old museum. Without moving my chin, I picked up the remote: on BBC News, people carried bodies from a blast-scarred building. An angry woman vowed revenge. It occurred to me that I didn't even know what side I'd be on if I had to choose; though probably the woman hadn't had a choice herself, but it was weird: she was Alicia's age. In her situation, I'd be screaming and cursing, too, obviously—but what then?

Alicia had taken the barbell out of her tongue. She hardly spoke, unless to say something like "I'll bruise if you touch me. Sorry: I think I'm ill." All she seemed to want to do was sleep.

Someone—and this made me really sad—had taken a pair of pliers and crushed Alicia's hourglass. She'd showed me the little wad of wreckage, the twisted silver, the burst glass, and just looked at me. There were tears in her eyes, but she'd refused to cry. Anyway, we both knew it wasn't me.

Marcia was busy emailing everyone using her *phone*—it would cost more than our house when the bill came. I skipped from channel to channel until I found an old American movie dubbed into Italian. A boy hid in a schoolbus from some kids who wanted to beat him up. *Now what? How do I get out of here? What do I do?* But I knew the answer: you just have to wait.

I poured a glass of wine and sat with it. I'd never had wine all on my own. I took a sip: it was a different kind, dark red, and I absolutely *hated* the taste. It was practically poison, it could do you harm, you had to force yourself to like it—so of course it was part of being an adult.

Dad drove us to the airport. No one talked. Mom would be staying on for a week (if you believed what she and Dad kept telling us in serious tones), so she could "wind up some important business in Rome." When I finally saw the sign they'd been joking about—

INVERSIONE

DI MARCIA

—no one even noticed. We passed old walls, umbrella pines: I was going to miss Italy.

There was snow all over Connecticut—filthy mountain ranges at the edges of parking lots, lumps and crusts still glittering in the woods—but it was easy to be back: I went to school, hung out with friends, used my phone and laptop like a regular person, and glided along in the familiar strangeness of being myself. I tried to take things as they seemed to want to be taken, which wasn't quite so easy anymore. In school, on the bus, at volleyball, during meals, I'd think of random things that had happened (or almost happened: always more of those), and the oddest moments would come back: my sulfury chewing gum. The sparker wand. That irresistible arch. My taste of hot tongue. How easy it was to drive. The old man in Terracina (when we finally got there) who wanted to know why we'd bombed the town in 1944, *after* the Germans had left, and killed his girlfriend? He showed us a colorless, scallop-edged photo of a girl my age and looked intently at each of us in turn.

An older boy—in Marcia's class, actually—started calling me. I wasn't sure about him, but we texted all the time and talked for hours very late at night. Or we'd be silent and listen to the connection, which had its own sound sometimes, like faraway surf. I'd lie on my back, fingers laced across my stomach, phone propped up by my ear, and fall asleep listening to him talk.

I still drink the occasional glass of wine.

Of course Mom *did* come home from Italy after a week and everything was fine, or seemed that way to me. They would *never* get a divorce—I was right about that.

Once there was no one around to impress, Marcia stopped being so mean, but we're not close; maybe I know too much. Anyway, I just went ahead and decided that I would treat her as an adult and expect the same, which means we don't talk a lot right now unless there's a reason.

In April, Alicia's mom fell asleep while driving on the Turnpike. After the funeral, Alicia left school, moved to Texas, and got a job as a bartender. Maybe she read her philosophy book on breaks. Maybe the book was right, at least as an approach to certain things? Or anyway better at asking questions than forcing a definite set of answers. I actually do hope she's OK. I wouldn't mind getting to know her again someday, once she figures out how to be herself without driving herself crazy, and how to get along in this weird civilization of ours without giving up her own idea of life (probably most people need to figure that one out).

I'd been sure she was going to mock me without mercy when they found me sitting by the road in Tuscany, a vomity, grubby, drunken mess, but Alicia had dropped her bag in the grass and put her arms around me, vomit and all; when she let go, she was crying, too. "I'm so sorry," she kept saying. I refused to go back to that house, and she agreed, and Marcia had nothing to say about it, so we all sat by the blue metal gate to someone's farm, ate the bread and olives and apricots they'd bought, and laughed about all the wine and the boiling tongue and my introduction to the kind of thing every woman has to deal with in one way or another—which isn't fair, gentlemen. Really.

Of course I'm exactly the same as I was before, only maybe I understand a few more things. And when you understand a thing it's yours, even when it stays a little bit out of reach. When I think of our trip now—about how it felt to be kissed for the first time; to stand on the spot where a huge temple had been; to get a pretty good sense of why a panicked nymph, her bare feet pounding the dirt, might beg to be transformed into a tree; or just to pass through an old arch again and again, until the villa, our beds, our belongings, even our *selves*, began to seem mysterious and out of reach—I feel a kind of nostalgia for the future. It's like knowing that something quite important is already mine, but having *no idea* how to get to it. Or anyway how to *wait*. The way a bus driver probably feels at the start of a shift, passing her lover's house along the route. I mean, seriously, I'm ready. Put a red slash through it, let's get on the road. +

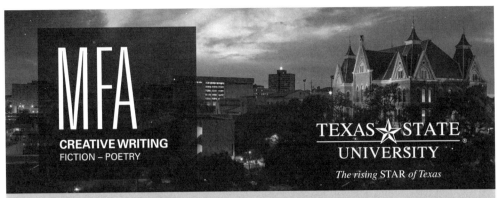

HANNA LIDEN, *PYRAMID MATCHES II*, 2016, C-PRINT. 60" × 48.25".
COURTESY OF THE ARTIST AND MACCARONE, NY/LA.

THE LAST LAST SUMMER

Joshua Cohen

JULY 5, 2016

THE GOVERNMENTS that get themed into casino-hotel-resort properties tend not to be democracies, but oligarchies, aristocracies, monarchies, Africa-and-Asia-devouring empires. Pharaonic Egypt, Doge-age Venice, imperial Rome, Mughal India. Atlantic City has incarnations of the latter two—Caesars Atlantic City and the Trump Taj Mahal—with the Taj being the last property in the city to bear the Republican candidate's name, though it's owned by distressed-asset czar Carl Icahn, who also owns the Tropicana, a crumbling heap styled after the *Casa de Justicia* of some amorphous banana republic. The worse the regime, the better the chance of its simulacrum's survival. Atlantic City's Revel, a hulking fin-like erection of concrete, steel, and glass that cost in the neighborhood of $2.4 billion, opened in 2012 only to close in 2014, which just goes to show that an abstract noun, verb, or imperative in search of punctuation (Revel!) doesn't have quite the same cachet as a lost homicidal culture.

Today, the fake ruins of Rome and India are among the cleanest, safest havens to be found in the real ruins of Atlantic City—a dying city that lives for summer. I was returning there, to my family there, still unsure as to whether this summer would be my last or its last or both.

Now, given the fact that AC's been so perpetually press-maligned that I can remember nearly every summer of the sixteen I spent there being deemed, by someone, "crucial," "decisive," "definitive," or "the last," this suspicion of mine might seem, especially to fellow Jersey

Shore natives, irresponsible and even idiotic—so I will clarify: I don't mean that I thought that after this summer of big media scrutiny but little new money the city would burn, or that the Atlantic Ocean would finally rise up and swallow it. I just thought that, come Labor Day, the city's bad-luck streak would only break for worse and no one would care.

After the legalization of Indian tribal and nontribal casinos in Connecticut in the 1990s and in Pennsylvania in the 2000s; after the legalization of tribal casinos in upstate New York in the '90s and of nontribal casinos in the 2010s; after the damage done to the city by Hurricane Sandy in 2012 and all the myriad, still-ongoing depredations of the global so-called Great Recession that resulted in the closing of four of the city's casinos in 2014 (the Revel, the Showboat, the Atlantic Club, and Trump Plaza), leaving AC with the highest rate of foreclosure of any urban area in the country between fourth-quarter 2014 and the present; this summer—the summer of 2016—already felt like the fall. Maybe this wouldn't be the last summer that White House Subs or Chef Vola's would ever be serving, but it might be the last summer that I, as a sane, unarmed, and relatively pacific human being would still feel comfortable traveling to them for a cheesesteak or veal parm on foot—taking the stairs down from the overlit Boardwalk to the underlit streets of what's officially become the most dangerous city in Jersey, now that Camden has stopped reporting its crime statistics to the FBI. It occurred to me that if and when AC is ever visitable or enjoyable again, my parents will probably have retired south to Cape May, and the few acquaintances of mine who still live on Absecon Island—the island of which AC is the northernmost town—will probably have left.

But what ultimately had me convinced that AC—whose historical cycle of boom and bust recapitulates each year in the cycle of "season" and "offseason"—would not be the same, or even recognizable, was the perfect-storm convergence of a few maybe-related, maybe-unrelated events.

First, the budget deadline: if AC couldn't produce a balanced budget for state approval by October 24—and most residents here were convinced that it couldn't, and that Governor Chris Christie wouldn't let it—then the State of New Jersey would assume control of all its offices and operations, commencing with what AC's mayor, Don Guardian (and the ACLU, and the NAACP), regards as an unconstitutional takeover of city government. Should this happen, AC would be the first city in Jersey history to be run from Trenton (besides Trenton). The state would have the power to renegotiate all of AC's contracts, including its union contracts, and to privatize, meaning to peddle, its assets—like the water company, the Atlantic City Municipal Utilities Authority, and the defunct airport, Bader Field—in the hopes of paying off the city's $550 million debt and reducing its $100 million budget deficit.

Second, the ballot referendum: on November 8, two weeks and one day after this likely state takeover, Jersey voters would go to the polls to decide whether or not to approve the New Jersey Casino Expansion Amendment, which seeks to expand casino gaming—until now restricted to Atlantic County—to two other Jersey counties able to provide suitable casino siting at least seventy-two miles from AC. If the amendment is approved—and as of this writing the opinion split appears to be 50/50—get ready for grand-opening celebrations of casinos in the Meadowlands. The logic is that AC has already lost about $2.5 billion in gaming revenue to neighboring states over the past decade, and it's only a matter of time before some enterprising schmuck puts up a betting parlor in Manhattan; the establishment of new casinos up north along the Jersey side of the Hudson might forestall that. Or it might not—but it would certainly ensure that the citizens of the largest city in the country will stop trekking almost two and a half hours on a defunct-bathroom Greyhound, or almost three hours on an Amtrak that because of track deficiencies must be routed through Philly, to lose their shirts.

Of course, November 8 would bring another decision, and not just for Jersey.

I called Mom and Dad, fueled up the car, and left New York, driving Turnpike (Exit 11) to Parkway (Exit 38) to the AC Expressway. There wasn't any traffic.

BACK IN THE (Bill) Clintonian 1990s, when the billboards flanking the Expressway and the Black and White Horse Pikes weren't bared to struts or advertising YOUR AD HERE, when my father made his money suing the casinos and my mother made hers giving accent-reduction lessons to South Asian immigrants who worked at the casinos, when my parents' friends and professional peers and just about every other adult bowing to my left and right and in front of and behind me in synagogue either regulated the casinos (for the state's Casino Control Commission and Division of Gaming Enforcement), managed the casinos (their gaming floors, food and beverage, and entertainment), or supplied goods and services to and for the casinos (ice, linens, waste management), AC—the city itself—remained a mystery to me, a paradox. It was a place where everyone made a living, and yet where no one liked to live. A place of fantasy (strippers!) and yet of bewildering strictures (you can purchase alcohol 24/7 in stores and bars, but not in strip clubs, though you can BYO alcohol into strip clubs!).

It was, to my teenage self, about a two-dozen-block strip of Boardwalk and two major if seedier streets, Atlantic and Pacific, which I'd visit for fun or trouble before heading out for the less crowded, less polluted beaches or home, making in the course of a single weekend night the same trip that most of the adults I knew made every weekday: between AC (population 39,260) and the whiter, more affluent Downbeach towns of Absecon Island or the whiter, more affluent mainland. The adults were just going to work; their children, or I'll just speak for myself, had drugs to buy and girls to meet.

I also became a casino employee, but only after I was sure I was leaving. The summer of 1998, the summer between high school and college, I worked at Resorts, a casino that lacked an apostrophe so as to appear, I'm guessing, less possessive: of my time, and of the customers' cash. I was a coin cashier, and my job was to stand, fully tuxedoed, inside an excruciatingly bright and noisy barred cell furnished with a tiny surface of faux marble (because marbling camouflages grime, and cash is grimy) and a small round aperture through which slots players handed me their buckets, white plastic troughs emblazoned with the Resorts logo and surfeited with their winnings. I would dump each bucket's lode into the churning maw of my automatic counter, which, while it tallied up the coins, also separated them, shunting the nickels and quarters—the preferred denominations of slots—into vast plastic bags that hung to the floor like the distended gullets of pelicans. I'd read the total from the counter's display and pay the players their rightful take in whichever form they requested it: bills, or—I was supposed to encourage this—chips, which at the time were regarded as the easiest monetary substitutes for players to immediately put back into circulation and thus be parted from. Fiat currencies would soon leave the slot floor altogether, with the introduction of new self-service machines that wouldn't take or pay out with coins at all, but instead took, and paid out to, casino-issued credit cards. At that point, in the mid-2000s, the honorable trade of the coin cashier, like that of the blacksmith (who now only posed for photos at Bally's Wild Wild West Casino) and the riverboat captain (who now only posed for photos at the Showboat), just vanished.

It should be noted, however, that before the casinos phased out coins and we coin cashiers were replaced with self-service machines, we spent all our shifts servicing our lesser machines, trying to declog them—especially on the graveyard shifts, when more and more players came in with buckets they'd use as ashtrays, so that their coinage was interspersed with butts (smoking was banned in 2008), and when more and more players, too late for the dinner buffet but too early for the breakfast buffet, came in with buckets of fast food they reused to hold their jackpots. They'd sit at the slots, pulling the levers or pushing the buttons while poking around in their buckets for fried-chicken drumsticks or BBQ ribs, and shake off the stuck metal before indulging. Coin cashiers were trained to contain these situations, and so were expected to go sifting through the winnings to remove any bones and burnt ends and shreds of skin and breading. Those were the simplest things, the simplest of the foreign objects, to watch out for, mostly because they came in buckets from KFC or in foam clamshell containers from Burger King or McDonald's. Other containers, such as shoeboxes or backpacks, were tougher to monitor, and if I—in the over-air-conditioned heat of the moment, under verbal fire from an interminable line of intoxicated zombies—ended up missing anything, any non-coin article, especially if I ended up missing something sizable buried at the bottom, like a wristwatch or a phone or a med-alert bracelet, it would (usually) announce itself by jamming up the counter, and clearing the jam would (usually) blank the total, in which case I'd have to pay out a quarter-bag's max: $100. Obviously, then, it would be in a slot player's interest, if he or she hadn't won quite $100, to make sure that stray cutlery or a spare key or other sabotage debris were always lurking below the coinage. Obviously too, the casinos knew this trick, and we coin cashiers knew that we were responsible for catching it—that we were being camera-surveilled from every conceivable angle and so might be disciplined, or terminated, for not catching it. But still: I was leaving for college in the fall, and there were midnights, there were dawns, I was finding bloody Band-Aids. Shift after shift, my totals rarely matched up, the amount in coins I'd taken in always considerably less than the amount in bills and chips I'd paid out from my drawers, because I kept having to hand over the $100 black chips or, more often, the crisp, sharp Franklins. Though I hate to credit a Philly boy, it was Franklin who put it best: "Neglect is natural to the man who is not to be benefitted by his own care or diligence."

On breaks I ate in the Resorts basement at the employee buffet—which was "free," because it featured leftovers from the customer buffets—and after my shifts I hung out with the only two cashiers around my age, the only two who after clocking out wouldn't dash for the jitney home. Everyone else I worked with was older—nice people, family people, immigrant or first-generation Indians, Pakistanis, Bangladeshis, Vietnamese, and Thai, who weren't going to squander their precious off-time arguing with pizza-faced white coworkers over pizzas at Tony's about what was better, hand jobs or DIY jerking.

Some nights I'd blow all my earnings at AC Dolls or Bare Exposure (which enigmatically, or out of legal exigency, once briefly called itself Bare Exposures). Some nights I'd blow just half my earnings on a room above the Chelsea or at the El Rancho (the one motel that'd never carded me and yet is now, deliciously, called the Passport Inn)—a room from which I'd call a few friends (males), who'd come and drink and smoke pot with me; a room from which I'd call a few friends (females), who'd never come.

Such are my memories, or at least the ones I've offered around like cocktail franks to folks in New York and other cities I've lived in, whenever someone asked where I was from and I answered AC and they said, "Hey, that must've been interesting," or, "Wow, that must've been nuts." With age, and after becoming assimilated to circumstances I'd never imagined for myself as a kid from the Shore (in Europe! with a girlfriend! as a journalist! as a novelist!), I realized that I'd unintentionally adopted their perspective myself—a sense of the Shore in general and AC specifically as strange, even freakish—and so made a habit of sharing, of performing, only the extremes. I gratified what I perceived to be my more sophisticated audiences with only the most outlandish anecdotes of my immaturity there, never mentioning, for example, that I was educated at the island's particularly good Jewish school and not in its particularly bad, racially tense public school system, and that my parents were—are—kind, pleasant, generous, intellectual people who weren't always 100 percent aware of—because I wasn't always 100 percent transparent about—all the nose-dirtying I got up to after-hours.

Now, having returned to the city—to what AC's Chamber of Commerce used to call America's Playground and now calls, with depressing deprecation, the Entertainment Capital of the Jersey Shore—I found that my feelings had flipped. What I'd been conditioned to regard as a madcap, hedonistic outlier of a place, an utterly, even excessively incomparable place, now struck me as not exceptional at all, but emblematic, not merely of the rest of the state but of the rest of the country off whose coast it floats. The city of my youth had seemed like a flounder in summer, that bastard flatfish that local fishermen call a fluke. AC 2016, however, was coming to seem like America's bowrider: what captains call the dolphins that swim in front of their boats, riding the wake off their bows as if heralds.

I FIRST NOTICED this sea change last fall, when a certain type of red-faced, overweight, whatcha-gonna-do-about-it New Jersey/New York male commandeered our national politics. Both Donald Trump and Chris Christie were talked about in my family constantly—Trump since before I was even in utero, and Christie since George W. Bush appointed him US attorney for New Jersey in 2001, and especially since he became governor in 2010. But it was only after suffering through their schoolyard-bully penis contests during the 2016 Republican primaries that I began to recognize how similar they were, how alike in personality and in unctuous, disingenuous style. If I hadn't detected their toxic resemblance before, it was only because they'd been menacing different playgrounds: Trump having always been nominally private sector, brandishing the better, or just more recognizable, brand; Christie having always been nominally public sector, an elected official who must be held to higher standards. The ongoing SEC and congressional and New Jersey State investigations into Christie's alleged misappropriation of Port Authority monies, his allegedly having made federal emergency-relief funds available to Jersey cities affected by Hurricane Sandy contingent on city-government support of unrelated state-government initiatives, and, finally, his allegedly having ordered the George Washington Bridge closed as an act of political retaliation against the mayor of Fort Lee—and so snarling a major artery from Manhattan—will likely continue beyond the conclusion of his term in 2018. Jersey's governor has always been such an unmitigated prick that what stunned me most last spring wasn't Trump's emergence as the GOP front-runner, but Christie's dutiful dropping-out and endorsing him—his assuming a role, even after Trump passed him over for VP, halfway between that of a catamite butler and a henchman capo, the butt of Trump's insulting fat jokes and the fetcher of his milkshakes and fries.

The Republican primary debates marked the televised degeneration of their friendship—or whatever a friendship can mean in politics—which began only in 2002, when Trump's sister, Maryanne Trump Barry, then a Philadelphia-based judge on the US Court of Appeals for the Third Circuit, nominated to that position by Bill Clinton, introduced her brother to the governor. The Christies were invited to Trump's third wedding, to Melania; the Trumps were invited to Christie's first inauguration. A year into Christie's first term, and six years after the State of New Jersey had started to pursue collection of the almost $30 million in back taxes owed by Trump's casinos, the State suddenly reversed course and settled for $5 million. Trump contributed an exceedingly modest share of the money he saved to the restoration of New Jersey's historic gubernatorial residence, Drumthwacket. New Jersey's near-miraculous tax forgiveness must be understood in the same way as its governor's near-miraculous abjection: neither are demonstrations of Trump's master outmaneuvering, but rather of Christie's cravenness. Christie will do anything to win, or be on the winning team. If he can't be President, or VP, he'll plump for chief of staff, or attorney general, or even just settle for a monogrammed-T swag bag with a Trump hat, Trump Steaks, Trump wine. Christie's not only inept, he's also running out of options: there isn't much of his party left to knock around. Politics (budget meetings in the State House in Trenton) used to be distinct from entertainment (*The Celebrity Apprentice* in syndication), but no more. Christie seems jealous of Trump, not just of his financial success or his nomination but of how well and recklessly Trump, as a former/current reality-TV star, can lie. Christie has always just ignored, withheld, or fastidiously obfuscated. Trump, by contrast, can't afford not to be blatant or audacious in his untruths, so as to keep earning free airtime from the cable networks and radio stations whose ratings and ad revenues increase—blatantly, audaciously—in correspondence.

To me, Trump was always a blusterer, a conniver, a mouth: a cotton-candy-haired clown who crashed the AC party late and left it early and ugly. To my parents and their cadre, the Republican nominee was a more malevolent breed of fraud: a dishonest client and dysfunctional boss. I spent my first weekend in AC persuading my parents to introduce me, or reintroduce me, to their casino friends, acquaintances, and colleagues, and spent my first week explaining my presence to many concerned and baffled adults, to people who didn't recognize me from childhood, to people I didn't recognize from childhood, and to strangers and all and sundry who'd make the time to talk Trump with me. The word I heard most often in reference to the GOP candidate—from Steven Perskie, the former New Jersey assemblyman and state senator whose original gaming referendum brought casinos to AC in 1976; from Nelson Johnson, the New Jersey superior court judge who wrote the book version of *Boardwalk Empire*; from Don Guardian, one of the few AC mayors in my lifetime not to have been charged with corruption; from Ibrahim Abdali and his cousin who'd only identify himself as Mohammed, Afghan refugees who sell pipes and bongs and martial-arts weaponry on the Boardwalk—the word I heard most often was *failure*.

Every Trump account I was given in AC described a man so extraordinarily bad at business, or at being anything besides a business celebrity, that he was forced to switch from building casinos to branding casinos with his name, that polysemous pentagrammaton he charged his partners to use and then sued them to remove once the decaying properties became a liability. In the 1980s and '90s, the casinos with which Trump was associated constituted between a third and a quarter of AC's gaming industry. The Playboy Hotel and Casino, which was founded in '81, became the Atlantis in '84, and went bankrupt in '85, was acquired by Trump in '89 and renamed the Trump Regency; he renamed it again as Trump's World's Fair in '96, and it was closed in '99 and demolished in 2000. Trump Castle, built in cooperation with Hilton in '85, was rebranded as Trump Marina in '97, was sold at a loss to Landry's Inc. in 2011, and is now operated by Landry's as the Golden Nugget. Trump Plaza, built in cooperation with Harrah's in '84, went bankrupt and shuttered in 2014 and now just rots.

And then there's the Trump Taj Mahal, which Trump built with the help of Resorts International in 1990 on financial footings so shaky and negligent that by the end of the decade he'd racked up more than $3.4 billion in debt, including business (mostly high-interest junk-bond) and personal debt, which he handled by conflating them. By lumping them together under the auspices of a publicly traded company, Trump Hotels & Casino Resorts, he dumped all his burdens onto the backs of his shareholders even as he continued to treat his casino receipts as profits, to be raided and reinvested in development in New York. Even while Trump Hotels & Casino Resorts bled an average of $49 million a year into the late '90s, even while its share price plummeted from $35 to $0.17 through the early 2000s, Trump himself continued to receive a salary in the millions, not to mention bonuses and the monies his personally held companies made from his publicly traded company leasing office space in Manhattan's Trump Tower and renting Trump Shuttle helicopters and Trump Airlines airplanes to fly around showroom acts and high rollers. Trump Hotels & Casino Resorts finally went bankrupt in 2004, and in its restructuring became Trump Entertainment Resorts, which itself went bankrupt in 2014 and was fire-sold to Icahn Enterprises, whose subsidiary, Tropicana Entertainment Inc., has run the Taj into a $100 million hole. Carl Icahn, the conglomerate's chairman, was once a wary adversary who now endorses Trump, though he's declined Trump's offer to become the next secretary of the treasury: "I am flattered but do not get up early enough in the morning to accept this opportunity."

On July 1, at the height of the season, the Taj's unionized employees from UNITE HERE Local 54 went on strike, demanding a wage increase and the reinstatement of health and pension benefits suspended in the transfer of ownership. Negotiations were never scheduled; Icahn and the union couldn't agree on a venue, let alone an agenda. In early August, Icahn announced that he'd be closing the Taj after Labor Day. And so the fall forecast kept getting grimmer, with the loss of the city's most prominent casino and more than 2,800 jobs.

The Taj's demise would be chronicled throughout the summer by the *New York Times* and the *Washington Post*, in articles framed as analyses of Trump's finances. These articles, like the leveraged-debt practices they documented, were virtuoso feats, given that they were researched without access to the candidate's tax returns. But reading the articles induced headaches: all those loans and defaults and shell companies shattered, keeping track of them was like counting the beach, grain by grain.

The main issue I had with this out-of-town finance journalism, however, was that it was finance journalism: none of its unbiased sums could account for Trump's meanness—that petty, vile villainy that was being described to me when I was casting around for a place to write.

Because my parents had remodeled my old bedroom into the room of dusty, disused exercise equipment, and because AC has no leisurely cafés or bookshop spaces and its public library is open only 9 to 5, I prevailed on my uncle to make me a key to the office of one of his companies, Fishermen's Energy, a consortium of commercial fishermen who are trying to establish what would be New Jersey's first offshore wind farm, in AC. The building was the Professional Arts Building, which went up in the 1920s and flaunts it; its windows gave onto Resorts. I moved into the conference room, adjacent to the cubicles of my uncle's three employees, who, given Jersey's disinterest in renewable energy, didn't have much work to do—or to put it positively, had the occasional leisure to talk.

The receptionist, Karen Carpinelli, previously worked for a family-run Atlantic County–based neon-sign firm that found itself working for Trump, who preferred to contract with family-run firms because they were easily abused. Trump consistently failed to pay the full amounts he owed, which forced the sign-makers to inflate their prices: apparently the totals didn't matter, only the discounts did, and if Trump paid at all it was usually half of whatever they billed him. Fishermen's Energy project director Tim Axelsson, who hails from a distinguished fishing family in Cape May, recounted to me how, in 1988, Trump had planned to arrive in AC for the first time in the *Trump Princess*, a $29 million yacht formerly owned by the Sultan of Brunei and, before him, by Saudi arms dealer Adnan Khashoggi. The *Princess*, however, being one of the largest yachts in the world at the time, was too large to navigate the channel, and so Trump paid to have the channel dredged, which it was, without any impact studies conducted or permits obtained (though the NJ Department of Environmental Protection did issue a belated stop-work order). Fishermen's Energy COO and general counsel Paul Gallagher, who prior to working for my uncle served as AC city solicitor, once served as manager of the Jersey-Atlantic Wind Farm, whose five inshore wind turbines, situated hard by the inlet, help power the city's wastewater-treatment plant. When that project went up, Trump made a call: there were five turbines, he said, as if he were counting up the notoriously short fingers on his notoriously small hands, and there were also five letters in his name—did Paul understand? Would the Jersey-Atlantic people be interested in festooning the poles of their turbines with T R U M P? Apparently, Trump would let them do it free of charge.

And this was just the lore to be found in a single office—the lore that was dumped on me about five minutes after moving in.

ALL ALONG the Boardwalk, the sun-bleached, tattered banners read DO AC—the city's latest marketing catchphrase. The Boardwalk was a scrum of such imperatives, with Trumps on every side issuing edicts and diktats, offering bargains. Trumps in toupees and with their guts hanging over their change belts, out on Steel Pier, out on Central Pier, trying to get me to try the ring toss, though the rubber rings always bounce off the rubber bottles, or to try the beanbag pitch, though the lily pads they're supposed to land on are kept wet and slippery with a shammy. Try Fralinger's Salt Water Taffy, which contains no saltwater. Step right up and I'll guess your weight, or at least I'll make your wallet lighter. What American literature taught me—what Melville taught me in *The Confidence-Man*, what Poe taught me in "Diddling," that imagination or fantasy can be a form a greed, even a uniquely American form—the shills and carny barkers taught me first, at $2 a lesson: I would never win that stuffed elephant.

The Boardwalk's kitsch, the kitsch of Trump's former properties along the Boardwalk, merely reinforce how retro a mogul the candidate is: a throwback who doesn't care he's a throwback, who's barely aware he is, dressed to impress in a padded Brioni suit and a tie with a scrotum-size knot. After a sham career spent endlessly lauding himself as the last great product of the last great era when our country still made things, when our country still built, he now spends what's basically his retirement—which he considers America's retirement, his and its mutual licensing age—wallowing in sentimentality and goading with nostalgia. He's a magnate brat who in an age of rapid computerized transactions and exponentially unaccountable ethereality didn't make his name, such as it is, or his fortune, such as it is, on Wall Street, but rather in the old-school outer boroughs, and later in schmancier Midtown, developing what he'd inherited. He deceitfully prides himself on having employed real, tangible workers (including illegal immigrants and Mafia contractors) to build real, tangible things (which tend to have structural insufficiencies, and the same black glass that's used in TV/movie evil-overlord compounds and fascist government architecture throughout the Middle East and Central Asia). Not for Trump any bundling, derivatives, or microtrades—just the anachronistic micromanaging of flamboyant chandeliers and ornate door handles. He's the steak-n-taters CEO, not an asexual vegan baby of the algorithm revolution.

Making my rounds of the Boardwalk bars, it was eerie: how every person's take on Trump was the same, or was so precisely contradictory. Locals—especially those who knew the candidate's business history—vigorously loathed him, while visitors—especially those who knew nothing of that history—were equally passionate in their admiration and praise. "He's just another billionaire." "He's one of us." "He's a liar." "He's so honest." Common to the heated speeches of both were the apparent influences of alcohol and fear. Everyone I was meeting seemed drunk on fear: of the candidate, of their country, of themselves.

The ambient scare that Trump has put into the populace, and the way his calculated swoops through the news cycle moderate or exacerbate this emotionalism, regulating it like a professional thrill, reminds me more than anything of gaming: of what it feels like to put my money on the line. It's as if Trump—this vanity candidate, famous beyond law—is offering all of us a wager: that he can inflame his rhetoric and press his luck without ever pressing it too far—without alienating all women and black and Hispanic voters, and without getting too many Mexicans, or too many Muslims, or even just some white Democrats, beaten up or killed.

This, of course, is the only type of wager that Trump can ever make: a bet against America, counting on our dumbness, counting on our hate. He'd never take a turn at one of the properties he's owned; he'd never belly up to one of the voting-booth-like slot devices on which his AC businesses were based. Trump, a man addicted to success, and—if his oration is any indication—a man with extremely limited reserves of self-control, can't ever gamble, because he can't ever lose. I'd bet that Trump is barely even familiar with the table rules, for the simple reason that he doesn't have to be; all he has to know are the odds to know that he can't beat them. Having owned the house, he'll never tempt the house. All he can do is torch it. Which is why Trump won't lose the election, at least not in the reckoning of his supporters. Even if Clinton is declared the winner, most likely even before Clinton is declared the winner, he'll allege some sort of conspiracy; he'll blame someone else; no failure can be his fault. He'll accuse the game of being rigged—he already has. He'll indict the nature of the game itself, calling the political process both overregulated and underregulated, prohibitive in cost, inefficient, and just plain evil, and the sad thing is, he's not wrong.

The saddest thing, though, is that the only place in AC—the only place in America, it seems—where you can go to escape his sped-up diet-pill tics and wiggy tirades is one of his former casinos. Two weeks into its union strike, two weeks before the announcement of its closing, the Taj was a mess of stained carpet, moldy walls, leaky ceilings. Regular maintenance personnel had been replaced by skeleton crews of temp labor, but since the dealers aren't unionized, the casino was open, and remained so locked down, so focused on keeping me unfocused and yet maximizing my TOD (German for "death," but also casinoese for "time on device") that none of its screens carried anything but ads for inoperative buffets and upcoming circus extravaganzas that would have to be canceled. No CNN, not even Fox.

The Taj, like most casinos, has primarily always been a slot palace, and any square footage given over to table games has to favor those that most favor the house: roulette, where the house edge is 5.26 percent, and craps, where the house edge is 1.4 percent, over the easier to understand and easier to play blackjack, where the house edge is .5 percent (slots are allotted a house edge of up to 15 percent). To put these numbers into words: you done never had a chance. But as long as your pleasure quanta (booze, food, shows, and carnal atmospherics) outweigh your pain quanta (your losses), research has demonstrated that you'll keep playing along, encouraged through every bad roll or spin or card by PR exhortations, or by the living example of Trump—whose image used to be everywhere in his former casinos; whose image is now everywhere except in his former casinos—telling average citizens that they too can beat the odds and become winners, the ultimate avatars of American exceptionalism.

This type of self-empowering yet self-sabotaging, ignore-all-the-facts-and-go-for-broke gaming faded from fashion through the '90s with the spread of numeracy through the internet. Data was suddenly determining, because it had suddenly numerated, everything, and I can recall how by the time I was working at Resorts it already felt ridiculous that anyone would go to a casino to play any game besides poker—a game in which players compete not against the house for its money, but against one another, for one another's money, with the house taking only a tiny percentage of each pot—the vigorish or rake (typically 10 percent, up to

$4). It follows that casinos don't make much money on poker, and so the few AC casinos that still provide a room for it do so begrudgingly, with the hope that the players' companions—their angry spouses and nursing attendants—will find their ways elsewhere in the casino, to the slots.

Of course, one of the beauties of poker is that it doesn't have to be played in a casino—it can be played anywhere, for cheaper. The first and last semiregular private game I ever participated in began at the Broadway Suites on W. 101st Street and Broadway in New York on some weekday in 1998—just after my summer at Resorts—and ended on that hungover, smoke-fogged day after Election Day 2000, when an art-history student left the table to hyperventilate on the floor by the poky Zenith TV and an ethnomusicology student went to find a dictionary—a paper dictionary—to check the definition of *chad.*

After the stolen election of *Bush v. Gore,* which was the first election I and all the other players in that game were eligible to vote in, it became normal for people of my generation—kinda-sorta millennials immersed in the mathematics of poker, who followed the Texas hold 'em tournaments just then being televised and played in online games between IRL games and participated in online poker tutorials—to also immerse themselves in all manner of election-relevant math, to memorize and rattle off how many electoral votes each state had, and to argue about which were the decisive counties or districts or, as in the case of Florida, precincts in each state; which percentage of overvotes or undervotes would have to be counted as legal votes for which outcome to occur and, of course, how the outcome would've been different if all the states, or if certain states, had split their electoral votes along the lines of their popular votes as opposed to awarding them winner-take-all—all of which were topics too specialized for, because too inaccessible to, prior generations of American voters, which kept up with the elections through the morning paper and evening news, without any interactive maps or regression analyses or aggregated (ranked and weighted) polling.

Of course, whenever you're reading a poll, what you're reading are odds, which you can convert yourself by flipping each percentage into a fraction, subtracting the numerator from the denominator, and dividing the difference by the numerator. For instance, if Clinton is leading Trump in the popular vote 48 percent to 42 percent, as she seemed to be throughout much of the summer, her odds of winning are 1.083:1 and Trump's are 1.38:1. However, with the electoral vote determining the presidency, each online bookmaking site projects its own 270/538 split to calculate its odds (for parimutuel betting, meaning, say, a bet that Clinton will beat Trump by any margin; and for betting the spread, meaning, say, a bet that Clinton will beat Trump by the exact margin of 330–208). Ironically enough, most of the more reliable sites that'll trade US election action for cash are registered in the UK, the Bahamas, or elsewhere abroad, because America doesn't quite approve of betting on politics—not because betting on politics is cynical, but because it's considered a variety of sports betting, which is illegal in all but four of the states.

America: a country in which even a noble law has to be justified through the drudgery of precedent and stupid technicality.

WEDNESDAY NIGHT, the Local 54 picket crowd chanting and waving placards outside the Taj was just about as sparse as its poker-room crowd and equally gloomy: "No contract, no peace!" "All day, all night, Taj Mahal is out on strike!" The poker room was all chairs, stacked and overturned and empty chairs, and two tables of half bachelor-party fools, half "grinders": pseudo-pros who if they'd been playing just against one another would've played tight, would've folded and waited, "grinded" in the interest of making a slow, steady profit. But tonight they were staggered between the bachelor-party fools, so the strategy was different, the tactics were looser. The old hands were taking advantage.

Out of shape, insomniac, amphetamined sharks, not circling, just sitting, around the circular tables, sniffing for blood or for related signs of weakness. They were waiting for a player—for a neophyte, a tourist in murky waters—to lose patience and bet, or to match or raise a bet of theirs or another's, not out of any discernible logic or psychology, but because discipline is boring, and no one comes to a casino to be bored.

That's the moment the bullying sets in—the daring, the teasing and taunting, which is often unvoiced, and often merely imaginary.

This was how it kept going down: an older, more experienced player would, after a period of concentrated play, without warning go all-in, which gambit the bachelor-party rubes would alternately take as a temptation and a test, a measure of their capacities and so of their manhoods: whether they had the balls to accept the challenge—because if they'd had the intellect, they might've declined it—or whether they were too cowardly, too womanly, too whipped. And so they'd let themselves go; they'd let themselves react—they'd become, I guess, reactionaries.

This whole circumaggravating and cumulatively gross situation of being provoked, or feeling like you're being provoked, and then having to resist responding to the provocation, and then not being able to resist responding because you're convinced that it's all just a bluff, seems to me quintessentially male. It forces its victims to choose—quickly, and in a sensory-overloaded, blinking, chirping environment—between the logical brain and the lower instincts, between getting out and getting even. Now, project all this parasexual, paraviolent incitement from the ludic, monetized poker table to the shouldn't-be-ludic, shouldn't-be-monetized political stage, and what becomes discernible is the liberal-conservative dilemma, in which the societal demands of social responsibility (folding) vie against the ego demands of animal appetite (staying in play and even raising the stakes), and reveal themselves to be zero-sum irreconcilable. This, I've decided, is Trump's technique: not numerically probabilistic or predictive (and so of limited use against the experienced), but a crude psychologizing that seizes on every weakness at the American table—all the poverty, ignorance, bigotry, and pride—and squeezes, until the electorate mans up and loses everything.

I tried bringing this up at the table, which consisted—at this ungodly and incalculable fluorescent hour of night/morning, of two grinders; two superdelegates, let's call them, who'd broken away from their bachelor party; and one guy who could've been anybody, in short-sleeved hoodie, board shorts, flip-flops, and wraparound sunglasses, who kept complaining about how difficult it was to get a proper martini during a labor dispute.

Grinder 1, Ricky from Philly, was annoyed and snapped at me: "No talking politics." Grinder 2, Bill from Bridgeton, said, rather mysteriously, "That stuff don't throw me none." Bachelor 1 said, "Fuck Trump, but fuck Hillary harder." Bachelor 2: "Bitch hasn't gotten it in a while—you can tell."

I left the table about $100 up after ten or so hours—$10 an hour being just about what I'd been paid nearly a decade ago at Resorts. I stumbled out onto the Boardwalk, into wan sunshine and mist, and found myself recalled to AC's marquee agon: what you're supposed to do with yourself once you're finished gambling. The only movie theaters left on the island were an IMAX, which was only showing *Warcraft*, and a filthy handful of XXX stroke rooms. The live-music scene is now dominated by dinosaur acts (Vanilla Ice appearing with Salt-N-Pepa and Color Me Badd; Rod Stewart: The Hits), and the art scene, which used to feature the paintings of Sylvester Stallone, has since been demoted to displaying the paintings of Burt Young (who played Uncle Paulie in the Rocky franchise). Also: it wasn't a beach day.

I got some (expired) yogurt and (unripe) plums from the Save-A-Lot, AC's only remaining supermarket, crawled back to the Professional Arts Building, and clicked through the news. There he was: Trump, the constant companion, the always-on, always-up-for-anything enabler. A link on the homepage of the *Press Atlantic City* brought me to a better-funded paper's lead item about Trump's campaign chest: Trump's campaign, it was being reported, had basically nothing left in the bank, and yet had paid out more than $1 million for each of the past few months to Trump's companies, for use of Trump Tower office space and Trump-owned transportation—this was the Taj scam 2.0. In an accompanying clip, Trump was asked for comment, and answered in incoherent banalities before swerving into remarks about terrorism—or what he always refers to as "Islamic terrorism." Unwilling to go to my parents' house and unable to sleep in the office tilt-and-swivel chair, I picked up the book I'd brought from New York: *The Theory of Poker,* a how-to classic of 1987 written by David Sklansky, a native of Teaneck, dropout from UPenn's Wharton School of Business (where he just missed overlapping with Trump), winner of three World Series of Poker bracelets, and arguably the greatest draw and hold 'em player of all time. In the very first pages of his book—which I must've read a dozen times before, for a reliable soporific—Sklansky lays out his Fundamental Theorem, which in my amped-up wakefulness now hit me like a law on the level of gravity's: "Every time you play a hand differently from the way you would have played it if you could see all your opponents' cards, they gain; and every time you play your hand the same way you would have played it if you could see all their cards, they lose."

Here, presented in sane, rationalist fashion, was the insane truth behind this race: that if Trump just keeps on being Trump, and if Clinton keeps pivoting and responding to his every move, he wins. The only way that Clinton can win, according to Sklansky's schema, is to force Trump to become inconsistent, but since Trump is already inconsistent—since he's consistently inconsistent—that's impossible.

As my uncle's employees dragged in for the day, I formulated what I'll call Cohen's Hypothesis, or the Cohen-Clinton Lemma: *If the game you're playing becomes impossible to win, then your main opponent is probably yourself.*

A TABLE, WHERE ANYONE can sit, where fortunes are exchanged: this was America, at least the East Coast white-folks version after the Civil War, when a limitless sense of economic growth seemed to derive not only from the Union's victory but also from the untrammeled expanses of the Western frontier and the prodigious influx of young single European males who kept washing up on the New York shore, including, in 1885, a 16-year-old from Kallstadt, Germany, named Friedrich Trumpf, who came here, as many have, and many will always, not to worship freely or speak freely, but to avoid his homeland's compulsory military service and try to make some dollars. Trumpf—father of Fred, grandfather of Donald—landed at Castle Garden, New York, America's first immigration depot, which processed more than 8 million people over its four-decade career. By the time Friedrich Trumpf had become Frederick Trump—by the time he'd become not just a US citizen but a prominent hotelier and brothel owner catering to gold rush prospectors and an elected justice of the peace—Ellis Island was open, and processing about 5,000 immigrants a day, not a few of whom would spend their dotages in the nearly 30,000 low-income residential units that Frederick's son, Fred, would put up throughout the New York outer boroughs with the aid of state and federal subsidies and tax abatement. Fred's son, then, came of age at a time in which about one-third of the country—over 100 million "ethnic whites"—had a parent or grandparent who'd entered this country through Ellis Island. These were Donald's people, well before he ever leveraged them into a voting bloc. After all, these were his tenants; he was their landlord. The Trump family's low-income, multifamily "projects"—in Flushing, Jamaica Estates, Bensonhurst, Sheepshead Bay, and Brighton Beach—were intended to be, and remain, substantially whiter than the projects of any other city developer.

Today, a hundred years after the peak of white ethnic pilgrimage to America, go to those projects—to those white ethnic enclaves that still exist in New York—and ask the people you meet where they're from. Poland, Ukraine, Russia, et cetera; the post-Soviets constitute the latest and perhaps last wave of Caucasian "pilgrims" whose acculturation and class ascension has been the dominant narrative in modern American life, until recently suppressing the narratives of forced immigration (black slavery) and genocide (Native Americans). I tried a version of this interview method at the Irish Pub on St. James Place in AC—one of the city's best, and only, noncasino bars—and about half of the people I asked said things like "AC," or "Brigantine," which is the next barrier island to the north, or else they just named the last bar they'd come from: the Chelsea, or the Ducktown Tavern. But the other half of the people—say ten or so—without any prompting answered my purposefully vague question of "Where are you from?" by offering "I'm half Irish, a quarter German, and a quarter French," or, the arithmetic be damned, "I'm half Dutch and two-thirds Italian." The people who gave me those answers were male and, respectively, 26 and 28 years old. In AC, the Irish Pub is festooned with Irish flags; the Italian restaurants and bakeries in Ducktown, the historic Italian neighborhood, are hung with Italian flags; and next to both the Irish and the Italian standards there's always the Stars and Stripes. In the Northside, which is the historically black side—AC is so confused that it's flipped the compass, so that the Northside is, in terms of true cardinality, the western-bay-facing side of the island—I didn't notice many flags at all.

These white ethnic roots—of "Italians" who don't'a speak'a Italian, of "Irish" who grew up in the Pine Barrens or on the Delaware River—creep into every element of Jersey life, even East Coast life, and if you try to resist their stifling, a gang of wife-beater-and-tracksuit-pants-wearing thugs always drives up to intimidate you with baseball bats and tells you to "suck it," in that rough, tough, I'm-from-a-cop-family-that's-also-a-crime-family accent that doesn't derive from any specific language or identity anymore, but rather from TV and movies and mongrel desperation. The sheer, shrill insistence on the continued relevance of these identities strikes me as a valid if annoying reaction to the fact that their progenitors—the immigrants themselves—have all just passed away. But with grandparents and parents gone, the identities they bequeath are perverted, which explains why first- and second-generation American ethnic whites have abandoned their forebears' traditionally pro-union, pro-welfare liberal Democratic politics, which were formed by the Great Depression, and amid the privations of the Great Recession found solace in the more medieval aspects of their

Catholicism: social conservatism and racism. The result is a Republican Party that's a caricature of the Republican Party, in the same way that Jersey Irishness is a caricature of Irish Irishness, and Jersey Italianness a caricature of Italian Italianness (don't even get me started on the Jews). With this swift deracination of ethnic whites, America will lose its last sense of white authenticity, of genuine white culture—of a whiteness that's always opposed and been opposed by the whiteness of the WASPs, the Puritans who once were this country's elite—and a massive segment of the populace will have to resign itself to an undifferentiated paleness: a whitehood-as-non-identity, that of a people from nothing, from nowhere, denied grievance. Ethnic whites are a dying breed, who've understood only just recently—historically speaking—that all they can be now is American whites, in an identity loss that they regard in their trauma as an identity theft—perpetrated by "minorities" and "illegals," and aided and abetted by that African Muslim Obama.

IT'S NO COINCIDENCE, then, that rage has become the prime political motivator of the white electorate today—given that theirs is both the last generation able to remember any ethnic white grandparents and the first generation whose standard of living has not appreciably improved on their parents'. Trump's supporters resent this so vociferously, it's as if a birthright's been revoked: this was not the country that "they," meaning "their ancestors," had been sold when they bought the boat ticket over. This was not what being white was supposed to be like, scrapping for the same scarce jobs with diversity-hire blacks and Hispanics and, worse, refugee Middle Easterners. Feeling wronged, feeling disillusioned, they retreat into mendacity and yearning—though because they have no faith in an economy that's betrayed them and have lost all belief in what their forebears called the American Dream, they yearn not for a better future, but a better past. This is what Trump means by promising to "Make America Great Again": promising to return us to a time that never once existed.

Call it the American Daydream, an idyll that's intimated and hinted at everywhere in AC: on billboards, on postcards, in the lobby of the Professional Arts Building, which is festooned with giant photomurals of all the old, since-demolished, European-style grand hotels that lined the Boardwalk at its bustling heyday, the totality of the scene captured in a black-and-white that's been touched up, that's been rosied, with pastels. Every day, taking the elevator up and down for cig breaks, I'd study these murals—I'd try to resist their calliope charms. Put starkly, the danger at the heart of sentimentality or nostalgia is how directly it's predicated on racism. That Great America that will be Made Again and the politics of racial oppression are, like the ingredients of any decent melting pot, inseparable.

AC was founded in 1854, just a year before Castle Garden opened in New York. Before then, Absecon Island was just a desolate sandspit that had been fishing-and-hunting grounds to the Lenni Lenape, and then a farmstead to the Quakers, and finally a minuscule, ramshackle village inhabited by the family of Revolutionary War veteran Jeremiah Leeds, whose cousin, "Mother Leeds," was said to have spawned the Jersey Devil.

The idea to turn the island into a faddish summer health resort on the Victorian British model belonged to Dr. Jonathan Pitney, a physician, while the financial support and practical infrastructure were supplied by Samuel Richards—the scion of a rich South Jersey bog-iron and glass dynasty—who built the Camden–Atlantic line, a railroad that connected AC with the cross-Delaware cities of Camden and Philadelphia. The railroad's engineer was Richard Osborne, who named the city after its ocean, and predicted that it'd become "the first, most popular, most health giving and most inviting watering place" in America.

But the city's first megahotel, the United States Hotel—in the mid-1850s the largest in the nation, with more than 600 rooms—was initially mostly vacant. The Philadelphia elite balked at the rude accommodations, the grime and smoke of the open-air train, and the rapacious swarms of greenheads and mosquitoes. However, the main reason that the moneyed set wasn't overwhelmingly attracted to AC seems to have been tradition: the good old families tended to already own good old second homes, to which they'd repair not for a weekend—because weekends, then, didn't exist—but for the duration of the summer. To give further context: beachgoing and ocean swimming didn't become established forms of recreation in America until well after the Civil War, and at the time of AC's founding the coastal towns that later became famous as resorts—the closest to AC being Cape May, but also Rehoboth, Delaware; Newport, Rhode Island; and Cape Cod, Massachusetts—were still significantly active as ports.

AC's regular clientele, then, turned out to be regular people, "redbloods" with "blue collars": people, usually of recent immigrant stock, who couldn't afford second summer homes and typically had short vacations, or just a short single day—Sunday, God's day—to profane with their pleasure. The first time a Camden or Philadelphia carpenter and his family could afford to pay another person to cook for them; the first time a Newark/Elizabeth or New York longshoreman and his family could afford to pay another person to eat and sleep in their house—to room and board in their roominghouse or boardinghouse—they went to AC: the only vacation destination on the East Coast to which there was direct rail service; a city clapped together out of water and sand and dedicated almost exclusively to making the Irish, Italian, and Jewish urban poor feel rich, or richer. This is the process that created the American middle class, which in America—unlike in Europe, where the middle class had always been a feudal characterization of artisans and merchants—became more of an ideology, or more of a delusion.

For nearly a century—the 1850s through the 1950s—new immigrants and their native-born children would come down to AC, dress in their finery, and stroll along the Boardwalk, which was invented to keep sand out of the hotels but became a lucrative commercial property that was also publicized as an education and an exercise. This raised wooden and later wood-and-metal midway featured displays of America's emergent production power (exhibitions of Edison's innovations stretching out over the piers) along with ample opportunities to consume (branches of the most fashionable Philly and New York boutiques selling ready-to-wear clothing at the very advent of mass tailoring), establishing in the imaginations of promenaders the commensality of industrial progress and personal, familial, and even ethnic progress. At its height—say the turn of the century—at the height of the day—say once the sun had tipped toward the bay—this grand boulevard took on the aspect of a nonstop parade route, a pageant of freshly minted Americans floating by, all showing off and being shown off to, mutually reveling in having "arrived," in having "made it."

Of course, this sense of success was premised on a fundamental injustice. Check out any of the old photographs, any of the old film reels, and note the rolling chairs—AC's signature white, wheeled wicker chairs that were first introduced for the use of the disabled back when the city was still being touted as a retreat for the infirm, but later adopted by able-bodied patrons. The people pushing those chairs are black—the only black people on the Boardwalk. In the surviving images of nearly all the early hotels, restaurants, and bars, it's the same: blacks in white uniform, their faces almost always averted from the camera.

At the turn of the 20th century, one out of four AC residents was black, a ratio that gave the city the highest per capita black population of any city above the Mason–Dixon Line—which, if it didn't take a sharp turn to form the Delaware border, would overlay the county line between Atlantic and Cape May Counties. Much of this porter and kitchen and laundry workforce was made up of freed slaves and their descendants, who came north because the hospitality industry was more profitable, and had more opportunities for promotion, than, for instance, sharecropping. What this meant was that black AC was occupied with its own—more precarious, more constrained—attempts at achieving upward mobility: compared with black communities elsewhere in America, black AC was prosperous.

These symbiotic or parasitic middle-class fantasies based on racial oppression were the great sustainers of AC—along with vice, which unites people of all colors. An economy reliant on seasonal tourism wouldn't countenance Prohibition, and from 1920 to 1933 the city just outright ignored the Eighteenth Amendment. Forget speakeasies and clubs: alcohol was sold out in the open in the city, whose wharves had ample docking space for bootleggers' ships. Opium dens and brothels were tolerated, but the numbers games were more popular, as were more formal card parlors. All this vice was allowed to flourish under the dispensation of the local machine, which was nominally Republican but operationally total: it had no opposition, and it even handpicked which Democrats would lose to it. The first boss of this machine was Louis "Commodore" Kuehnle, owner of Kuehnle's Hotel, and its most infamous was Enoch "Nucky" Johnson, who spent three decades remuneratively installed in the nothing position of Atlantic County treasurer. Kuehnle and especially Johnson exacted money from the rackets in exchange for police protection—turning the police into a mercenary force for the rackets—and after pocketing shares for themselves, invested the rest into purchasing peace from the state and federal authorities, and in acts of patronage both major (building Boardwalk Hall) and minor (charities for orphans and widows). This unlawful but effective arrangement wouldn't just grow in scale, it also served as blueprint for allied endeavors. In May 1929, the summer before the stock-market crash, Johnson assembled a conference in AC—the prototype convention of this convention town—that attracted the emissaries of organized crime from Philadelphia, New York, Kansas City, Detroit, Chicago, Cleveland, Boston: Al Capone, Lucky Luciano, Meyer Lansky, Dutch Schultz, et al. This was the founding of America's first national crime syndicate, and it was Capone who—in a late-life interview he granted the FBI from Alcatraz—most succinctly summarized their agenda: "I told them [in AC] there was business enough to make us all rich and it was time to stop all the killings and look on our business as other men look on theirs, as something to work at and forget when we go home."

Capone's statement was prophetic—just not for the gangsters, or the "illegal" gangsters at least. Hard times came to AC with Prohibition's repeal, and were compounded amid post-WWII prosperity—under the machine of State Senator Frank "Hap" Farley, and the more independent and so less effectually venal city governments that followed—with the gradual nationwide legalization of nearly every vice that previously had been most safely and most dependably available within the city limits. More than the rise of air travel or the proliferation of private car ownership and the interstate system—more than the miracle of air-conditioning—this was the greatest threat to AC: permissiveness abroad, as municipalities throughout the States became more accepting of sin, or just more interested in taxing it.

Nevada approved gaming in 1931 in response to the crash. By the end of the '50s, Las Vegas had emerged as the gaming capital of America, and by the end of the '70s—when New Jersey finally caught up and officially approved gaming in AC—the precedents were already in place for the rash of both tribal and nontribal approvals that followed.

And so the continued expansion of casinos, and the continued extrapolation of casino principles into governmental policy—into the scaffolding of a state that can deny its citizens all but the barest amenities of welfare and health care, only because it sanctions their conviction that they're all just one bet, one lever tug, away from becoming rich, chosen, elect, the American their ancestors had aspired to be, the American that God had intended.

○ ○ ○

I FOUND MYSELF—America finds itself now—at the very end of the Boardwalk. The very end of this immigrant's midway lined with cheap thrills and junk concessions, pulsating with tawdry neon and clamoring moronically. The end of this corny, schmaltzy Trumpian thoroughfare that entertains us with its patter and enthralls us with its lies.

And yet we stay here, on the Boardwalk, because it's safer than stepping down. Because we trust the Boardwalk, at least we trust that it can't be trusted, and so we're reassured by how straight it seems, how direct it seems, the way it lulls us back and forth. We're threatened by the pavement, by the city that we might find there. The ghost streets off Pacific Avenue and Atlantic Avenue, off Arctic and Baltic—all the broken roads and dead-end alleys left behind by Wall Street, which underlies every street of the Monopoly board.

Here, unlike on the Boardwalk, everything is real. Here everything is both ghostly and real. Vacant houses. Apartments boarded up to protect against squatters. Eviction and foreclosure papers flap from the doors like tongues. NOTICE TO CEASE, NOTICE TO QUIT, papers keeping the sun out of the windows. The apartment houses rubble away into empty lots pierced by wind and drowned in the shadows cast by shuttered penthouses. Empty lots spontaneously converted for parking, a sign in the windshield of a Saturn: PLEESE DONT TAKE ME. Walking between the Boardwalk and the Professional Arts Building, walking between the Professional Arts Building and my car spontaneously parked in a dirt and, after the rain, mud lot, meant passing the porn store, which, especially if I was making the trip after sunset, meant getting accosted. By men who slept on the beach and spent their waking lives on the street, where there were fewer police and more chances to hustle. Corner of Pacific and MLK Jr. Boulevard. Guy trying to bum cigarettes. Guy trying to bum a dollar for booze. Guy trying to deal to me. "Yo, got coke, yo." "Molly, molly." "Got syrup." Taking my money and not coming back. Trying it all over again the next day unabashed, and then when I told him I'd rather just talk, he got in my face, called me gay, called me a cop. A woman telling me how the check-cashing place would only cash checks made out to people with addresses in Atlantic County by people or businesses with addresses in Atlantic County. Telling me she lived in Georgia, or had once lived in Georgia, and her only hope of returning was this check from her cousin in Camden. "Ain't Camden Atlantic County?" "No." "What Camden then?" "Camden County." "Goddamn."

Another woman giving me some woe chronicle of how she was running to catch a jitney and fucked up her knee, and how with this one knee blown and all the weight on the other, the other got fucked up too, and how she got laid off, either because of the injury or unrelated to the injury, and was homeless now, and how every time she went to the doctor's office she just got a referral to another office that was never open, and no lawyer would take the case and sue the jitneys. Man standing in the midst of the lot holding up either a raincoat or construction tarp, screening a woman squatting pissing or shitting.

Down at the Boardwalk's terminus, by Oriental Avenue, by night, the seagulls keep flying into the Revel and dying. Or they flap and limp around a bit before dying. You never see or hear the impact, you just get what happens after. Immense white gulls, flapping, limping, expiring. They fly into the Revel's giant vacant tower of panes and break their necks, because without any lights on, the glass is indistinguishable from the sky.

OFFSEASON

On November 1, the New Jersey State Department of Community Affairs rejected Atlantic City's budget and rescue plan. On November 8, Election Day, the New Jersey Casino Expansion Amendment failed. New Jersey itself went for Clinton, but the country went for Trump. The morning after, while Clinton delivered her concession speech, New Jersey's Local Finance Board voted 5-0 to approve Governor Christie's immediate takeover of Atlantic City. I am writing this on that morning—it is November 9. A gray day, humid and rainy. My parents called to say that it was the anniversary of Kristallnacht. +

DAN IVIC, *SUNRISE*, 2012–15, OIL, ACRYLIC, OIL STICK, AND COLLAGE ON CANVAS. 96" × 70".
COURTESY OF THE ARTIST AND LYLES & KING.

OLD SHIP

Kristin Dombek

This is the fourth print installment of Kristin Dombek's advice column. Questions can be sent to askkristin@nplusonemag.com.

DEAR HELP DESK,

I spent the past decade going to war. Seven times, not that I think the number of times matters.

Everyone who's been to war has their own perspective on what it was and so it means different things and has different effects. Whatever it did mean—and I'm not sure it meant anything, though it did have a certain purity—the war experience has produced some consequences for me which I need help figuring out.

The problem is that I've come out of adjustment. There are lots of ways to describe it, but to put it simply I'd say that most things about life feel pretty pointless and the outcomes trivial. Even though the outcomes are not trivial at all. It just feels that way. Everything feels stupid and lame and disconnected from me. I guess there has been a kind of desensitization or something.

It's more than a purely conceptual problem, however. There is also the drinking, sleeplessness, drugs, violence, and contempt for everything, including the future. Though I believe these are all just symptoms of that first thing, the weird alienation.

I woke up last week in a pool of blood. I don't remember how the night ended, but I do remember a brutal fight with a drug dealer that didn't end well. The head wound and all the broken stuff was fine, I was just thankful it wasn't worse. I mean, it could still get worse.

How to rehabilitate? I'm not sure. Getting more war feels like the best option, but that can't be right. That's why I think it's not PTSD. It's more like post-traumatic stress dependence. Though I'm probably making that up. Either way, it's what happens to an adrenaline addict in the time after they hit their highest high. I want more.

Or maybe I want something else. Sometimes I say the names of friends who were killed, then I say my name. It is clear I would rather have their name. Looking back, I guess the preference might have been to die there.

But at the same time I don't now want to be dead.

What I want is to live in the moment safely. Currently, I feel like I might be so far in the moment that I have no connection to anything, past or future, or even right beside me. It's just me alone in the moment, being a dangerous idiot. Or maybe I'm living in the past. I don't know. Certainly, the problem is that I don't know. Maybe I'm just having a long tantrum.

I drink every night until things get ugly. Most of the people who knew me have left.

Perhaps the "stress" is what does this. Though it's not stress, really, it's repeated long-term exposure to the possibility of being blown apart suddenly. It's the length of the exposure that does it to you, I think. When you're living with that, it seems you have to stop planning for the future in order to face it. You can't have dreams and hopes and still operate in a world like that. At least I couldn't, though I didn't realize it at the time. Maybe it's just not that easy to live after you accept your death.

I loved my last girlfriend so much it felt like I wanted to consume her. Instead, she broke apart trying to keep up with me. She started as this beautiful innocent creature, but she spent two years trying to relate to me and then she was too much with me and she nearly did not pull up in time. It reminds me of a story about an American soldier with his Vietnamese girlfriend during the war there who responded to their issues by getting naked in the shower and fucking with a live grenade suspended between them, which they set off as they came. I wonder how much that girl really wanted to be there, objectively. She only wanted to be with him, and it cost her. I guess he consumed her. I hope she wasn't faking her orgasms.

Maybe it could be a problem of narrative. I was living a story and now the story seems to have stopped and I don't really care, that's what it feels like. Like an old ship rusting in a bay somewhere. Or maybe more accurately, just a car accident. I've come to a stop, metaphorically. That's what it feels like. What it looks like is also very much like a car accident.

I don't know what to do, is the point. What should I do, Kristin? Everything's all unhooked and I've become a hazard.

I'm not going to put my hand up for treatment, so don't suggest it. Medication isn't the answer, but it's the only answer the professionals will insist on. I'll figure this out or I won't, there's not another way, and it's not a big deal.

Let me rephrase the above: I know what to do—stop drinking, get clean, straighten up, move forward—but nothing I've found can make me want to do it. Or I can't do it. Maybe I'm just delaying the shower grenade.

Still, it feels like a philosophical problem to me. I tried to reread *The Myth of Sisyphus* but I couldn't figure out how to get past that first paragraph.

Signed,
Old Ship

DEAR OLD SHIP:

You say that this is a philosophical problem, and I will try to treat it as one, leaving aside the issues you raise and dismiss along the way: whether the number of times at war matters, what war is and what it means, whether you have post-traumatic stress disorder or post-traumatic stress dependence, whether it's stress or exposure or a problem with narrative, and whether you should be running, not walking, to whoever is left to watch over you through the seventy-two hours of shaking and sweating, the week it will take to glimpse what your mind might someday feel like at rest, and the year or so of learning to live in drag as a civilian in our dull kingdom while you build the fortress of friendship you'll need to save your life from that first paragraph of *The Myth of Sisyphus*, the one you can't get past, which Camus begins with bloodless certainty: "There is but one truly serious philosophical problem, and that is suicide."

I hadn't read the book, but because you couldn't, I've read it now. Suicide is the only "serious philosophical problem" for Camus because life, stripped of the old metaphysical reasons for living, is like pushing a rock up a mountain. At the top you watch the rock roll down, and return to the bottom to push it up again. You probably don't need to reread the book to remember: suicide is not, for Camus, an appropriate response to this condition. Awareness of its absurdity is. Accept the world's silence in the face of your nostalgia for meaning. Refuse hope, fraudulent transcendence, and religion wherever you find it (even existentialist philosophers who are not named Camus are too religious). Maybe this is the beginning of real thinking, the beginning of consciousness itself.

If I am tempted toward advice-column heroics by your question—and of course I am: Could I be the one to answer the question of why to live?—Camus cautions me. "One does not discover the absurd," he writes, "without being tempted to write a manual of happiness." He insists his book does not recommend a belief or a course of action; it merely describes "an absurd sensitivity that can be found widespread in the age," an "intellectual malady." But Camus does approve of some responses to the absurd more than others, which some people I've known have managed to adopt as a belief system. Embrace the repetition, get as much life as possible, count it up. Seduce lots of women like Don Juan, whom Camus admires. Write novels that really get at how hopeless the hopelessness is, as Camus himself did. Gather experience without pretending at meaning. There is an appealing intellectual self-sufficiency to this approach, which Camus suggests might even earn one a measure of contentment, as if Sisyphus at the summit, watching the rock roll down the mountain, "concludes that all is well."

It was 1942 when Camus published this book, 60 years after Nietzsche had declared God dead. What remained of the grand narratives and ideologies had shattered in bloody war. Twenty-four years later, *Time* posed the question anew on its cover: "Is God Dead?" If the question, put this way, is less in vogue now, Camus still describes so well the way the world feels when it rubs up against our nostalgia for the old meanings: silent. And empty; the "God-shaped hole," we called it in Sunday school, assuming this must be what the hearts of nonbelievers always felt like. In your case, I guess it would be a war-shaped hole. There are other names: closing time, the end of the party, the desert of the real. Because whatever the story was about—the God you'd get to be with later in heaven, the cause worth fighting for, your country, your art, your masculinity, your heroism (I don't know what you did those seven times at war)—it always runs out.

I don't know from war, but I know this about despair: its hegemony is to try to make everything look the same, to get you to mistake the hole at the end of one story for the whole world.

But life is so much more various than Camus describes. Some ways of living are more like pushing a rock up a mountain than others. And I don't think you would have written if you didn't suspect that this were true.

If you get high as fuck every night and follow the occasion to its logical and bloody conclusion, for example, your life will definitely feel like you're pushing a rock up a mountain over and over again. But let's say you stop doing that. Let's say you *stop drinking, get clean, straighten up, move forward*. Maybe you have to learn to do something difficult for you, so new it doesn't feel like repetition, at least for a while. Maybe it's a new job, and someone there befriends you; maybe you develop friendships with a group of people, and each friend has a life that is different from yours. Say you become as interested in their lives as you are in your own, and begin, despite your hopelessness, to support them. Maybe you even fall in love with someone who is not consumed by you but who is different from you and you can see it, who surprises you every day. Let's say you begin to find a calling, a way to make not just your immediate life but some broader world more hospitable, more meaningful, and safer for others than it would have otherwise been. At this point, your life won't *feel to you* so much like pushing a rock up a mountain as it did before, or not so much like a ship rusting in a bay, to use your image. I would argue that then your life *is* different, that you're *not* rusting in a bay.

Maybe from the satellite perspective of philosophical objectivity, you'll still look like a dude pushing a rock up a mountain no matter what you do. But let's look more closely. Go to street level, look again. Some rocks are heavier than others. So much so that some should barely be called rocks. There may be some allegorical resonance between the existential labor of making meaning of one's life and the actual drudgery of forced, repetitive manual labor, for example, but I doubt anyone who's actually doing forced physical labor, anyone consigned against their desire to domestic labor, any wage slave, would mystify the difference between the two.

You asked for philosophy and I am bringing it, late-night dorm-basement style. But I'm not just splitting hairs. This variety in our actual experience suggests—I think—that Camus got the question wrong, or that the question itself is the problem. The only important philosophical question isn't why we each, individually, might choose to live. It's how to live with each other, given that the facts of our lives are contingent on the facts of others'.

The truly depressing thing about the world isn't how quiet it is, in the face of our nostalgia for old-time religion and nationalisms and conventional gender categories and essentialist philosophies. The world is noisy, and overwhelmingly various. The truly depressing thing is our unequal access to the possibility of living free and in community, to finding meaningful work, to choosing to live in ways that are less like pushing a rock up a mountain.

Sometimes I say the names of friends who were killed, then I say my name.

I don't know what you mean when you call war "pure." But this may be one way in which it is: it lifts the veil, shows you're interchangeable, in a world that is heartbreakingly unfair. It could have been you at the other end of the gun, the drone, the bomb. It could have been me, exposed every day for ten years to the possibility of being blown up. But it wasn't, and if my life as it is now depends on it not having been me, it depends, too, on your suffering. Your friends who can no longer deal with your nightly car crash probably look at you and see it, too. Your anger, this accident you've become, could be theirs, and how then could they live? They turn away.

The question of suicide, Camus's question, turns away, too. It pretends it's your individual existence that's important, and isolates you from this truth of the world. To be a civilian depends on others going to war. The creation of wealth depends on the creation of poverty. The privileges of whiteness depend on the construction of "race" through violence both spectacular and banal. The heterosexual paradigm depends on the denial of the actual variety of our desires, and on and on—and you might have been born into any other position than the one you were. I'm ranting, I'm sorry, but my point is that any question that tries to isolate the individual from this mess—to pretend that anyone's position in the world is autonomous and individually earned—seems to me, right now, false. The mess is depressing, but the question that keeps us from living in it (Why live at all?) is a prison.

The better question is less elegant. Given the violent ways we as humans try to control our contingency and exchangeability and vulnerability, how should we live, and act toward others, whom we otherwise might have been? How do we shake the persistent illusion of our own unique centrality and stop fighting for it at the expense of others? It's a very big question about the world, but it's also a better question for you: how do you get to the end of the story of war, get the war out of your body, and yet remember what is important about what you have seen? *My friends' names, and then my name.*

YOU WANT a philosophical principle to give you some motivation to get out of the bay in which you're an old ship, rusting. You want the clarity, the rigor, and the strength of philosophy to give you a reason to do what you have to do next. But ever since I read your letter I have been thinking about poetry—specifically a poem by Mark Doty called "Visitation." In the poem, a man hears that a young humpback whale is stuck in a nearby harbor. The man is depressed, grieving something or someone. What he is grieving is unnamed in the poem. The world is "dark upon dark, any sense / of spirit an embattled flame / sparked against wind-driven rain / till pain snuffed it out." He assumes the whale is experiencing the same pain; it is stuck in the bay, helpless, its ability to navigate its way out confused by sonar or who knows what human technologies and environmental atrocities. In language that treats the whale as a metaphor, Doty shows us that the speaker is projecting only his own pain:

> . . . grief
>
> has seemed to me itself a dim,
> salt suspension in which I've moved,
> blind thing, day by day,
>
> through the wreckage, barely aware
> of what I stumbled toward . . .

But when he goes to visit the harbor, he sees the actual whale, and begins to realize that for the whale, it may not be "that way at all." He begins to perceive, or interpret, this whale's own experience, and realizes what he's witnessing might not be a helpless, trapped thing, but a joyful being. Maybe the whale is playing, greeting the humans gathered along the wharf by swimming near them and breaching. It teases the edges of the harbor, blows exuberantly, moves in ways the speaker can't help but recognize as pleasurable. "Enough," the speaker writes to himself, to his way of seeing things only in despair. When the young whale is done checking out the harbor, he or she swims out into the sea, not stuck at all—just visiting. And this visitation—*"Holy Infant, Little Marie"*—inspires the poem's ending:

> . . . even I
> couldn't help but look
>
> at the way this immense figure
> graces the dark medium,
> and shines so: heaviness
>
> which is no burden to itself.

And the last lines, which I have been wanting to write to you since I read your letter:

> What did you think, that joy
> was some slight thing?

For you, given what you've experienced—the war still going on in your body and mind, a war that demands repeating every single night—for you, joy would not be slight or sensible, either. I doubt it would be prefaced by some philosophical realization, some calm progression toward a principle that meant you, as an individual, should live. Compared with war, and in the context of the unfairness of the world, joy is ridiculous, impossible, unreasonable, absurd, an apocalypse of the way you're living now. It would be heavy and it might even be frightening. It escapes you now precisely because it is such a big fucking deal, because it doesn't make the kind of sense you want, because it is radically different from violence but also from certainty, from what you already know. And it will come only if you realize that it is not just about you, your life. It comes in being able to feel others again, as Doty describes feeling the whale, to recognize when others are visiting you. I don't know what to call this. "Communion," says my friend Matt, who is writing quietly, too, a few feet away. So let's call it that: communion.

I first heard this poem years ago, when I interviewed the poet Kathleen Graber. She is a friend, and I knew that in middle age she'd abandoned her job teaching public school and her well-appointed suburban home to live meagerly and dedicate herself to learning to write. I was interested in the question you're asking, at the time—how do people change their lives, their beliefs, completely?—and was interviewing people across the country who had. I knew that before this conversion experience there had been a series of deaths in her family, and then she herself had a cancer scare, but I didn't know what she'd say:

> I had been a philosophy major as an undergrad and I really, because my parents were so volatile and my mother was so . . . Reason had no impact on her, right? She was just not open, you could not reason with her. I had really dedicated my life to being a reasonable person.

One year she got roped into taking a bunch of kids to a poetry festival in New Jersey. At the time, she says, "if somone had come in and put a gun to my head and said, 'Name a living American poet,' they would have had to shoot me." After a long and complicated bus ride, she arrives at the festival and sees Mark Doty read:

> I remember very clearly—he read a poem called "Visitation," about a whale coming into a harbor at Cape Cod and being stranded, and his thinking that it could only end badly, and at the end the whale does leave the harbor, and it ends with the rhetorical question: *[with wonder]* "What did you think, that joy / was some slight thing?"
>
> And I think that what that poem did was it asked—there was something about that poem that was very, very wise, but it was a kind of wisdom that wasn't about logic. It was a wisdom that was of another species entirely. And I had not realized how desperately hungry I was for this other kind of wisdom that wasn't a wisdom that had its root in something you could reason your way toward.
>
> And I was just totally blown away by this poem, I just thought I want to learn to do that. Whatever that is—oh, that's a poem? I wanna learn to do that

As in Doty's poem, the change in Graber's story about Doty's poem comes as the result of a visitation, an illogical communion that introduced *a wisdom of another species entirely.*

Both Doty and Kathy were mourning. To grieve is to become vulnerable to feeling, to acknowledge what you've seen of the world's worst violence, to mourn the buddies you've lost. Mourning is awful, but it is also hopeful, because it acknowledges that a story could matter that much, that the lives of others matter that much.

You are asking how to get out of the bay, but you keep leaving it, choosing the car crash, the pool of blood. Your problem, I think, is not how to get out, but how to stay there long enough to let the story run out, so that you can actually begin to mourn. This is more hazardous than putting the bender on repeat, in a way. It puts you at risk of caring again.

YOU SAY YOU'VE COME to the end of the story, but I think you're stuck in the middle of one. And by writing me, you've written yourself into another story, in which an angry and despairing man (my father, a boyfriend, a male friend) calls on me (or so I believe) to name a philosophical principle that will make life seem worth living again. Can I be heroic, stronger than the woman you consumed, the one who nearly didn't pull up in time? Am I smart enough? Are real orgasms worth all the violence? Given the timing of your letter and the familiarity of its language, I suspected that you were not who you said you were, not someone who's spent time at war at all, but one of my depressed fiction-writing friends, fucking with me by posing the great white whale of advice-column questions: Why live?

For a while, I blocked this question, turned away from the temptation to pretend to know, better than you, better than anyone, why and how to live. After a while, I even asked my friend if he was you (he said he wasn't). But the suspicion, the way your letter was so familiar that it read like fiction, was what eventually helped me see: it doesn't matter whether you are who you say you are. Your story is familiar, whether it's fiction or not. If it's not fiction, it's still a story, you're still in one, and I have something to say in response. It's not that smart, what I have to say, and it's not that heroic. It does come from a place of knowing what it's like to wake up morning after morning unsure of whether it would be better to be dead or alive. It's that it's in precisely the vulnerability you're trying to escape, not in strength or certainty, that you might begin to see why and how to live.

Nearly every morning, bloody news. To love the world hurts the heart. Your letter hurt, and then, when I began writing to you, my boyfriend had just had a dark night of the soul, wishing for death, and the next morning I woke up and learned from the internet that an old, dear friend of mine, someone familiar with despair and with the logical conclusion of a bender, had disappeared completely. Then I learned that a man had walked into a gay club in Orlando and shot down half the dancers. Instead of writing to you, I had a go-to-pieces on the couch for a few hours.

Love is love: it began to flood the internet as I lay there. It's probably why there were religions in the first place. As if it's true, as it says in the chapter from 1 Corinthians I kept reading that morning as I watched the news scroll by, as if it could be true: *love never fails.*

I understand, as much as a coddled civilian can understand anything—my rocks are pebbles, kicked up the slightest slope—that it must feel the most compelling thing in the world to continue to choose violence, to your drug dealer, your friends, your mind, your own body. But sometimes we have to do things without knowing. With the body, at least for me, you have to take a leap, have faith that if you can hold on and make it one or two weeks without a constant hangover, you will know things you don't know now. There is a feeling in the body that is just the feeling of physical well-being and it connects you to all humans and other animals and maybe even trees. The war will always be there, but you have a choice of what to give your attention to. The familiar story, the car crash, or the thing more radical and more frightening and wiser than strength: to grieve, to renounce the story and that paragraph you can't get past, to make peace with your contingency and interchangeability so you can see the other side of it, to the connections that make it a joy, sometimes, to be alive.

In other words, it does sound like you need to get clean. But don't do it for the sake of health, or morality, or to submit to some new system of discipline. Do it so that you can begin to grieve what's happened to you, and what you've done, and the people you've lost, and the stories you've lost. Do it so that you can prepare your body and mind so that when joy comes, you'll recognize it. Do it so your friends return, and when they start to tell you why they don't despair, you can actually hear them. In place of the story that ran out, then—instead of crashing the car, instead of getting out of that bay—my suggestion is to find some way to stay in it. There's no other way to find out if you're just visiting.

Yours truly,
The Help Desk +

CLEON PETERSON, *THE PRACTICE OF MASTERS*, ACRYLIC ON 9PC. WOOD PANEL (FRAMED BLACK). 60" × 60".
COURTESY OF THE ARTIST.

DON'T BE SCARED, HOMIE

Sam Frank

UFC 194, LAS VEGAS, DECEMBER 12, 2015

THE FIRST TIME I BINGED on mixed martial arts, or MMA, was on a 2014 JetBlue flight from New York to California. Those take a long time. One channel was replaying UFC 168 and all that preceded it, including the eighteenth season of *The Ultimate Fighter*, the reality show created by the Ultimate Fighting Championship to promote new talent. The season's drama revolved around the *fuck you, bitch* animosity between the teams' coaches, Ronda Rousey and Miesha Tate, who had fought before in 2012. At UFC 168, they rematched in the cage. Rousey tripped and arm-barred Tate to remain undefeated, then refused to shake hands. Next, the best counterfighter of all time, Anderson Silva, who had just lost his title to All-American wrestler Chris Weidman, got his own rematch. In the second round, Silva aimed a left kick at the back of Weidman's leg, and Weidman lifted his shin to block. The impact snapped Silva's tibula and fibula in half. The fight was over. I glanced sideways to see whether my rowmates were judging me.

A year and nine months later, on a work retreat, I found my friend Matt hunched over his laptop watching 261-pound Roy "Big Country" Nelson get clinched up against the octagonal cage with a head underneath his chin, and collar-tied and foot-stomped and face-elbowed and gut-kneed and catch-wrestled and dirty-boxed for a sweathoggish twenty-five minutes by the merely 239-pound Josh "Warmaster" Barnett, Matt's favorite fighter. Two months after that, on a date late at night, I checked my phone on a street corner and saw Holly Holm triple-shatter

Rousey's jaw with her left leg in a hundreds-times-retweeted GIF. A month later, Matt was buying the José Aldo–Conor McGregor pay-per-view for his birthday. McGregor was the most marketable fighter in UFC history, a 27-year-old wiry Irish guy with a handsome beard, gaudy suits and tattoos, a talent for trash talk, and a wicked straight left hand—"the Celtic Cross." But McGregor was up against the terrifying Brazilian champion Aldo, who once trained acrobatic capoeira but had focused his game into a simple, punishing one: hard leg kicks, hard knees, hard punch combos; fundamental Dutch kickboxing plus the best defense in the sport. They had spent a year feuding after fights and at press conferences—McGregor playing Mystic Mac to the crowd ("It will be done in one"), Aldo, who barely speaks English, steely with a scar across his cheek from childhood. I read an oral history of Aldo via his former opponents that was eight thousand words of "That dude will, like, cut your muscle" and "That was actually the most pain I've ever been in, because it was all soft tissue" and "softball-sized welt" and "I literally could not feel my fingers rubbing against the skin of my leg because the nerves were dead" and "My sternum hurt for, like, *almost two years.* I'm not even sure what happened." By this point I had started training at a Brazilian jiu-jitsu academy. The ref says, "Let's get it on!" Aldo jumps in with a left hook chin-first but McGregor's left beats him to it, the punch, the punch, Aldo's chin and body falling forward-left stiff into the mat. In thirteen seconds Aldo has lost for the first time since Jungle Fight 5 (yes) a decade earlier, McGregor has the 145-pound featherweight belt and is sitting atop the Octagon, Matt is like speechless, and there it is, I am a fan of MMA.

UFC ON FOX 17, ORLANDO, DECEMBER 19, 2015

THE FIRST ULTIMATE FIGHTING CHAMPIONSHIPS, in the early '90s, were freak-show tournaments of all sizes and styles: shootfighting vs. kung fu vs. savate vs. kenpo vs. wing chun vs. pencak silat vs. aikido vs. ninjutsu vs. Brazilian jiu-jitsu. There were no time limits: the ref didn't stop the fight until someone either gave up or was knocked unconscious. For the first few tournaments, BJJ won. That is, the not particularly athletic Royce Gracie, through his command of mechanical and positional advantage, took down and controlled, then submitted via stranglehold or joint lock, much more imposing men. In fact, Royce's half-brother and UFC co-owner Rorion chose Royce to compete precisely because of his scrawniness compared with their studly brother Rickson. The Gracie family, based in Rio, had invented Brazilian jiu-jitsu, Japanese judo adapted for self-defense on the ground against bigger opponents; seventy-odd years later they set up the UFC to showcase what it could do. (John Milius, who cowrote *Dirty Harry* and directed *Conan the Barbarian* and *Red Dawn*, came up with the idea for the cage.) In his first fight Royce Gracie took down an American boxer (wearing only a single glove, in case he had to tap out with his other hand) and submitted him. Then he choked out Ken "The World's Most Dangerous Man" Shamrock, a pro wrestler who'd cut his MMA teeth in Pancrase, a Japanese promotion that had former fake wrestlers fight for (mostly) real. In the final he faced a Dutch karate champion who had viciously beaten a giant sumo wrestler and an extra-large kickboxer. But Gracie calmly body-locked him, tripped him, rolled him over, and strangled him. Temporarily it was settled: BJJ was king.

Then Olympic-style wrestlers and Red Army–style sambists, grapplers as well but much better athletes, came in with adequate submission defense, and they could take anyone down and pin them forever—"lay and pray"—or, better yet, control them while hitting them in the face: "ground and pound." By UFC 5, Ken Shamrock had tightened up his anti-submission game; he fought Royce Gracie to a draw by lying on him for half an hour. After that, Royce retired and Rorion sold his share of the business. For a time wrestlers dominated, but eventually kickboxers and boxers learned how to sprawl—when a sweaty man dives for your legs, you jump your own legs back and drop your chest on his back—and how to stand up when someone was on top of them. This was "sprawl and brawl." The arms race continued from there, a layering of styles and moves and countermoves.

Meanwhile the UFC was professionalizing. It replaced *Bloodsport*-like tournaments with boxing-style match-ups, introduced judges, weight classes, and five-minute rounds, required gloves, banned Speedos, fish-hooking, head butts, and groin strikes . . . and still only New Jersey would sanction events under these new Unified Rules. In 2001, a company called Zuffa (Italian for "fight"), founded by Dana White, supposedly a former boxer from Boston, and the Vegas-casino-owning maybe-mobbed-up Fertitta brothers, bought out the promotion for

$2 million. They used television strategically, broadcasting some fights and *The Ultimate Fighter* on male-oriented Spike TV, and later on Fox and its cable channels. They bought out competing promotions and worked to get the sport legalized nationwide. They strengthened drug testing and secured a Reebok sponsorship, a raw deal for fighters, who used to get five figures for an Xtreme Yogurt logo on their shorts' ass but now had to wear a standard-issue kit in exchange for a few thousand bucks. And thus the UFC halfway cleaned up the mess that is two people giving each other brain damage in a cage.

By late 2015, the pay-per-view UFCs were approaching number 200, and the company had launched parallel series on network TV (UFC on Fox) and cable and streaming (UFC Fight Nights on Fox Sports and UFC Fight Pass). UFC on Fox 17 features Michael Johnson, among the fastest guys in the sport and the big favorite, against Nate Diaz, a year removed from a loss by unanimous decision to 155-pound Rafael dos Anjos. Diaz had come in injured, undertrained, and five pounds overweight, which cost him 20 percent of his purse; dos Anjos kicked Diaz's lead leg till it almost fell off, then beat him up on the ground.

Nate is the younger brother of Nick Diaz, a UFC fighter with perhaps the sport's biggest cult following: in the ring and out, he enacts most transparently the psychodrama of professional combat, which he lives and bleeds and hates. The brothers grew up poor in Stockton and trained for the burritos the older guys would buy them after practice. They learned jiu-jitsu from Cesar Gracie (it's a big family) and boxing from Richard Perez, who had coached a local-hero world champion. They're triathletes and quasi vegans. Nick, born in 1983, turned pro in 2001 and became World Extreme Cagefighting champion two years later, after which he began bouncing between the UFC and competing promotions; Nate, two years younger, followed in 2004. In 2006, Nick lost to Joe Riggs by decision, then fought him again in the hospital ("He came to my side of the hospital"). In 2007, Nate won *The Ultimate Fighter* and a UFC contract, while Nick was in Japan brawling with Takanori Gomi, who hit him with "some little *hadouken* fuckin' punch" that unleashed a blood river from under his eye before Nick suddenly choked him out with his shin, a *gogoplata*. This victory was overturned by a pot test, no contest, six-month suspension. In 2008, Nate triangle-choked Kurt Pellegrino—legs figure-foured around his neck and left arm—while giving him the finger with both hands; Nick almost started a fight with K. J. Noons after a fight with Muhsin Corbbrey by taunting Noons, "Don't be scared, homie." A year's pot suspension for Nick in 2012. Then in 2015, after lying down in the cage because Anderson Silva wasn't fighting him hard enough, five years and $165,000—again for marijuana metabolites. Afterward Nick gave a harrowing interview to Ariel Helwani, MMA's fanboy Studs Terkel, in which he talked about forced ADD drugs and constant childhood uprootings and his girlfriend killing herself after his first pro fight, and how "I'm the original Conor McGregor. . . . He wouldn't be who he is if it wasn't for me. Nothing against him. I'm the original real deal. I never did steroids in my entire life. I had to learn how to fight the real way and the right way. That's why I'm the best fighter in the entire world," and, more than anything, how awful he feels that he made his brother into a fighter too. "I got us in this, and if I don't make any money, I don't have any way to get us out."

So Nate Diaz is in it, and now here's Michael Johnson. Two long, slim guys at 155 pounds, Diaz left-handed, smooth rubbery muscle tone, goatee, no tattoos, punches himself in the chin eight times when his name is called. Like a boxer, heavy on the lead leg, which Johnson tries to kick out from under him as dos Anjos had, but Diaz picks it up to check with his shin. It's back and forth for two minutes. Diaz almost whiffs on a hooking right and turns it into a slap—the patented Stockton Slap—to get a few extra inches. No huge pain in it, just humiliation. Diaz ducks and mocks, puts his hands out like *What*, waves his hands *Get at me*, throws the 1–2, left jab–right cross, shakes his head *Naw*, 1–2, arms down by his sides and shoulders shrugging, leans back and crosses his arms in B-boy stance, punches and slaps, occasional kick, ticky-tack stuff, 1–2, "I hurt you," points at him, slaps him harder and shows him the palm that perpetrated, head kick, hands behind Johnson's head in a Thai clinch and knees him, Johnson's coach yelling "Don't give up" (don't ever say that to your fighter), and with ten seconds left Johnson actually takes Diaz down, jumps on Diaz's back as Diaz stands up, Diaz does a forward roll to shake him as the bell sounds, and then for ten seconds more the fight is done but Diaz is somehow still working on a knee bar while sticking his hands up to celebrate and Johnson's just kicking at him in frustration.

The judges give the fight to Diaz unanimously, and Joe Rogan, the blocky bald comedian and UFC color commentator, enters the cage for the postfight interview. "This was a beautiful performance against a very tough guy in Michael Johnson," he says. "How do you feel about it?" What follows on television is one long bleep, but it can be reconstructed. "Fuck that," Diaz says, a mouse forming under his left eye. He points his finger—in the air, at the camera. "Conor McGregor, you're taking everything I worked for, motherfucker. I'm going to fight your fuckin' ass. You know what's the real fight, what's the real money fight. It's me, not these clowns that you already punked at the press conference. Don't no one want to see that, you know you beat them already. That's the easy fight. You want that real shit, right here." And now both hands are up to point at his own shoulders: this fucking guy. "Hey, and another thing . . ." At which point, feeling bad for the network censors, Rogan takes the mic away.

Backstage, Diaz talks to Helwani about McGregor. Diaz: "When we fight, we're going to fight. Fight-fight. For-real fight. He thinks he's the ninja. I'm the ninja. *Ninja Gaiden*. *American Ninja*. Real motherfucking ninja. This ninja martial artist right here, I started that shit. That shit came from Stockton. . . . *Double Impact*, *Lionheart*, *Armageddon*, all this. American ninja, Irish ninja, represent your shit, homeboy." The perfect monologue from a kid raised on Van Damme movies and video games who used to have *sai* fights with his brother in their mom's living room and is now, finally, coming into his own. What's the key to beating him, Helwani asks. "Train hard and ninja his ass up."

BELLATOR 149, HOUSTON, FEBRUARY 19

THERE ARE MANY PROMOTIONS besides the UFC, in America and worldwide, but at this point only one even notional competitor: the Viacom-owned Bellator, which lately has been making fights with UFC castoffs and occasionally outbidding its rival for a legitimate talent. Bellator 149 is the former, a B-roll headlined by the third fight between Royce Gracie, now 49, and Ken Shamrock, 52; and co-main-evented by Kimbo Slice (Kevin Ferguson), 42, and Dada 5000 (Dhafir Harris), 38, former street fighters from Florida, where Kimbo became famous a decade ago for his backyard-brawl videos.

This is the kind of fiasco the UFC is good at avoiding. Gracie knees Shamrock in the balls, then TKOs him—the ref hadn't seen a thing. Shamrock afterward: "There's no way I'm going to fight from that point.

I just can't, because my boys are not where they're supposed to be." But before that, Dada and Kimbo, two overstuffed middle-aged men, Dada with a neon-red Mohawk, lying almost still on top of each other and unable to stand up, or clinched and panting asleep on each other's shoulders, or throwing slow wild punches between deep breaths and zombied half-alive on their feet, until finally in round 3 Dada gets punched once more and staggers halfway across the ring and collapses like a cliché of a dramatic death scene. Twitter is quick to call it the worst or best fight in MMA history. Shamrock and Kimbo pop for steroids.

In April, Dada went on ESPN Radio to say he'd had kidney failure caused by rhabdomyolysis from his forty-pound weight cut, and two flat-lining heart attacks in the cage. "I was dead. When you talk about your spirit leaving your body, looking at the light, but it's not your time to go, and you actually get brought back, that was my situation." Supposedly everyone's medicals checked out beforehand, but then they were fighting in Texas, whose commission is notoriously one of the worst in the country. There's a death or two a year in MMA, and none yet in the UFC. (By comparison, there were 923 recorded boxing deaths between 1890 and 2007.) Some MMA deaths are, predictably, due to brain hemorrhage, others to undetected heart conditions, and others to weight-related kidney issues. More deaths occur in unregulated fights than in regulated ones: on Twitter there are sometimes clips of small-promotion fights that the ref hasn't called off even after a guy has been strangled five seconds past pass-out and you wonder that more people haven't died, but somehow the fact is they haven't, it isn't like boxing, where you can be up against the ropes getting pounded in the head for rounds upon rounds. In that sense it's slightly more humane.

UFC 196 LAS VEGAS, MARCH 5

IN THE UFC, YOU EAT what you kill. You're an independent contractor, and the basic contracts suck, starting at around $10,000 to show up and another $10,000 if you win, out of which you pay your team and for expensive medical exams. The payout escalates a few grand with each win, and gets negotiated higher only if you have leverage. Which means that you have to "move the needle," which means that you sell $60 pay-per-views, which means that the UFC tracks your social-media metrics to see what kind of money you're making them. Based on that, you can *maybe* get a percentage of the PPV money and a bigger base rate (there's no fighters' union to keep the UFC honest). Ronda Rousey and Nick Diaz move the needle, and all-timers Georges St-Pierre and Anderson Silva and Jon Jones move the needle, and Conor McGregor moves the needle more than any fighter the UFC has ever had. He knows how to sell himself and sell a fight, and he makes millions and brags about making millions and has license to do almost whatever he wants, especially because he fights frequently and takes opponents on short notice and knocked out one of the five best MMA fighters ever in thirteen seconds.

So now McGregor wants to be 145- and 155-pound champion—no one's held two belts simultaneously—and he's booked to fight lightweight champ Rafael dos Anjos, but dos Anjos breaks his foot two weeks out. Everyone wants this fight—McGregor is a multimillion-dollar payday—but Nate Diaz, no top contender, is the name on fans' lips: because of his post-Johnson call-out, and because he's a Diaz, even though Nick has always been the star. UFC president Dana White once infamously said, "Nate Diaz is not a needle mover. . . . His numbers, he doesn't pull the numbers in." But Nate planned it this way with his brother, he took the fight with Johnson just so he could call McGregor out afterward, and now Nate finally has his leverage. He even tweets, about McGregor, "He's going to have to get on his knees and beg." The UFC kneels. Negotiations drag on, and Diaz doesn't have time to cut to 155 anymore, so they settle on 170 instead—welterweight—and sit down for a press conference. McGregor: "I should create my own belt. I am, in myself, my own belt. It doesn't matter if it's featherweight, lightweight, welterweight. It's the McGregor belt. That's it." Diaz: "You fight midgets. You knocked out three midgets, and you're pumped up. I'm a real motherfucking fighter, fighting grown-ups, all the time."

A lean and muscular man (for women it's more complicated) can drop about 10 percent of his body weight by drinking too much and then too little water and cutting out carbs for a few days—every gram of glycogen in your muscles holds three grams of water, and your muscles hold thirteen-odd grams of glycogen per kilogram, and your liver holds some more, and essentially if you watch your levels for two weeks before a fight and then jump in and out of a sauna and wrap yourself in towels and get the shakes maybe just slightly you can dehydrate yourself very efficiently. If you're good at weight cutting, like McGregor, you can drop more like 15 percent and go to your weigh-ins looking like a skeleton in a skin suit. Lightweights weigh in at 155 the day before their fight; otherwise they're normal-size men, who are nearly six feet and walk around at 175 or more, and thus lightweight is the deepest and best division. Welterweight is for big normal men, and featherweight is small normal. (Then there's heavyweight contender Stefan "Skyscraper" Struve, seven feet tall, 265 after a cut, and flyweight champ Demetrious "Mighty Mouse" Johnson, five-three and 125.) Diaz was being hyperbolic about midgets, but four of McGregor's previous five victims at 145 had been five-seven or shorter.

McGregor, barely five-nine, eats himself up to 168 pounds without a weight cut and looks muscular but sort of puffy. The six-foot Diaz is skinny-fat fresh off vacation in Cabo and enters as a gigantic underdog. The head games continue; McGregor has met someone who gives less of a fuck than he does. They're interviewed on CNBC, and McGregor's in a tailored gangster's suit and Diaz is in his usual black T-shirt, and the host and McGregor are ganging up on him.

HOST: What are your financial dreams? What, to you, means you've made it? A mansion, a Ferrari?

DIAZ: I don't know. I don't care.

MCGREGOR: Say it like it is, Nate.

DIAZ: Who gives a fuck? What the fuck is this, the money channel?

And walks out. Although CNBC is the money channel.

McGregor basically has one weapon—a great left hand that he times and places often perfectly—which he disguises behind looping karate kicks and crazy pressuring footwork, and for the first round and a bit he bloodies Diaz up with it, this hand loaded up to take a head off. But Diaz is rolling with McGregor's punches, deflecting their power; he's bleeding badly, but he has scar tissue, he bleeds easy, Diazes don't get knocked out because they train with real boxers like Olympic gold medalist Andre Ward, and they know how to take a punch. Conor is explosive but Nate's a triathlete, and no one can stand and trade at pace with a Diaz—their whole thing is to taunt opponents into brawls and then pick them apart with their infinite gas tanks and little half-powered punches. The first round is all McGregor, and so are the first two minutes of round 2. Then Diaz slaps McGregor, tags McGregor, slaps him some more, taunts him some more, knees him up against the fence and begins to open up, McGregor has one more flurry in him but Diaz hits two more combinations and McGregor has given up, he's hurt and tired, McGregor shoots a shitty panic takedown and Diaz sprawls, rolls him around, punches him a few times to expose his neck, and strangles him seconds later. It's over—everything changed in two minutes. Diaz walks around flexing like Gumby, mean-mugging with his face masked in blood, and rubs Joe Rogan's belly. "Nate Diaz, you just shook up the world. How's that feel?" "Eh, I'm not surprised, motherfuckers."

UFC 198, CURITIBA, MAY 14

McGregor, "obsessed," demands a rematch with Diaz, for UFC 200 in July. But then as the fight approaches he pretends to retire because he doesn't want to interrupt his training to do a press conference. His tweet to this effect—"Thanks for the cheese. Catch ya's later"—is retweeted 161,776 times. He's pulled off UFC 200: the UFC showing they're bigger than he is. You can't skip your promotional obligations just because you want to train hard and get your revenge. Nate Diaz spends his downtime training with Jean-Claude Van Damme and feuding with Justin Bieber; McGregor pimps a fight with unhittable retired boxer Floyd Mayweather. It's a stupid joke, a publicity stunt, an attempt to regain leverage—everyone should know that even McGregor's untested grappling would smother Mayweather if they fought using MMA rules, and McGregor's leg kicks would chop Mayweather down if they kickboxed, and only a mild stroke from Mayweather could allow McGregor to land a meaningful punch if they boxed; and also it's a guaranteed UFC lawsuit. Of course plenty of suckers bite. But finally Nate–Conor 2 is announced for UFC 202. Mayweather will have to wait.

In the meantime UFC 197 is a drag, and UFC 199 is the most unexpectedly violent and thrilling card of the year, and UFC 198 is held in Brazil, with at least one Brazilian in every fight—the kind of thing the UFC likes to do to shore up a national market ("World Fucking Domination," as they put it in 2013)—and I mention it only because of Demian Maia, a beautiful man. In 2007, he won the Abu Dhabi Combat Club championships—some sheikh decided to make grappling his country's national sport and fund the world's most prestigious no-*gi* tournament—and then signed with the UFC. His jiu-jitsu got him to 11–0. But then Nate Marquardt knocked him out in one punch, and Maia refocused on kickboxing; he lost a few more fights as opponents brushed off his weak jiu-jitsu takedowns, so he started training American wrestling more seriously; at age 38 he's become a complete fighter, disguised as a fourth-degree BJJ black belt. And now he does just enough striking, or striking footwork, to get in on your leg, chain-wrestle you down, float over your guard, take your back, and strangle you or crank your neck till your nose starts bleeding. It's become inevitable. He makes it look easy. Here at 198, against Matt "The Immortal" Brown, Maia does it again, backpacking Brown for two rounds before pretending to be hurt, luring him to the ground again, and locking in the rear naked choke. It's a masterpiece. The current trend in jiu-jitsu is toward dynamic submission-hunting from anywhere. But Maia shows that the old Gracie style—proceeding step by efficient step through increasingly dominant control positions—works if you perfect it. No one who hasn't taken BJJ likes watching him fight. I hope he'll be welterweight champion, and not only to annoy them.

UFC FIGHT NIGHT 90, LAS VEGAS, JULY 7

DANA WHITE LOVES, *loves*, to go on ESPN to break news, but that's the closest MMA comes to a normal media environment; otherwise the UFC is off on its own. Its subscription streaming service Fight Pass, on which this card is being shown exclusively, has every UFC fight ever, and it's a record of what a force the UFC has become. It includes the libraries of World Extreme Cagefighting, which had a lot of great light fighters, and the Japanese promotion Pride, where all the top heavyweights once were (including Fedor Emelianenko, who never fought in the UFC), and Strikeforce, which had Ronda Rousey and Miesha Tate as well as good big male fighters. This is because the UFC bought out all of them, took their assets—fighters as well as old fights—and shut them down. Fight Pass also shows Glory, one of the best kickboxing promotions, and the women-only Invicta, and Eurasia Fight Nights, which has a Russian announcer who can be counted on to say things like "That was unexpectable" and "Excuse my French, ladies and gentlemen. This is nearly terrific," and rusticated amateur hours like the Alaska Fighting

Championship (there's a raffle), and the Eddie Bravo Invitational, the most exciting grappling event going. There are of course many dedicated MMA news sites, and ESPN has ramped up coverage, but the best discourse takes place elsewhere. Half of what I've learned has been from podcasts like *Heavy Hands* and *Fights Gone By* and pseudonymous YouTube analysts and a Twitter user handled @GrabakaHitman, who's devoted his life to GIFing every last fight anywhere anytime. Exemplary tweet: "Can someone find a Fuji TV One stream so I can watch a Russian hand-2-hand combat expert fight a Mongolian wrestler on a moat at 4am? Thanks."

And of course, "Train by day, Joe Rogan podcast by night, all day!" That was Nick Diaz in the cage to Rogan at UFC 137 after beating B. J. Penn. What do you know about Joe Rogan? My sister used to watch *NewsRadio*, and Phil Hartman was amazing, and Andy Dick and Dave Foley and Maura Tierney and Stephen Root and Vicki Lewis and Khandi Alexander were very good, and Rogan was fine; who had any idea that he would become a paragon of some new American masculinity after a stint on *Fear Factor*, that show where people ate bugs? Now he has an incredibly popular hours-and-hours-long YouTube podcast where he sits around with his flat-earther friends and drinks Budweiser and talks DMT and flotation tanks and libertarianism and kale shakes and fighting, and he's likable despite himself and adjacent in confusing ways to other very contemporary ambivalent figures like Sam Harris the anti-Islamist meditating neuroscientist and Tim Ferriss the Silicon Valley lifehacker and Jocko Willink the Navy SEAL business consultant who wakes up every morning at four-thirty to lift weights and GET AFTER IT; the next thing I need ("need") to do is figure out what Rogan and Marc Maron think of each other. (On the other hand, Rogan and Ira Glass interacting is unthinkable.) Rogan, lately, is backing away from UFC color-commentary duties, and it's not that he's exactly been great at that job, but he is wildly enthusiastic, especially about jiu-jitsu, and manages to ignore or shout over his idiot partner Mike "Goldie" Goldberg, usually with an "Oh, he tagged him, Mike!!" It's a shame that Phil Hartman isn't around to replace him, or Orson Welles. During the events Rogan isn't working, he and his pals livestream alternate commentary.

Rafael dos Anjos's broken foot has finally healed, and here he is to defend his lightweight title, not against McGregor—who's now slated for his Diaz rematch—but Eddie "The Underground King" Alvarez, a boxer-wrestler from Philly whose wife sits in the crowd screaming *Eddie!* What a fight. I head to Twitter, where @GrabakaHitman has already synced up the video with the voices of Rogan and Joey "CoCo" Diaz, a comedian from Alvarez's neck of the woods. Here's what it's like (Rogan in italics):

> *Dos Anjos caught him with that left high kick. And that's what I'm talking about, he can add in—* [Alvarez feints left, loops a right hand through dos Anjos's guard, wobbles him.] Oh Jesus Christ. *Oh, he almost slipped him!* Oh Jesus Christ. *Dos Anjos is in big trouble!* Oh Jesus fucking Christ. Oh Jesus fucking Christ. *Alvarez is all over him.* [Alvarez is winging wide lefts and rights, but dos Anjos somehow stays on his feet.] Oh Jesus fucking Christ. Jesus. Oh Jesus. Fucking. Christ. *He's gonna win.* Jesus fucking Christ. Oh my God. Oh my God Jesus. This is fuckin' tremendous. *Oh! He decked him again.* This is heart against fuckin' skill, Joe Rogan. *Oh! Flying knee!* [Dos Anjos is backed up to the cage and Alvarez jumps into his head knee-first.] Nothin' but fucking heart. Nothin' but fucking heart. *Oh no! He went down like this.* [Alvarez falls down after the knee and dos Anjos climbs on top.] Oh Jesus. *Side control.* Yeah, but he don't know where he is. *Alvarez back up!* [Dos Anjos is obviously stunned, and can't keep Alvarez down.] He doesn't know where he is. *Alvarez is back up and he takes him down.* [Alvarez quickly double-legs dos Anjos and keeps punching him in the face.] He doesn't know where he is! This is heart against fuckin' skill! I'm telling you cocksuckers! I've been waiting for this fuckin' fight for three fuckin' months! This is what I'm talking about! This is what the fuckin' problem is with the UFC! [Dos Anjos has somehow stood up again, and still Alvarez is punching him.] *Look at him going to the body.* Every once in a while, you run into a brick fuckin' wall! This guy, Diaz, these people are savages! *Ohhhh!* [Alvarez is knocking dos Anjos's head into orbit with uppercuts, but the champ stays standing.] Look at this shit! You gotta kill this motherfucker! [Referee jumps in, waves the fight off.] That's it! It's fucking over! [CoCo Diaz, pounding the desk.] There's a new one fifty-five! Where's Conor McGregor now? Where's Conor McGregor now? This kid's Philadelphia. You dumb motherfuckers. *Eddie Alvarez.* [Coach Mark Henry jumps on Alvarez's back in celebration.] This is crazy. I told you this was the fight of the fuckin' year, you fuckin' momos. *Holy shit.*

○ ○ ○

THE ULTIMATE FIGHTER 23 FINALE, LAS VEGAS, JULY 8

WOMEN'S MMA IS a few years behind men's. Ronda Rousey remains the second most famous fighter in the world, after McGregor—she got incredible mileage out of her Olympic judo and pure bullying aggression, until Holly Holm, twice *The Ring* magazine's best female boxer, kept her distance, took her time, and showed up Rousey's limitations by breaking her face at range. Only a handful of other women rate with ranked men. Cris "Cyborg" Justino weighs too much to make 135, which is where Rousey and Holm fight, and the UFC has so far refused to start a 145-pound class. Then there's Joanna Jędrzejczyk and Claudia Gadelha, by far the two best 115-pounders. Gadelha has muscles that make you think steroids. And Jędrzejczyk (she likes Joanna "Champion," the Internet likes Joanna "Violence"), 11–0 and belt-holder since 2015, is a slightly built kickboxer with brutal elbows—one of the top strikers in the sport. Gadelha wrestles Jędrzejczyk down for two rounds, but Jędrzejczyk keeps standing back up, and by round 3 Gadelha is gassing out (big muscles guzzle fuel: the dangers of being jacked) and Jędrzejczyk is snap-kicking her in the face, elbowing her in the clinch, teeping her so Jędrzejczyk's toes dig right up under Gadelha's sternum—hitting her almost at will. Jędrzejczyk even, in a flourish, takes Gadelha down. When Gadelha waits on her back, legs up in guard, Jędrzejczyk kicks Gadelha's calf dismissively, walks away with her back turned, and pumps her fist in the air like a . . . violent champion. After losing the first two rounds, this stylish, evil woman wins the next three going away. Who the hell's gonna beat "little Joanna from the hood"?

UFC 200, LAS VEGAS, JULY 9

DIEGO SANCHEZ HAS BEEN FIGHTING approximately forever—since winning *The Ultimate Fighter* season 1 in 2005, and before that three years in King of the Cage and Aztec Challenge and Ring of Fire—and he thought he might have chronic traumatic encephalopathy from too many head blows. Nope, false alarm, he tells an interviewer for fifteen run-on unblinking minutes: "I'm sharp, I'm fast, I'm primed, I'm prepped, and I'm peaking . . . Cerebrum Brain Health Centers got this [points to his head] back to optimum . . . look at me, I don't look 34,

I am alkaline, alkalized, I'm on point, and I'm coming to dominate and destruct . . . I got my brain fixed, I got this shit balanced . . . the left side of my brain and the right side of my brain . . . blood tests where we ran my blood for 250 different cooked and uncooked foods . . . zero inflammation in my body, zero inflammation in my brain . . . three hours a day meditation . . . I was in the sauna doing eye exercises . . . the eyes are the brain and the brain are the eyes . . . I got away from the meditation because I'm all about Jesus Christ . . . but it's not the devil . . . this is training . . . now when all the guys at the gym are, *Waah, my body's catabolic, I need food, I need rest before my next training session*, Diego Sanchez is at the gym, outside, in a balance pose, in the ice bath, meditating, I mean Sanchez is on point, Sanchez is coming for the belt, I'm outside saying *Yes, yes, yes, yes*." Then this MMA Molly Bloom gets in the Octagon with Joe Lauzon, whose cauliflower ears make him look like Bat Boy, and is TKOed in two minutes.

Nate Diaz is interviewed cageside. McGregor's trash talk can't touch him. "There ain't nothing to say. The reality of it, in times of war he ain't even alive." What's the point of a rematch when you already could have strangled someone to death?

REPUBLICAN NATIONAL CONVENTION, CLEVELAND, JULY 19

After months of rumors, all of them denied by Dana White, the UFC gets sold for $4 billion to Ari "Brother of Rahm" Emanuel's WME-IMG talent agency: a two-thousand-times return on investment, of which the fighters see nothing. "The feeling I have is that I had a son, and they adopted it, sent him to study at Harvard, and now my son controls Wall Street," Rorion Gracie says proudly.

WME-IMG makes White's staying on a condition of their purchase. His role in the UFC is peculiar. He's a combination Vince McMahon and Don King: promoter and matchmaker and hype man and negotiator, hero and heel. He feuds publicly with troublemaking fighters, cursing at them for not fighting often enough, or fighting boring fights, or refusing fights on short notice, or trying to earn full market value. He pretends to reward company men, but screws them over, too. He's been on the cover of *Men's Fitness* more than once, most recently its Special Success & Big Muscle Issue: "Sculpt Huge Arms, Get Shredded Abs, Kick

Ass Like HIM!" In the accompanying interview, he gives an echt-Dana quote: "Believe me, the guys who deserve the money are the ones you don't hear bitching about money." He's petulant and straightshooting and a pathological liar and almost the biggest personality the UFC has. He loves *Family Guy*.

So guess who shows up at Donald Trump's GOP convention. "What's up, GOP?" White's more than a little shouty in his jacket and open-collar button-down, but his four minutes onstage are almost charming and almost plausible (this is the Dana paradox). In 2001, when all of America and John McCain hated this "human cockfighting," Trump called White and made an *actual* good deal for presenting UFC 30 and then 31 at the Trump Taj Mahal in Atlantic City. "Nobody took us seriously. Nobody. Except Donald Trump. Donald was the first guy that recognized the potential that we saw in the UFC, and encouraged us to build our business. He hosted our first two events at his venue, he dealt with us personally, he got in the trenches with us, and he made a deal that worked for everyone. On top of that, he showed up for the fight on Saturday night and sat in the front row. Yeah. He's that guy. He shows up." And, wouldn't you know it, "I've been in the fight business my whole life. I know fighters. Ladies and gentlemen, Donald Trump is a fighter." I would definitely pirate that pay-per-view.

UFC FIGHT NIGHT 92, SALT LAKE CITY, AUGUST 6

I SHOULD FEEL BAD about liking fighting, or liking fighters who are violent and ugly in their everyday lives, or liking fights until the moment when the referee *should* have stopped the beating and only then turning on my disgust. And I do, sometimes. But usually I just wish the fighters got paid better.

"We all fight to get paid," Nate Diaz has said. "But I'm also fighting for myself. If I'm not fighting, I'm dying." Lots of guys talk about how fighting saved their lives. Matt Brown is nicknamed "The Immortal" because he clinically died from heroin before being resuscitated, then moved on to OxyContin; when three acquaintances died in three months, he joined an MMA gym. Mark "The Super Samoan" Hunt's memoir is called *Born to Fight*: his father beat Hunt and his brothers with brooms and branches and for twelve years raped their sister; Hunt himself went to prison twice before he was persuaded to take up kickboxing and God. Besides barbed wire and the fighter's nick- or given name, God is a big tattoo theme in the UFC—angel wings and crucifixes and belly text reading GOD'S GIFT—and He makes His way into half the postfight interviews. For the faithless, on the other hand, fighting competes mostly with fucking. Georges St-Pierre is equanimous: "There's three things in life that excite me," he told Ariel Helwani. "There's a woman, of course; dinosaurs; and the violence of the Octagon." But then there's Nick Diaz: "What can I say. For me this is a curse, you know. I haven't been fanatical about being an MMA fighter since I turned pro. People are always like, 'Oh, so that's your passion.' I'm like no, it's not my passion. Women are my passion. Or at least, maybe, well, one woman. Potentially. I suppose." Teruto Ishihara, an unranked young featherweight from Osaka with cornrows and a septum ring, is with Diaz: "I don't like MMA. I don't like boxing. I don't like wrestling. I don't like grappling. I like only bitches. I don't want to fight. I really don't. I'm not trying to get fans or be different from anyone else. I don't want to fight. I do this because it's the best way I know of to get girls." In Salt Lake City, he gives free tickets to the first three women to kiss him on the cheek outside My Thai Asian Cuisine. While retreating at Fight Night 92 he plants his back leg and knocks Horacio Gutiérrez down, then jumps on him with hammerfists and gets on the microphone: "Party tonight! Come with me, Salt Lake bitches, baby! Today, my mother happy birthday, I love you!" That night he is Instagrammed in bed with four women. Everyone has their clothes on.

UFC 202, LAS VEGAS, AUGUST 20

FINALLY CONOR MCGREGOR and Nate Diaz are due to fight again. McGregor has moved his whole operation from Ireland to Iceland to Las Vegas at the cost of $300,000: coach, assistant coach, movement coach, performance coach, nutritionist, masseuse, cardio expert, jiu-jitsu and boxing sparring partners, videographer for his new lifestyle channel, fast cars, mansion, bespoke training facility with kettlebells and battle ropes. Diaz meanwhile does curls at a globo-gym. The buzz around the fight is strangely muted, until McGregor shows up to the prefight press conference half an hour late. And suddenly Diaz says,

"Fuck your whole team, how 'bout that," and walks offstage at a sign from his brother. Their crews start throwing water bottles and Monster Energy cans at each other, and a solitary cup of Starbucks. Nick Diaz immediately Snapchats himself with a small smug girl who claims McGregor clocked her. "That's fucked up. Bro. Why you hitting. Kids with bottles?"

I run around looking for a sports bar. The first one I try is filled to capacity; at eleven-thirty, I walk into Bleachers on Flatbush, and order myself two Bud Lights for about twenty bucks as the DJ plays "Mo' Money Mo' Problems." The card has gone by superfast. The guy standing next to me runs his hand across his throat—a twelve-second decapitation by Anthony Johnson of Glover Teixeira in the co-main. He is the only one around me not in a pro-wrestling shirt: NWO, SUPLEX CITY, THAT'S ROODE—some multiracial crew rolling deep. Five minutes later it's fight time.

McGregor walks out wrapped in an Irish flag, to "The Foggy Dew/Hypnotize," Sinead meets Biggie, and swaggers about the cage like he owns it. Diaz enters to Tupac (his bulldog is named Makaveli) and stalks around, glaring. They don't touch gloves. Mike Tyson is cageside. Round 1, McGregor isn't fighting McGregor-style. He's throwing efficient flat-footed Muay Thai leg kicks instead of bouncy wasteful karate kicks; he's counterpunching instead of just loading up his left hand—more willing to adapt than his bluster would indicate. A counter left knocks Diaz to the ground, and Diaz throws up guard, but McGregor doesn't take the bait, doesn't rush in for a knockout and risk getting submitted. Round 2, McGregor's left hits Diaz twice more, and twice more he goes down, the guard comes up, and McGregor just beckons Diaz back to his feet. Diaz's face is a mess again, his front leg is chewed up. But he keeps walking forward. And halfway through the round, maybe a minute later than McGregor gassed last time, again he loses steam. Diaz starts pressuring. Now he has his hands out, *What?!*, wiping blood off his face, pawing in flurries at McGregor. Round 3, Diaz is out for the kill. McGregor runs away to reset his position, and Diaz points at him for cowardice. They're up on the fence, in the clinch, and Diaz gives the finger to McGregor's corner; the cage mic gets him saying, "Fuck all of you." *Fuck your game plan.* He slaps McGregor, catches his leg but can't get him down—Diaz has never been a wrestler, he's a boxer who uses his BJJ if you panic-wrestle, and McGregor has enough counterwrestling to defend. He runs, Diaz points. Diaz hits 1–2, 1–2 against the fence, to the body and head, knees and uppercuts, and McGregor is saved by the bell. Round 4. Now Diaz is the tired one—is that possible?—and McGregor has recovered, as if round 3 was all rope-a-dope. Diaz can barely see. Is the fight tied at two? Is McGregor up 3–1? Diaz probably needs to finish him. Round 5, and Diaz flexes for the crowd. McGregor is running again, and again they clinch, and again Diaz can't take him down. McGregor walks away, and Diaz gives him the finger. Diaz clinches him up again, elbows and knees, and judo-trips him with eleven seconds left. The bell sounds. Diaz helps McGregor up and they hug for a second. Diaz's face is dripping blood; McGregor is limping. One judge has it a draw, but the other two give three rounds to McGregor. Conor: "Surprise, surprise, motherfucker. The king is back." It feels rehearsed. Nate: "I thought I won that fight. They can't have a motherfucker like me win, I'm too real for this sport. . . . I didn't get to train, I had injuries. Fuck that, I ain't into making excuses, but he should have finished me off. I want number 3. I gave him number 2 the second day, so I'm ready to go again." One of the wrestling fans gives me dap, and I walk out high on violence. +

IN TBILISI

Victoria Lomasko

INTRODUCTION

Victoria Lomasko is an artist, activist, and independent journalist based in Moscow. Her works of graphic reportage, drawn live on the scene, focus on minor or oft-neglected figures on the fringes of contemporary Russian society: migrants, the LGBT community, juvenile prison inmates, sex workers.

The following is an excerpt from "A Trip to Tbilisi" (2015), in which Lomasko visits the Georgian capital. Although Georgia has been an independent republic since 1991, it continues to have a tense and complicated relationship with Russia. Georgia was incorporated into the Soviet Union in 1921. On April 9, 1989, the Soviet Army fired on anti-Soviet protesters in Tbilisi, killing at least twenty people. The "Tbilisi massacre" was a turning point in the relationship between the two nations, paving the way for Georgia's declaration of independence from the Soviet Union via popular referendum in 1991. Since the collapse of the USSR, Georgia and Russia have been engaged in a conflict over the regions of Abkhazia and South Ossetia. The conflict came to a head in the 2008 Russo-Georgian War, which resolved in Russia's favor, fueling further tension. However, 2012 saw a renewal of diplomatic relations. Russians may now even visit Georgia without visas.

In Tbilisi, Lomasko spoke with historians, artists, journalists, activists, squatters, and a prominent local priest about the country's political climate. Among the issues facing Georgia are homophobic violence ("I think if they had caught up with us, first they would have raped us publicly, then killed us," said an activist of the mob that came out to oppose an LGBT rally in 2013), the religious majority's suppression of women's rights ("Google is a substitute for gynecologists, priests are a substitute for psychologists," one art student said), poverty, homelessness, internal displacement, and gentrification. *Other Russias*, a book of Lomasko's collected work, is forthcoming from n+1.

—*The Editors*

THE SOVIET PAST

ALMOST ALL Soviet symbols have been dismantled in Tbilisi, so I was surprised to find a militant Soviet monument two steps away from Rustaveli Avenue, in April Ninth Park.

LET BANNERS WAVE ON HIGH

The monument was erected to mark Georgia's entry into the Soviet Union. Its title, *Let Banners Wave on High*, refers to the poem by the famous Georgian poet Galaktion Tabidze:

> The day has dawned: A sun of fire glides up.
> Let banners wave on high!
> The soul's athirst for liberty and right

A friend explained to me that Tabidze wrote the poem in 1919, when Georgia declared its independence from tsarist Russia. The date of the poem was changed in Soviet times to 1921, "the year the Bolsheviks occupied Georgia."

The Stalin Avlabar Illegal Printing Press Memorial Museum survives in Tbilisi: golden hammers, sickles, and stars glitter on its red gates. The underground printing press operated from 1903 to 1906. Georgian Social Democrats, among them the young Joseph Stalin, descended into an underground vault through a well to print revolutionary newspapers, leaflets, and books.

"What can I say to great Russia from the American colony of Georgia?"

These days the museum has no ticket office, schedule, or employees. An elderly Georgian man named Soso, who introduced himself as a former KGB colonel, guides the tours. Soso said that when he returned to Tbilisi from Moscow after the collapse of the Soviet Union, he was unable to obtain a pension or an apartment, so he moved into the museum. He survives on donations from tourists.

"There are sometimes no tourists for two weeks," he complained.

While we were talking, kids from the neighboring houses dashed into the museum. They said it was the first time they had seen the museum's gates open, and they wanted to see what was inside. They looked at the numerous portraits and busts of Stalin and Lenin.

"Do you know who that is?" I asked, pointing to a bust of Lenin.

They said they didn't know.

MISHA, GEORGY, AND NIKA. NIKA: *"Is Lenin a poet?"*

In parting, Soso advised me to stop by the Stalin Garden Museum, opened by a former cabdriver in the courtyard of an apartment building.

USHANGI DAVIDOVICH DAVITASHVILI, proprietor of the Stalin Garden Museum, is 86 years old. When I asked him about life under Stalin, he recalled annual decreases in food prices and showed me display cases in his garden containing printouts of Stalin-era prices for all kinds of goods.

Ushangi Davidovich created the museum by himself. He gradually bought the historic photos, portraits, and busts, made the model of Stalin's house in Gori with his own hands, and brought Soviet helmets and grenade fragments back from Stalingrad. A stone slab in memory of his dead son also stands in the garden museum. An old photograph of his parents hangs next to a formal portrait of Stalin. The walls are decorated with bunches of garlic and dried flowers and fruits.

"I ask my neighbors who are afraid of being fired, 'Is life good for you under capitalism?'"

Framed black-and-white portraits hang on the wall where the museum display begins. The young, attractive faces in the photos belong to the protesters who were shot in Tbilisi after the Twentieth Party Congress in 1956, where Khrushchev famously criticized Stalin. Following the Congress, unrest broke out in Tbilisi.

"There were rallies at the monument to Stalin every day," recalled Ushangi Davidovich. "We demanded explanations. On March 9, Khrushchev ordered the troops to open fire on us. They fired without warning. I had stepped away to get a bite to eat, so I survived. Twenty-seven people were killed; the youngest was 15. There is nothing in the history textbooks about it."

He began to assemble the Stalin museum immediately after these events.

Ushangi Davidovich invited me to his flat to drink homemade *chacha* (Georgian vodka) and warm up. He showed me one of his museum's eighteen guest books, featuring comments from Stalin's daughter and tourists from all the Soviet republics. When I came to visit a second time, Ushangi Davidovich wasn't home. He was at a meeting of a new communist party, Russia Is Our Friend.

WHENEVER I ADDRESSED someone in Russian, elderly Georgians took it as an occasion to chat about relations with Russia. In Tbilisi, there are many pensioners working as cabdrivers, and almost all of them said something like this during our ride:

> Seventy percent of Georgians believe it is better to side with Russia than with Europe or America. The West sends subsidies, but they all end up in the pockets of the ruling elite, not ordinary people. There is nothing to do in Tbilisi because of unemployment: nearly all the factories are idle. In Soviet times there was work, and people were taken into greater consideration. Is it possible to live on a pension of 160 lari?

The cabdrivers would ignore my remarks about the economic crisis and political crackdown in Russia: "Would that we had a president like Putin!"

One pensioner, a refugee from Sukhumi, struck up a conversation with me on the bus:

> In Soviet times, I was not a Communist, and I criticized the regime. Now, looking back, I realize it was better. Free education and medical care for everyone. My son fought [in the Abkhazian-Georgian war] and was shell-shocked, but the state did not give him medical treatment. I am very angry at the authorities.

REFUGEE FROM SUKHUMI: *"The people who said 'Georgia is only for Georgians' are to blame for the war."*

The guard at one of the European organizations in Tbilisi wanted to talk with me. He asked that I not give his name or draw him in uniform. Working in security was tiresome, he said, but there was no other work to be had.

"I don't want a visa-free regime with the European Union. I want a visa-free regime with Russia," he said.

When Georgia was part of the Soviet Union, the guard said, he didn't like that all decisions concerning Georgia were made in Moscow. He dreams of good relations between Georgia and Russia, but on equal footing.

"I'm against the European Union, because to join it you have to accept same-sex marriages."

When older people wanted to interact, they gave me a gift or treated me to some food. When young Georgians heard me speak in Russian or in Russian-inflected English, on the other hand, they often behaved in a deliberately cold way.

I mentioned this pattern to Nino, director of the Heinrich Böll Foundation office in Tbilisi, who offered a possible explanation:

> Russians have a lopsided attitude toward us. Either they embrace us and say, "Remember what good friends we used to be?" or they accuse us of falling out with them. It is a postcolonial complex: we enlightened you, but you do not appreciate us.

"Even human rights activists come to Georgia as if they were coming on vacation: girls, wine, and khachapuri . . . All the clichés."

ARMENIANS IN TBILISI

GEORGIANS AND ARMENIANS converse differently. During my trip to Yerevan, the Armenian capital, I noticed that Armenians tended to analyze all phenomena: they immediately noticed when an argument lacked logic or the facts did not add up. What matters in Tbilisi, by contrast, is to entertain and be entertained, to be lively and artistic. My new Armenian friend Luz, who had recently moved from Yerevan to Tbilisi, agreed with this impression.

LUZ: *"If I let my guard down I'll turn into an outcast. It's forbidden to be sad here."*

I showed my portrait of Luz to Georgian friends. Here are their comments:

> Yes, it is forbidden to be sad in Georgia. Anger is the only negative response that is more or less acceptable. We have not learned to cope with sadness. If you delve into your emotions, you might find even more terrible things.
>
> Acting happy is part of your social status. If things are OK, you don't whine or cry.
>
> Georgians don't like weak people. It's part of the culture.

Armenians are the second-largest ethnic minority in Georgia. They make up 5 percent of the population, while Azerbaijanis make up 6 percent.

The ancestors of many local Armenians were refugees from the genocide in the 1910s. Yana is an Armenian woman born in Tbilisi: her great-grandparents fled to Georgia during the genocide. Yana grew up in a Russian-speaking family. She learned Armenian and Georgian in college.

YANA: *"Tbilisi in the 1990s was like* adjapsandal, *a dish in which all the vegetables are mixed together. Nobody knew anybody's ethnicity."*

Modern Georgians have a chilly attitude toward Armenians. In my conversations with Georgians, the most common explanations went something like this:

> Before the revolution, there were more Armenians in Tbilisi than Georgians. They controlled commerce, and Georgians came from the countryside like migrant workers and worked for them.

> Georgians do not live in Armenia, but lots of Armenians live in Georgia. They own real estate and businesses. The large Armenian diaspora is a potential threat

Almost all the activists and artists I met in Yerevan travel to Georgia several times a year. There are many more Western foundations in Georgia and therefore more prospects. Many of my young friends in Tbilisi had never once been to Armenia. When I asked them about Electric Yerevan in 2015 and other protests in Armenia, they said they had read more about Turkey or the protests in Greece.

In Tbilisi, I was involved in *Working Agenda of Amirani/Mher*, a project organized by the Georgian artist Lali Pertenava to strengthen ties between artists and activists from Georgia and Armenia. The Georgian participants said it would be wrong to be separated from Europe.

"We must appreciate the European experience. We have a global future."

ARMENIANS AND GEORGIANS. ARMENIAN WOMAN: *"We're supposed to present on how well we learn from the West?"*

"In all the discussions, the Armenians were pressured recognize that the European way is the right way and that it's bad to be dominated by Russia," Zara, an activist from Armenia, said afterward.

Young progressive Armenians have a negative attitude toward Russian influence in Armenia, but they do not idealize Georgia's dependence on Europe.

AZERBAIJANIS IN TBILISI

THE ARMENIANS INVITED their Azerbaijani friends to the project's farewell meal. In Tbilisi, I heard repeatedly from Armenian friends that despite the ongoing conflict between their countries, Armenians and Azerbaijanis understand each other better than they do Georgians. There were no people closer to them, the Azerbaijanis told me, than the Armenians.

Among the Azerbaijanis who joined us was the writer Seymur Baycan. He gave me his novel, *Quqark*, about the Nagorno-Karabakh War. In *Quqark*, Seymur recalls the first skirmishes between Armenians and Azerbaijanis in his hometown of Fizuli in the early '90s: the town's transformation into ruins, and his family's move to Baku. The hardest passages to read were not the war scenes but the scenes of domestic violence. The beating of wives and children in Azerbaijani families is described so casually.

Seymur was part of the Baku cultural scene in the '00s. Since 2009, the regime has been pushing active members of the creative intelligentsia out of Azerbaijan.

Later, I met Seymur's friends, a young married couple forced to leave Baku under pressure from the authorities. Günel Mövlud is a journalist and poet. Haji Hajiyev is a doctor.

SEYMUR

Günel started out as a blogger. After publishing a series of critical texts on the problems of Azerbaijani society, she became one of the most widely read writers in her country. Günel now works as an editor at Meydan TV, an online media platform created by Azerbaijani dissidents in Berlin.

GÜNEL, HAJI, AND NADIR. GÜNEL: *"Azerbaijani women in Georgia are completely isolated from public life by their families. You only see them selling herbs at the market or working as nannies or maids."*

Most of Günel's reports deal with women's rights in the South Caucasus.

"The lives of Azerbaijani women living in Tbilisi are different from those of Georgian women," she said. "Azerbaijani girls are taken out of school by their families in the ninth grade and married off at the age of 14. If Azerbaijani girls resist, it's suicide. Our child's nanny became a grandmother at 32. Talk to her."

Their nanny, Renka, agreed to pose for a portrait and talked a little bit about herself.

She was married at 13 and had a daughter when she was 14.

RENKA: *"It was hard. I had help from an older girlfriend, who had a child already, and a little from my husband."*

At 19, she had a second child, a boy. For a long time, Renka kept house and took care of her children, going out into the city only with her husband. She began working as a nanny recently. She really likes her job.

Renka said this of unmarried women who earn their own money: "They have money, and they live the way they want. In my opinion, that is better."

IN THE CAUCASUS, there is a term for correct behavior on the part of the individual in society: *namus*, in Azerbaijani and Armenian, and *namusi* in Georgian. For men, namus means honor and conscience. For women, namus is bound up only with their sexual behavior, with their availability to men. In the North Caucasus, it is believed that a man whose female relative has been sleeping around can cleanse his namus only by killing her.

Seymur says that namus can be bought in Azerbaijani society. If a woman—an actress or singer, for example—brings a lot of money home to the family, she can come home late at night and bring a different man with her every time.

WRITER SEYMUR AND JOURNALIST GÜNEL. SEYMUR: *"Namus is for the poor."*

Günel told the story of a girlfriend, an unmarried university student. Guys in the neighborhood monitored her appearance and threatened violence if she did not observe namus. Once, when a male acquaintance was walking her home, they were both beaten up. The same guys completely ignored other female neighbors who wore miniskirts and had breast implants: they were the kept women of rich men.

NOT ALL YOUNG AZERBAIJANIS are willing to lead the lifestyle imposed on them by society. Four kindred spirits—Ruslan, Lala, and Emin, from Baku, and Elvin, from Tbilisi—have organized an activist project called the Thinking Citizen. They rent a space in Tbilisi and hold educational lectures there twice a week. They are interested in grassroots efforts and cultural development in the South Caucasus, as well as such taboo topics as domestic violence and the role of Azerbaijani women in society.

EMIN, LALA, ELVIN, AND RUSLAN. ELVIN: *"In the '90s we were doubly stigmatized, as a different ethnic group and as Muslims."*

Elvin said that even Georgian journalists find it difficult to do stories about Georgia's Azerbaijanis because they are such a closed community.

RUSSIANS IN TBILISI

FRIENDS IN TBILISI have noticed that young people from Russia, disappointed and unhappy with events at home, have begun to settle in the city in recent years. For now, they are few in number. The ones with whom I spoke chose Georgia because Russians don't need a visa to travel there; it's warm, cheap, and close to home; lots of Georgians speak Russian; and there is much in common between the cultures. They weren't sure whether they could put down roots in Georgia, but they weren't ready to go back to Russia, either.

Jan, a former Moscow activist, is one such semi-immigrant. "Georgia is like one big village. The mores are patriarchal and relations between people are more heartfelt than in Russia. There is less aggression, but the irresponsibility of Georgians is annoying," he said.

JAN AND ANI. ANI: *"Most Georgian men are sexists."*

Jan rents a flat with his girlfriend, Ani, whom he met in Tbilisi, and her brother, Nodar. Like many young Georgians, Nodar does not speak Russian, and our conversation did not go well in broken English. I asked Nodar to write his thoughts about Georgian society on the drawing.

JAN AND NODAR

Jan reads the news from Russia less and less, but when he does he's glad he managed to escape the "total madness."

Russians can always be found at the Kiwi Café in downtown Tbilisi, Georgia's first vegan café. It was opened in 2015 by a international crowd: Georgians, Russians, an Iranian man, and a Swedish woman. The original idea was to cook very simple and cheap food, but the café gradually turned into a tourist hot spot. Activists from Russia, hanging out in Tbilisi indefinitely, work part-time in the kitchen there.

The Kiwi Café holds regular film screenings and discussions, and talks and lectures on social and political topics. I attended a lecture on the struggle of the Kurds for their rights, which was given by Alexei, an activist from Yekaterinburg.

LECTURE AT THE KIWI CAFÉ. ALEXEI: *"Barzani is like Putin. He's also permanently in power."*

Alexei had come to Tbilisi with a group of friends: "We have been here for two months already, and not once have we encountered a policeman or an official. In Russia, you get the feeling they're everywhere, and you are superfluous."

Oleg, a former Moscow journalist, is a co-organizer of the Kiwi Café. He spoke about his two most recent trips from Georgia to Russia. The first time, Oleg crossed the land border at the checkpoint in the village of Verkhny Lars: "I was led away for a special check by the FSB. They suspected I was an Islamic State fighter."

The second time, he flew into Moscow with a Ukrainian friend. His friend's Ukrainian passport, Transcarpathian registration address, and tattooed body were sufficient grounds for detaining and deporting him: "You haven't even managed to enter the country before you realize where it is you've come back to!" +

OLEG: *"I've never been homesick for Moscow these past two years. But if an opportunity to go back arises, I'll go."*

—Translated by Thomas Campbell

AMALIA PICA, *RECONSTRUCTION OF AN ANTENNA (AS SEEN ON TV)*, 2010, FOUND METAL, WOOD, WIRE, CABLE, AND CEMENT. 96" × 64" × 41". COURTESY THE ARTIST AND MARC FOXX, LOS ANGELES.
PHOTO: ROBERT WEDEMEYER, 2010.

I DIDN'T TALK

Beatriz Bracher

Beatriz Bracher, born in 1961 in São Paulo, is an editor, screenwriter, novelist, and cofounder of Editora 34, one of Brazil's most respected literary publishing houses. She published her first novel, Azul e dura (Blue and Hard), *to critical acclaim in 2002;* Não falei (I Didn't Talk), *excerpted here, was published in 2004. In 2016, Bracher won two of Brazil's most prestigious awards, the Rio and São Paulo literary prizes, for her fourth novel,* Anatomia do paraíso (Anatomy of Paradise, *2015*).

Bracher came of age during the Brazilian military dictatorship. Like the nameless young woman who wishes to interview the narrator of I Didn't Talk *about his involvement in the resistance movement, Bracher's memories of that time intersect with the lives of people whose friends and lovers were tortured, exiled, and killed, as well as those who may have done the killing. As Brazil's fortunes have risen and fallen over the past two decades, Bracher's voice has remained steady and restrained, her eye critical and alert. Now, as the nation is roiled by political unrest, memories of the authoritarian past, both mournful and nostalgic, torment the historical imagination of a nation lurching in an uncertain direction.*

IT HAPPENS EVERY DAY. It has to be among strangers: that's where things emerge. It's how they become known. Stories are the shape we give things to pass the time in line at the bank, on the bus, at the bakery counter.

I asked, what do you do for a living? And he told me, I'm retired. Twenty years ago, at a motel café table, I found the answer unhelpful.

His wife, all in white, looking like a nurse—an impression aided by her husband's physical defect—worked in the navy. I was a school principal. Jobs help us make assumptions about people, the same as wrinkles on a face, the color of someone's skin, the clothes a person wears, the way they butter their bread. "Retired" tells you nothing. A retired doctor, retired garbage man, retired president, retired manicurist, not simply "retired." But today, yes, now I understand: retired is right.

Look, I was tortured. They say I snitched on a comrade who later died by soldiers' bullets. I didn't snitch—I almost died in the room where I would've snitched, but I didn't talk. They said I talked and Armando died. I was released two days after his death and they let me stay on as the school principal.

Eliana was in Paris. Our daughter, Lígia, was here with my mother, in this empty house which then was full. After I was imprisoned they arranged Eliana's trip to Paris. They didn't arrange for me to go anywhere. Eliana died. My father, sick and retired. My sister, Jussara, still a girl, was finishing school and doing a free test prep, studying all day. The family could never really count on José. Eliana died in Paris, she's buried there. I talked to her on the phone after they released me. It was summer here, and she was in Paris, trembling with cold, and complaining a lot about it—she wanted to see her daughter, bury her brother, take care of her mother—her voice trembled on the broken public phone I would use to get a connection without paying. I imagined her with purple lips, inadequately clothed. She couldn't come back, and I understood she couldn't take it, she always felt the cold more than I did—but she couldn't come back, and that was all that remained of her.

Armando, my classmate, was her only brother. Luiza said that Eliana died of pneumonia without ever finding out that I'd said what I never said. I don't trust Luiza. How does someone die of pneumonia in Paris? She stopped eating. Yes, but weren't there friends around to feed and clothe her? I was furious. Luiza told me to remain strong for the revolution—she hesitated, her metallic voice taking on the electricity of the military shocks, and to make things worse, I'd gone deaf in my right ear—no matter what happened to Armando you're still one of us, not everyone can withstand it, not even the strongest, Eliana died without knowing, don't worry. Dona Esther went crazy over the death of her children and wanted to hang on to her grandchild. I didn't go crazy and I couldn't touch Lígia. I found her baby babble intolerable.

Francisco Augusto, who'd recently left med school, reset the bones in my fingers, taped them to splints that I tore off a week later, confirmed permanent deafness in my right ear, and recommended a dentist friend I should see about my two lost teeth. But I didn't go. I didn't tell him about my nightmares or the impossibility of sleeping for more than fifteen minutes straight. Nightmares, we all have them, and I couldn't go insane.

Dona Esther killed herself, but not without paying us one last visit, embracing her granddaughter, Lígia, whispering in her ear a final goodbye mantra and looking at me with disappointment: Armando trusted you even more than he trusted me.

At the café table in that inland motel, the girl from the navy told us they were newlyweds. Eliana had been dead for ten years and I said, I'm a school principal, and the husband said, "retired." I could have also said biologist, or linguist, or educator. I had a full set of teeth again and was spending the holidays with Lígia and her friend Francisca in the "historic cities" of Minas Gerais.

As though only some cities were historic. The present history of São Paulo is so violent that it occupies space in possible pasts and futures. Unable to look forward or backward or to the side, we stare at our feet. When Lígia was 10, São Paulo still had the possibility of history. We'd go to the São Bento Monastery, the Pátio do Colégio, the Ipiranga Museum, the Consolação Cemetery. Usually she could go by herself to buy bread at the bakery. She knew Dona Maria the grocer, Senhor Ademar the shoemaker, she played with the neighborhood kids. I've been the victim of an urban pastoral that I don't like at all. My lack of belief in the impossible is yielding. I'd rather not believe it and argue with Lígia about it. The move to São Carlos is the next phase in my career. I'm not giving up, as she alleges. I'm going to dedicate myself to Lucilia's project at the university, her study of language-acquisition difficulties. Lígia thinks I should have accepted the post at the Department of Education, or at least continued directing the program in professional development and responding to requests for talks and seminars. I'd like her to come with me. The university there is very good—her husband would have no trouble getting in and, more important, my little granddaughter Marta could go out by herself to buy our bread. Not yet, she's only 3, but she'd come with me, she'd get to know the baker, the neighbors, she'd pay attention to the color of the sky, the winds that bring the rain. No, there's nothing pastoral, I try to tell myself, about this empty house.

We finally sold the house. I have a few months left before I have to give it up. I'm looking over the pieces of furniture that are coming with me. José, Jussara, and Lígia took what they wanted after my mother's death. Jussara took only a few small things: some shirts, the oil painting of a little boy drawing, and the vanity mirror in the ugly mahogany frame, the kind there were in so many homes on Rua Teodoro Sampaio. It was Vóana's but beloved by my mother—it was where she stuck little notes to remind herself what she had to do the next day. Jussara grew up to be a beautiful, tall young woman, very thin like our father, but even so she took some of her short, plump mother's shirts. She said she'd wear them around the house. I never went to visit her: she raised her family in London, is a respected psychiatrist, her children speak Portuguese with an accent. But she says she wears Dona Joana's clothes whenever she's home alone, especially a wool-gauze dressing gown that our mother often wore. I had to shrink Jussara a bit in my mind, imagine her compressed, or else the gown was too short on her, too indecent to be something from Dona Joana's collection.

My mother was an excellent seamstress. She acquired important clientele, people from outside the neighborhood. "Important" was how she put it, and we knew who she meant, something that wouldn't happen today. I wouldn't know how to place names or faces or occupations if someone said "important clientele" to me now. Obviously they weren't people from the neighborhood. When I went to elementary school, I had to take two buses and get off downtown, and I could tell it wasn't enough to be from outside the neighborhood to be considered important. My mother treated all her customers the same way, their clothes all done with the same care, the prices fixed. The importance of the customer only altered the quality of the cloth and my mother's patience. The important ones—my mother would say as she prepared dinner at the stove, as José and I did our homework at the kitchen table and Jussara, the baby, ten years younger than José, slept in her crib—are the most distrustful. They explain every detail because they're afraid I don't know the names of the stitches. My mother found this lack of trust to be reasonable: shoddy workmanship is rampant across the world. Ignorance has no fixed address, no mark on its forehead—she'd listen attentively and humbly repeat the details. It's just, she'd say, that some of the important customers use the terms incorrectly: they want a ruffled skirt but they say pleated, they want a three-quarter-length sleeve and they say half sleeve. You can't correct them, mainly because it doesn't get you anywhere, poor things, so assured in their mistakes, so I have to show them with fabric how it will look, find a photo of a similar model. Only then can I know for sure what they want. But one must understand that these people never had the opportunity to learn.

The late Dona Joana was a very intelligent but unambitious person. She regarded both stupidity and ambition as birth defects or characteristics acquired through mishaps in life, and felt it necessary to have as much patience with such people as when dealing with the blind and the deaf.

Armando liked Dona Joana. We were classmates in elementary school and again in high school. He'd come have lunch with me in the weeks leading up to our exams and we'd study together until late afternoon. Francisco Augusto was Armando's classmate in med school. He's a good doctor—as Armando would have been, I suspect. I studied biology, and after that education, then linguistics, and now I'm going to São Carlos. Armando used to talk to my mother. About seasonings, recipes, little things about the city and its characters. Some dishes were renamed "Armando's." We'd had them all before: pasta with meatballs, sautéed squash, baked rice without olives but with real corn, toast with creamed spinach and minced hard-boiled egg. Only now they were Armando's meatballs, Armando's rice, the same old thing, but under new ownership. José, Jussara, our father, and I—we didn't have dishes named after us, although we ate them with pleasure. I think that sort of praise wasn't part of our language—maybe that's what it was. Sometimes I got caught up with something downtown and stayed there, annoying Armando. He didn't want to miss out on Dona Joana's food. Later he learned how to get there himself and would go on his own. He'd say he could only study law while listening to the *tac-tac* of the sewing machine.

I'm healthy, the illnesses I get come and go without steady medication, I cost very little. My mother and father are dead. Jussara has taken care of herself for a while now, Lígia and her husband have found their footing, Renato is no more, and so with my retirement money I have more than I need. I don't have a car with taxes or registration, no microwave or any other useless machine, only a computer that crashes sometimes, meaning I then have to call the ever-stranger Alexandre, the grandson of my ancient neighbor, Dona Eulália, and he comes over and futzes with it and forgets to charge me. The house, which is old, needs constant work: a burst pipe, burned-out wiring, a door that squeaks but won't shut anymore. It's all going to hell, so I have an agreement with Tobias, a thrifty handyman. He tells me gently the house needs a complete renovation, the pipes have to be replaced, the wiring requires this and that and who knows what else. I bravely resisted for these past thirty years, ever since I got out of prison, ever since Eliana died and I moved back here. At first I had my father's firm support. But after he died I had to keep up the fight alone. Lígia, Jussara, and my mother all took Tobias's side and wanted to do the renovation, the remodeling, change everything, but my team prevailed and the house was allowed to age in peace. Now a developer will tear it down, like all the other old homes nearby, and many families will live off this plot, including Lígia's. I put my part of the sale toward an apartment for her and there was still enough left over for a small house with a yard in São Carlos.

José was here a few days ago, he slept three nights in our old bedroom. I sleep in our parents' old room. He came to meet with his editor and with people from the newspaper and the magazines he writes for. He saved the last night for us to eat together. That was how he put it: I left Friday free for us to have dinner, you have any plans? Aside from sleeping, no sir, I said, like I was one of the neighborhood clients responding to one of the important clients. He found this funny—he knows I'm too lazy to go out at night, the farmers' hours I keep. We barely ran into each other on Wednesday and Thursday. He has his own key and knows where to find sheets and towels, and despite his criticisms he makes do with my jam-jar glasses, my mismatched plates and bent silverware. It was the last month of the professional-development courses for teachers, and I still needed to show up for meetings at the DOE to prep for next semester and to attend commencement ceremonies. Good-byes were said, homage paid, as if I were leaving for another planet whose wizened inhabitants, having forsaken the flux of São Paulo, are put out to pasture. The past tense triumphed in each tribute, and I left more irritated than when I arrived. This live burial annoyed me. It was an elegant and efficient way to stop listening to what I have to say, of reading what I write with glazed eyes. How can we give courses in professional development if we're the ones who need to be brought up to speed? I don't believe in this any longer. But Professor—with that awful little voice of respect that I can't stand—it's what's practical. I think I got tired of the practical, it doesn't interest me anymore. Anyway I'm finishing something off with this move: it's certainly an ending. I am killing something, I don't know what, maybe ambition, since Dona Joana couldn't stop life's mishaps from infecting me with it.

I went to the university early on Friday to clear out my office, submit grades for all the stragglers, sign off on all the necessary bureaucratic things to formally dissociate myself, and have lunch with Teresa. Early that morning, when I put the bread and newspaper on the kitchen table with an automatic gesture whose predicate is to turn toward the stove, take a pot, fill it with water, set it to boil, et cetera, I gave a start, and the bread and the newspaper nearly broke two teacups, two saucers, and two small plates from the old china set José took after our mother died, which were now placed neatly on white napkins. There was a vase with flowers and a package wrapped in gold paper with a note from my brother. My first reaction was to look around to make sure I wasn't in the wrong house. Then, irritation with this invasion of my breakfast ritual, with my coffee in a glass, sweetened coffee in the pot, my baguette with butter and crumbs on the old table. In the rage and confusion of these last days, as so many around me were calling them, I pushed it all to the corner of the table, took out my cup, pulled apart my bread, and read my newspaper. The sports page, an old habit of Armando's that I'd taken up over the past few years, as though I'd always done it. I threw the package from my brother on my bed and took the note with me to read on the bus, en route to the university.

Mine, mine, mine. Like a little child learning the language of the tribe, I find myself in the acquisitive phase of a new language. At the same time the old one, the one I knew and used, seems sterile. It was now my cup, my bread, my rage, my 64 years of age. As though I needed once more to name and own what I was taking with me. Return to the first person and to the possessive, the twin juvenile plagues that modernity bequeathed us and against which I had struggled sincerely. José's note spoke of the same necessity, but in a completely opposite sense. He wrote of reminiscing and I think of creating; he wrote of discovering and I need to be establishing. The note brought me peace, banished the childish indignation I'd suffered in recent days that had obstructed my ability to reflect and left me frivolous, orphaned, left to pure reaction.

His Machadian* tone—which José cultivates in a way that borders on plagiarism yet somehow remains, paradoxically, his own—revived my happiness in the same way that, when absorbed in some specific and complex composition, we're surprised by the sound of birdsong. Maybe the bird had been singing for a while, maybe its song just penetrated the machinations of logic. But we perceive it suddenly, born alongside our own unexpected joy at hearing it. It pulls us out of ourselves, destroys the train of thought we'd been following without leaving a trace, leaves us only the pleasure of listening to the bird. When we realize we're happy and have lost our train of thought, we sigh, resigned to the idea of starting over again, and the solution appears as clearly and as unexpectedly as the birdsong. As José wrote, "*This is what happens to me, as I go about remembering and shaping the construction or reconstruction of myself*" (Machado, as written by José).

As I go about remembering, what a beautiful thing. I need to reread Machado, retrieve the unexpected things I no longer remember. Unlike José, who tries like Dom Casmurro to construct a past that will be kind to him in the present, I look for my errors, I kick stones and send the cockroaches running, I walk through spiderwebs that spread across my face and ask every smug milestone I've passed, What purpose do you serve in my life? Did you manage to hold firm, emit light, make noise, serve at least as a pillar to sustain the person who made you, or are you already so spoiled by applause that the flick of a finger could send you tumbling over a cliff into the calm and muddy river of the satisfied?

Inside the gold package tossed on my bed were the first chapters of a new book that José was writing, the first, I read in the note, of an autobiographical cycle. It was an advance copy and he wanted my opinion. Although it was artfully written, the request was sincere; it moved me, but I couldn't help but find it amusing. José had already exposed himself and our family in his first book, his most experimental and the one I like best. None of the others is straightforwardly bad—they all have their charm and depth. But for all the styles he's tried—detective stories, historical fiction, even his critical essays—there's something predictable that I find off-putting. I know where he wants to end up: they are, in fact, long explanations in which his sexuality plays an increasingly important role. But his note moved me. I think it's the first

* Joaquim Maria Machado de Assis (1839–1908) was a Brazilian novelist and is perhaps Brazil's most venerated writer. The title character of his novel *Dom Casmurro* (1899) is referenced in the next paragraph. [Trans.]

direct request I've received from my brother in many years. Even in his most dire straits, he never asked us for anything, never let down his guard or allowed us to help him. He moved away a long time ago. He was a hippie in Arembepe, saw a flying saucer somewhere in the central plains, went backpacking in Machu Picchu, got stoned in California, until, like a holdout convert, he became an academic, a man of letters, got a fellowship in Germany, then in Spain, and finally returned to live in Curitiba. After our father's death he came to visit more frequently. When our mother got sick, five years ago, he moved back home, and for the two months before she died he took care of her. You couldn't call it a reconciliation, because there'd never been a fight. *Reencounter* is the right word, from José's point of view.

Me, I lived practically my entire life with Dona Joana. I could never reencounter her. The truth is our mother could never reencounter José either. Her son had gone through so many transformations since he left home at 17 that her affection for that matured man was the kind you might feel for the friend of a dead son who reminds you, with his presence, his age, and his stories, of the dead child who no longer exists. "The teacups," the note continued, "are part of the set we used to use when we were little, and which I took with me when we split up her things. I thought of all the reasons they're so special to me and why I wished to share with you, my older brother, something that time divided, but all these reasons would deeply annoy you, no matter how sincere. We've never spoken about it, but I can imagine your opinions about keepsakes—I'm aware of your aversion to junk and your preference for coffee in a jar. I ask only that you accept them, with my sincere affection."

I agreed to have lunch with Teresa because I enjoy her company, a feeling I think is mutual and that allows us to enjoy an understanding, stimulating even when it comes to discussing academic concerns. This time there was no concern, just an end-of-year lunch for two. We agreed to meet in the department café and then go somewhere nearby so we could eat well, with some peace and quiet. She was with a young woman who looked like an undergrad student of mine. I don't remember much about her, only that she was charming—but then there were so many. I didn't catch her name, Ercília or Marília, or something like that. It turned out she was writing a novel that took place in the '60s and '70s, when she was only a child, and she wanted to interview me. She'd already interviewed others and Teresa had suggested my name.

Her protagonist was more or less my age, was imprisoned, became an educator. She needed information about the period, about the education system, the details of daily life in public schools and prison. She said she'd already read my books. I think she was studying pedagogy or anthropology, I didn't quite catch it. She didn't know that I'd been a prisoner, had participated in the movement. I didn't participate, I said. But Teresa made a pouty face, like I was being difficult or modest. I didn't want to upset Teresa, but the situation really bothered me. The girl sensed this and was intimidated. She's interesting, this girl. I mean. I mean, no, that's just it, she's pretty, serious, and this wasn't idle curiosity. Finally Teresa asked her to say more about her book. The girl said she'd just started working at a public school and was impressed by the "aggressive emptiness" she felt between the teachers. In the novel she wanted to portray a time when education still seemed to have an explosive meaning, a detonating force—and where this eventually led. She'd already read books about the history of education, about the repression of the resistance movements, she'd seen the films, heard the songs, but she said she needed to interview people because her book wasn't about politics or education, but about something she wasn't quite certain she understood yet. Now that I think about it, she's pretty bold, this girl. I knew exactly what she was talking about, because I'd done all this plenty of times already, and I don't like being the raw material that somebody else sucks dry.

But at the time I found it charming. This shameless inquiry into my life, so transparent, utilitarian. She said she needed to know the lingo from the time period, details and nuances that you can't get from reading books. She admired my ideas, that I understood, but ideas weren't what she wanted—none of them mattered. She wanted my age. To ferret out words from those years that still lingered in the speech of older men. A Trojan horse, this gift from Teresa. And I can't get it out of my head, this girl and her interview. She even ended up with my phone number, though she hasn't called yet. I hope she doesn't call. It's a bad time. I told her I hardly remembered anything and she said she wanted those, too, broken memories, the scrambled view of what remained—what was vanishing in the midst of all that aggressive emptiness.

She said she'd like to read some of my more recent work before doing the interview, and Teresa mentioned the reports and letters I'd sent not long before to the Department of Education, in which I'd offered my unsolicited opinion about the latest direction teaching had taken. I ended up telling the girl I'd send them to her, even though they weren't public documents. What was her name? Josefina? Maria? There's no way I would call Teresa to ask. When the girl calls, she'll say her name. It's not good, this business of forgetting even recent things. I jotted down her email someplace, but I think it was only her initials. I wrote it down so I would remember to send her the letters and reports, but I haven't had time.

I'm disorganized, forgetful, which is why I created a rather rigid methodology, external to me and from which I wouldn't be able to escape. I became what appeared to be a punctual, organized, and responsible person. *Appears* is the right word, but without its insinuation of falsehood, which is connected and consecutive to superficial or incomplete knowledge. He appears generous, but once you really get to know him—you can't even imagine. This would actually be a good way to teach Portuguese. Take an expression at random, one that arises in a trivial classroom conversation, when we're not—when we appear not to be—teaching. In those innumerable instants when the teacher speaks about their spouse or against the government, or when a student—but rarely does the trivial conversation come from the students. In those moments we can interrupt our speech and call attention to the word being used. It's the birdsong. Or the appearance of a priest in a church when we're only there to see the stained-glass windows. That moment in which we perceive another dimension to the thing we're doing, the object we're examining, the instruments we're using. The value of error, this is precisely the value of error. Yes, because the birdsong in the middle of muddling through Kant is certainly an error, as much as when a flesh-and-blood priest appears right beside you as you're going on about the Baroque. It skews our thought, distracts. And such is the magic of errors: we return from them changed. Like an errant trajectory, suddenly on the wrong street. Only then do we stop to think about the general design of the streets and their layout and determine the most interesting path, which may or may not be the shortest. Then the teacher uses the word *apparently* in an unusual way, stops and says, how curious, we sometimes use *appear* to say that something is false, that it seems to be something that in reality it isn't. But when you think about it, we also use it to say that something appears to us in such a way, in such a form, and it's the only way we know it, the way in which it appears. Because we aren't sure if it will remain, over time, in the same way that we see it now. Or perhaps we suspect it will be able to change, so we say that it now appears. But could it be that when we say that something appears, what we really mean is that it's false? Or do we only use it to express our hesitation, one that may not be motivated in any way by the thing in itself? And then we can open the dictionary together with the students to find out if *apparent* has any relation to *parent*.

I was always favorable to the presence, in every classroom, of a Portuguese dictionary, an etymological dictionary, a Latin dictionary, a Greek dictionary, a common grammar, and a dictionary of verb and prepositional correspondences. And not in some corner of the room, but on my desk, to be handled at all times, without formality.

I say I appear organized because that is how I've become in relation to the world, without having changed my nature. Thus: *apparently*. I am organized to everyone who comes into contact with me and apparently organized only to myself. But I didn't send those report-letters to that girl of Teresa's. Not because I lack discipline, or because she didn't deserve it. I left it to the end of the week to determine what I would send her, and ever since, I've hesitated. The dinner with José came in between.

Eliana died at 25. Tomorrow she'd be 59. I don't think there was a suicidal vein in the family—Dona Esther's melancholy was more Lusitanian than depressive. She was widowed young, with small children, and sold her father-in-law's bakery, which her bohemian husband had inherited and never knew what to do with. She bought two houses to rent out and went to work for a Catholic ladies' association. As Dona Joana would say, she had the opportunity to learn, and learn she did. When I was young, I was envious of Armando, of his mother who worked away from home, of his father's absence; he had the family apartment to himself and all the responsibilities of the man of the house. It all seemed modern and adult in comparison with our little clan huddled under Dona Joana's wing and my father's black umbrella. When I first met him, Armando would go to get his sister at her day school every evening at five. I never heard him complain the way I did on the few occasions my mother asked me to watch Jussara. He didn't regard what he did for his mother as a favor; it was part of his household duty, like going to the bank to pay the bills. The house was an apartment and it was his: he had a set of keys, his mother consulted him on the best way to manage their domestic budget. In my house there was no space beside Dona Joana to assume such a role.

Compared with José, I was apparently a very independent young man, an appearance that my contact with Armando cracked open to reveal a mama's boy. It was a bitch, but nothing could be done about it. When I looked after Jussara so my mother could go out, or when I brought her some kind of fastening from the notions store downtown on the way home from school, she'd tousle my hair in return, the smile on her face expressing pride in her little boy, all grown up. It was so different from the way Dona Esther treated Armando when he gave her the receipts from the bills he paid at the bank, along with her change. She didn't thank him. She sighed, remarked on how costly life was, she praised God that she had a job and, unlike the women she served in the institution where she worked, she didn't depend on others for help. The scholarship Eliana received to study in the Catholic school weighed on her pride. She and Armando decided that the way to set things right was for Eliana to attend the same public school that Armando did when she got to high school. By then she'd be old enough to catch the bus by herself and make her own lunch.

Eliana, who would be 59 years old tomorrow, was passionately devoted to her brother. Armando—a loudmouth, a truant who always got away with things, a ringleader, a prankster, a mediocre center striker, a foul mouth, mediator of various factions, spokesman for all our student demands, merrymaker, glutton, and miser—he felt part of any group that life set before him, claiming the role of brother or father no matter where you put him. Eliana on the other hand belonged to only one group: her family triad. A chosen people, bearers of the mark. It was necessary to deserve it, the mark, which she daily mastered through her dedication to her studies and in the seriousness with which she measured her thoughts and actions. Francisco Augusto says that love triangles hold more love than duets. He says that the desire to defeat and dominate is what preserves it. Eliana was possessed by the obligation to serve and to live up to a certain level. She couldn't fail. Up to the level of her mother, first of all, and then, forever and always, her brother. She wasn't timid, submissive, or defensive. She was delicate. She had that joy of the very serious. She died without knowing, Luiza said, don't worry.

I hesitate not because I fear the exposure of my incoherence. Retired, said the man who moved with the help of a walker and his new wife. I'm in the navy, said the wife in white, and we're newlyweds. We don't know anything about the people we see and when they tell us what they are—retired, in the navy—we're surprised because without realizing it, we already knew the entirety of their lives: something inside us has woven their stories and relationships. Mainly about the things they don't tell us. In the bakery, that pretty girl with the bags under her eyes, I think—she's married, she's nursing and doesn't sleep much at night. She proudly displays her weariness and the stain of leaked milk on her low-cut dress. She has the voice of a queen and her gaze is distracted, she loves and is loved and the love flows into the bread, the butter, the milk, the baker, and transforms even the famished gaze of the little urchin on her breast into an homage to maternity—and this is how we make people known and familiar, enclosed in a story that doesn't threaten us. When the girl in white at the motel said, I'm in the navy, she guided my thoughts, fixed a prearranged path—that of the nurse who'd used her husband's infirmity to make herself indispensable and loved, a love always threatened by the possibility that her companion would be cured. I don't know whether this information about her was enriching or limiting.

Life is full of surprises. I'm in the navy, said the girl in white. This cancer, it's already taken my breasts and given me these silicone tits, it's eating me from the inside and I want life, bread, the baker, and the desires of this little boy, said the girl from the bakery. The danger, when confronted by these surprises, is to say to ourselves, oh yes, now I understand, and to halt the process of imagination, deactivating it. To accept Navy and Cancer, to archive them in pigeonholes called Soldier and Death, is to discard, as error, Care and Maternity.

Oh, how thought betrays. Next to error, betrayal is my engine. I was going to talk about two beautiful women who attracted me, like someone who means nothing by it, only to illustrate a prosaic analogy, and I've returned to soldiers and death. Soldiers and death. Where along the way did I lose the dark, shining skin of my domineering nurse and the pulsing tenderness of my new mother? Soldiers and death. Left, right, left, right, march little soldier, in your soft beret. The trick is to accept these betrayals of reality and thought, incite them, remain open to receive them, but never submit to them. +

—Translated by Adam Morris

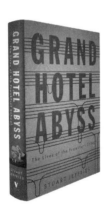

JULIAN CHARRIÈRE, *POLYGON XXVIII*, 2014, MEDIUM FORMAT BLACK-AND-WHITE PHOTOGRAPH, DOUBLE EXPOSURE THROUGH THERMONUCLEAR STRATA, ON PHOTO RAG. © JULIAN CHARRIÈRE, VG BILD-KUNST, BONN.

WARD'S FOOL

Caleb Crain

I DREAMED LAST NIGHT that I crossed the river and visited the tall ruins. In waking life I've only ever admired them from this side of the water. The quiet over there must be impressive; the only thing to hear would be the wind, and maybe now and then an ache or creak from one of the structures as they continue to settle.

A part of me has always wanted to go—are there raccoons?—but I never have, in part because of the first memo I ever wrote for you. You may not remember it, but it has come back to me, as a sense-memory almost more than as an intellectual one, every time I have sat down at this desk, because it was the first thing I wrote with a manufactured pen after coming to Drayton—an amenity that brought home to me what being at Drayton meant. The memo established—fluidly, blotlessly established—that there was every reason to believe that the rumors *weren't* true and that the levels across the water were indeed as high as the holding authority then said they were, and subsiding no more quickly than the authority maintained. I never went, too, because such a visit would have been against the law, and I have always been deterred by respect for the law, or at any rate by fear of fines or detention should any boatman I approach for a ride turn out to be an undercover police officer. And in part, finally, it has to be said, I didn't cross the water because for the past twenty years I have been in your service and conscious of your investment in me, financial and human. I used to go so far as to think that if I ever wanted to run a risk that large, I would owe it to you to ask first—which would mean, of course, that I would never run the risk, because for my sake you would say no.

By now you have probably guessed why I introduced this memo with my dream. My long-standing wish to visit the ruins and the long-standing obstruction of my wish rather neatly illustrate the most common questions about free will, the topic you have asked me to explore. If I know better than to visit the ruins, can it be said that I am not free to visit them? If an instrument of governance forestalls a visit that almost any rational and informed observer would consider misguided, is my freedom impaired in a way that I ought to mind? And if my contractual and (we might as well call them) emotional obligations are incompatible with a visit, and if it is never, at any time in the course of my life, in my interest to repudiate these obligations or otherwise divest myself of them, is it the case that I have been kept by them from visiting? In this matter, do I have a will of my own? A delicate question for someone in service to be asked to investigate, but the delicacy is not irrelevant, and you have always allowed full license and expected complete candor in the course of research. I suspect, moreover, that one need not be in service to be troubled by the question, or by its fellows. After all, although the motive behind your request twenty years ago for a memo on the ruins, at the time still fairly raw, may have been mere curiosity, the philosophy of your system of memos is by and large pragmatic—a memo aims to present the best pertinent counsel obtainable by a proportionate effort within an appropriate time span, according to the formula that I repeat at least once a week to one or another of the younger members of the staff—and so perhaps I may infer that on your part, too, there is a wish to visit, or at least once upon a time there was. Twenty years ago. For you, too, such a wish, if it did once exist, will have been obstructed, if not stopped, by prudence, law, and a sense of responsibilities owed elsewhere.

I'm making a speculation about you personally only in order to suggest the universality of the issues. ~~But no doubt these sentences are so irremediably orotund and cautious that you will over~~

There is a further challenge to free will to consider, one that is a little theoretical and therefore somewhat harder to see. Suppose that tomorrow morning the appeal of a visit to the ruins strikes you as worth the price, at last. Is going to strike you as worth the price. And suppose, too, that a scientist of the old days watches your brain, overnight, as your valuations of the alternatives are shifting. We can imagine him using one of the real-time scanners that doctors used to be able to call upon, plugged into the best of our generators here at Drayton, which, we can further imagine, is by a miracle giving us the steady voltage, within narrow tolerances, that the fine devices of the old days seem to have preferred. Since we're in the realm of the hypothetical, why not also suppose that the images produced by the scanner are sharper than anything the scanners of the old days were able to achieve, and that we have somehow found a computer with unmelted circuits as well, and that we are tasking the computer with keeping an inventory of the locations and directions of all the electrons in your brain as they tumble along your neurons, so as to extrapolate their future paths. If, at two-thirty in the morning, the computer tallies that when you wake up at nine you will choose to cross the water despite penalties and losses, is it correct to say that you will choose freely upon waking? The computer will have predicted your choice more than six hours before.

A quibble of this kind was the challenge to free will of most concern to philosophers explicitly so called in the decades leading up to the final presidency. It is hard to take seriously now, but progress in instrumentation and artificial intelligence was so rapid in those days that perhaps the prospect of a complete monitoring of the biological substrate of a person's interiority did not then seem entirely theoretical. There is some reason to think, after all, that the nature of people's concerns about free will varies with the epoch. In the nineteenth century, as the flames of religion were apparently being extinguished in the superior dawn of science, the great worry was how to reconcile free will, imagined as spontaneous, with morality, imagined as immutable and absolute. Was a person who understood the nature and worth of virtue ever really free to choose something else? By the time the twentieth century was yielding to the twenty-first, the worry had been replaced by one strangely analogous: Was a rational agent ever really free to choose a course of action that failed to maximize his economic self-interest? It was to politics that people generally went for an answer for the latter question, in those years. The philosophers were, as I say, then preoccupied by the problem of the hypothetically powerful computer. They feared that once the computer was armed with a perfect knowledge (equally hypothetical) of the world as it existed at a particular moment, there would be nothing it couldn't predict—no decision it couldn't undermine by knowing of it in advance—by simple calculation of that moment's consequences. Even in the library we have assembled here at Drayton, discussions of the threat are so extensive that I find myself worried about falling—almost against my will, as it were—into the error of awarding the topic an amount of attention proportional to the attention awarded to it by earlier writers, rather than the amount I myself think it deserves.

A shortcut, perhaps: Do you remember Alan Burns? While he was in service here as your chauffeur, almost fifteen years ago, he let a number of people know that he thought there was still a place in the continent for a republic and that he was going to fight for it. He wasn't shy about it; a report of his intentions must have reached you. He was resourceful, as a chauffeur has to be, about foraging and bargaining for parts as well as about making repairs, and I think he was so sure of his value to you that he didn't care if you heard. You probably remember that I came and told you that I wanted to follow him, without telling you (but without much disguising from you) where I thought he was going and why.

I had never taken much interest in politics before. You told me that you believed I wouldn't go. ~~I think you understood that I was in love.~~ You acted, in other words, a bit like the hypothetically powerful computer. And in fact, by the time Alan was ready to leave, I had decided to stay. Out of my wages I bought him provisions from our storehouse—a smoked gigot, jars of preserved plums, a wheel of cheddar—left them next to his pack on a side table in the front hallway, and went for a walk around the fields on the north side of the refectory, which had then just recently been put under tillage. I had chosen items that I thought wouldn't go bad quickly. When I came back in from the walk and saw them still sitting on the side table, my heart leaped into my mouth. (Odd turn of phrase. Like a little frog that I wasn't then able to swallow again.) I asked Sidney, at that time already our head steward, if perhaps Alan hadn't left yet. He said there hadn't been enough room in Alan's pack.

It would be unfair and a little delusional if I were to claim that you deprived me of the freedom to follow Alan merely by happening to know me better than I knew myself. ("So ask him for the money for your kit" is what Alan had said to me when I told him about your prediction. "He'll probably give it to you if he doesn't think you'll go." But I didn't think that would be right.) This anecdote doesn't feel personal to me, by the way, and I trust that it doesn't to you. The past, after enough time goes by, resurfaces and becomes available for an almost objective re-examination, as if it belonged to someone else. Of course it doesn't ever belong to anyone else; one is the only custodian.

~~A body brought in at Pembroke last February is thought to have been Alan's, by the way. I sent for details and received a letter last week from the runner who made the~~

I'm tempted to declare my shortcut by anecdote a sufficient refutation—I expect you'll agree that it would be unfair of me to claim that your prediction fettered me—and I might even end the memo here if it weren't that one of the threads running through the tangles around the hypothetically powerful computer seems to be attached to, of all things, your system of memos. I wouldn't be looking out for your interests, in other words, if I didn't go at least a little further into the matter. (The risk that you run that I might *not* look out for your interests, by the way, is also bound up in the tangle, as I'll explain shortly.)

In the greater philosophical tradition, the original form of the theoretically omniscient computer was, of course, the mind of God. A god's powers are magical and exempt from scrutiny; one doesn't ask how a god would come to know the events of the future. But a computer, even an imaginary one, must have technical specifications, and it's evident by inspection that the computing power necessary in this thought experiment isn't trivial. In the limiting case, the map probably has to be as large as the territory: the only computer capable of predicting every action in the universe throughout all time is the universe itself, acting over the course of all time. And even if the scope of prediction is narrowed to your decision, Mr. Ward, to cross or not to cross the waters tomorrow morning, the tasks of monitoring the electrons that constitute your decision-making process and forecasting their paths inside your brain likely exceed even the total computer power available at the time of the final presidency. Philosophers of that era who tried to poke holes in the imaginary computer objected not to its size, however—it was too easy to imagine a larger one—but to its speed. Would it be able to finish calculating your decision before you yourself had made it? Or they doubted the resolving power of its attendant microscopes, or rather, doubted that any resolution would be of use. Since ancient Greece, in fact, there had been an idea that some of the smallest particles of matter were unpredictable and therefore, somehow, a refuge for free will. If, at a deep, invisible level, the elements of matter were fuzzy and chaotic, then perhaps among them one could escape observation and tracking? So went the hope.

In the stratum where humans live, however, we interact with subatomic particles only when they are massed together in such numbers that the laws of probability make their coordinated motions as regular as those of billiard balls, the ivory toys that you must remember since I still do, so smooth and symmetrical that even a novice student of Newtonian physics could predict their neat collisions. A freedom to be chaotic, moreover, isn't the kind of freedom anyone wants, as the pleasure given to one's ear by the orderly click of one billiard ball against another used to suggest.

~~Is freedom no more than a matter of scale? While I write this, leaves of mint are drifting in my white porcelain cup as if at liberty, but the cup is sitting on this grand desk, which used to be yours, beside quires of paper that you have also provided. A generous~~

The whole problem of foreknowledge seems to me factitious. I wonder if it's a residual cognitive artifact of the percept formerly known as God, which hasn't really been superseded, after all, if philosophers continue to believe in the capacity to see time the way God was supposed to have seen it—on a long, unrolled parchment, the past next to the present next to the future.

What if that's not possible? *What if time is real?* What if the future doesn't exist yet, and the past no longer does? Almost immediately, from the moment I saw the provisions still sitting on the side table and realized, at the same moment, that I desperately wanted to hear that Alan was still on the grounds somewhere and knew, also at the same moment, that I was wanting it too late, that I was wanting it because it was too late—almost immediately I made a conscious effort to become the sort of person who would have gone with Alan instead of the person who didn't. This person, the person I wasn't, would be freer than I had been, and happier, even if he would never have Alan again any more than I would. What I felt was that even if I never had Alan again I would be freer and happier if I didn't make any consolidation of my personality around the decision that I happened to have made to stay. *I had made a mistake.* I don't mean that I pretended not to have made the mistake. Having stayed, it made sense to continue to stay. But I was going to make a different choice the next time. I made calculations about what the person who would have gone would have felt if he had stayed. I decided he would sometimes become sad about the error but wouldn't let himself become embittered or cynical about it, and so I tried to keep a kind of openness in my sorrow.

If any of the philosophers of the old days were still alive today to read this memo, they would probably ask why I was so confident that the future doesn't exist in a way so different—so much more multiple—than the way the past doesn't exist. And if billiard balls were the only structures of interest in the universe, I would probably have to concede that I am sentimentalizing—that steeling myself in later years was no more than a compensation for, or even just a reflex to, my earlier failure of nerve—that I am only pretending to be responsible for the alteration in myself, like the rider in the well-known thought experiment (or thought non-experiment, rather) who persuades himself that he wants to go in the direction that his horse is already headed. Maybe I am mistaken even in thinking that an alteration in myself has been made. I think, however, that the old philosophers suffered from too little faith (ironically, considering their attachment to a godlike conspectus). As I see it, every life is both an experience and a repetition of experience. Even the simplest organism rehearses the species memory written in its genome, and a human being has four additional kinds of memory: a limbic system, which associates arousals to situations; task memory, which acquires skills like driving or tennis; culture, including language, which pools wisdom in impersonal forms; and personal recollection of one's individual history, which in time one almost stands apart from. I believe that human beings are unique because their memories rehearse the past but not fatally; during a repetition the mental representation of an experience may be altered by study, practice, correction, new associations, interpretation, comparison, and error.

Is it more implausible that information about the future could come into existence before the future itself does? Or that a being with the endowments that I have described might be capable of sometimes learning from mistakes?

~~(manic?)~~

Lacking such faith, the old philosophers had to square the circle. Through clever redescriptions, they tried to make free will seem compatible with an immutable future. Life, in their subtle but not commonsensical understanding, became an experience somewhat like that of reading this memo. By the time the memo reaches your hands, the choices made by me (and by you) that went into its formation have already been made. Any suspense you might feel while reading is an illusion, a side effect of its communication to you through words, which your mind, like all human minds, must understand in sequence. While you're reading the words at the beginning you don't yet know the ones at the end. But your ignorance of the words at the end does not mean they haven't already been chosen. Even for me, in the experience of writing, I'm aware of constraints, especially if I choose to limit myself to telling you what I believe. I have no control over what I believe; no one does. All I can choose is whether to lie or whether to put a little more effort into thinking my thoughts through or into expressing them more clearly or more cogently. I seem, strangely enough, to have free will chiefly over the aspects of writing that might be labeled aesthetic.

And even in the realm of the aesthetic, your patience, you might wish to remind me, is for me a limit. With your patience in mind, I want to assure you that I haven't digressed as far as I may seem to have, because a coordinate strategy, among the old philosophers, was to turn the problem on its head and argue that in most cases, a rational person doesn't want free will, anyway. One doesn't really want a free choice between taking Maple Avenue or Hapgood Drive; one wants to take whichever route is faster. One doesn't want a free choice between a hempen or a flaxen rope; one wants to be told which is stronger and lighter. Free will, in this understanding, is a last resort—not a boon but a crisis. If a person can afford to, say, hire a staff of researchers to map out all his paths ahead of time and write memos on every crux he faces, thereby allowing him to restrict his exercise of free will to as few decisions as possible, his life will be greatly improved.

~~But if a larger and larger proportion of people are induced to believe that the only meaningful choice is one that maximizes the economic benefit to them, and if they are encouraged to slot their desires into a smaller and smaller number of approved cubbyholes, and ignore any invitations by or tendencies in others to wish for anything outside these cubbyholes, it will be as if all the chaotic particles in the world were conjoined into billiard~~

~~(mania a defense against loss)~~

It's me, by this logic, who has been sapping your free will all these years—Ariel as the jailer of Prospero . . .

~~I seem to be saying good-bye.~~

But it's a serious question, actually, whether the system is in your interest. Maybe not all that serious if what's at stake is the selection of a rope, but suppose you ask the staff to read novels for you so that you will never have to waste time on one you don't like. (A double hypothetical, since you prefer nonfiction.) How could we predict what you will like or not like? We might be able to find a certain type of novel that pleases you, but how could we find a type of novel that neither you nor we yet know you like, or a novel that breaks out of type altogether, other than by taking the risk of recommending one you might not like at all? In aesthetic matters it may not be possible to minimize free will. What if a crucial life decision is more like an aesthetic discovery than like the choice of a radio? That is, a decision that is also about the grounds of decision. Necessarily it runs the risk of complete failure.

If free will is only exercised in the absence of adequate information, then perhaps one is only really free if one leaves the world of facts for a world that is not-real. Not-real the way that the self that I decided to become, even while staying here, has been not-real. Acknowledged not to be real. Fiction being perhaps the highest form of repetition with alteration. I could have chosen to imagine, for example, that after Alan left, he decided to live in one of the empty structures across the river.

In the mornings, before you came down, he drank his coffee on the settle in the front hallway while he read your newspaper, folding and unfolding it with the care that is prudent when one is doing something for which one doesn't have permission. "Here's the man who's going to solve the world," was his line for me, whenever he saw me. I was very young and I liked it that a man with a beard was calling me a man. There's a fear that people like me sometimes have that they'll go from being a boy to being a little old ex-boy without ever having been a man in between. One day I got up the nerve to ask him to come look at a map with me. You were considering some property, I told him, and I wanted to ask about the roads to it. Of course what I really wanted was to see what we would say to each other when it was just the two of us. And when we were alone, after he told me about the roads, what I said, very stupidly (but in my own conceit, very boldly), was, "Why do you say I'm going to solve the world?"

"Do you mind?"

He seemed to know that I didn't.

"Aren't you going to?" he went on.

"Are you going to fight?" I asked. He was kind of an asshole, in a number of ways. I think that was a part of what I ~~admired~~ liked about him. The inconsideration.

"Once I've saved up for a kit."

"How will you provide for yourself?" I asked.

"Listen to the way you talk," he replied. And then he asked what I was doing that night and whether he could visit me, but those weren't the words he used, and so the risk that I had taken in talking to him had been worth it—even beyond the exhilaration of the risk-taking itself—everything had succeeded—the next two months—

It was about a year later that I was invited into your bed, which didn't last any longer.

~~Please don't think that I don't appreciate everything you've~~

Did you decide to assign me this question because you had heard about the kit that I put aside for myself last month? Maybe this memo should be understood not as an answer but as a bet between the two of us about the answer. +

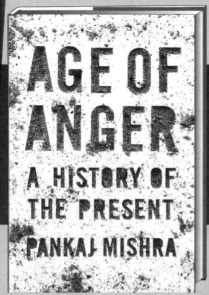

ASA NISI MASA

ACE HOTEL

New Orleans Pittsburgh Los Angeles London

Palm Springs New York Portland Seattle

REVIEWS

A. S. HAMRAH

All That Counts Is Getting to a Normal World

The New York Film Festival, 2016.

IN HIS 1987 FILM *SOIGNE TA DROITE*, JEAN-LUC Godard explained that the hardest thing about the movie business was carrying around film cans. In the digital age, that problem has been solved, for better or worse: films are now portable media packages. It's the audience, not filmmakers, who face cinema's big challenge: figuring out where to see movies. If you are lucky or foolish enough to live in New York City, you can turn to ScreenSlate.com and always find a movie worth leaving the house for. If you live anywhere else in the US, it's not as easy. This is where film festivals come in. The big film festivals in North America, unlike those in Europe and Asia, bring masses of people to places most of them would not otherwise visit: Telluride, Colorado; Columbia, Missouri; Toronto. Film festivals, as much as music festivals, have led the way in the professionalization of experience into creative-class gatherings and industry conferences. Before there were TED Talks and South by Southwest, before there was Coachella, there was Sundance.

The New York Film Festival has always been a little different. Since 1963 it has been the premier yearly showcase in the US for serious cinema of all kinds. Held at Lincoln Center over two and a half weeks in late September and early October, the festival concentrates on a smaller slate than other festivals but is nonetheless huge. It is divided into somewhat blurry categories: twenty-five Main Slate features, fifteen documentary features (although some Main Slate features are docs), eleven additional Explorations and Special Event features, about twenty revivals of older films, thirty shorts, more than forty Projections films representing the nonnarrative avant-garde, and a section of virtual-reality items called Convergence. There are also, of course, parties, Q&As with filmmakers and actors, and "An Evening with . . . " events. This year's were with actors: Kristen Stewart, who appears in three films in the festival, and Adam Driver, star of Jim Jarmusch's new film, *Paterson*.

Many of the films have already shown in festivals around the world, and some go into general release soon after they screen. The New York Film Festival serves as their official introduction to the US, in which the tony setting of Lincoln Center confers on them the status of worthy and serious works. The Main Slate films represent a set of features not just for cinephiles but for any cultured person keeping up with the movies—anyone who is interested in film as an art form that will survive the big-studio superhero infestation and the burden of quality TV.

Before and during the festival, about fifty films are screened during the day for the press. I saw forty of them. I missed one because of a therapy appointment. (Even though I am a film critic, I hope to be able to have normal relationships someday.) I missed another because I had a hangover and couldn't face the hour-long trip to Lincoln Center from my apartment in Brooklyn. Two I paid to see, and went on Sunday afternoons after buying tickets using the festival's complicated and anxiety-inducing website, with its countdown clock.

THE PRESS SCREENINGS began as President Obama arrived in town for his last visit to the UN General Assembly the Monday after a bomb went off near Chelsea. It was mid-September and New York was a humid mess, with extra police presence, traffic jams, spottier-than-usual subway service, and the lurking shadow of a possible Trump presidency making everybody nervous. None of that stopped film critics from arriving at Lincoln Center an hour before showtimes to make sure they got good seats in the Walter Reade Theater.

Standing in line at Lincoln Center with other journalists at 9 AM brings into stark relief the difference between artists and critics. Because Juilliard is at Lincoln Center, each morning dozens of young drama students pass by the festival press line on their way to class. An inordinate number of film critics are men, and young men are especially overrepresented. The drama students, among whom young women seem to be equally overrepresented, pass by in a parade of youthful vigor, unaware they are strolling by their future judges. This daily nonmeeting of the two groups made me want to donate money to a feminist film critics' organization.

Sitting in the auditorium, I learned that some of the young critics were Airbnb'ing from out of town to attend these screenings, while others were commuting daily from other states. Seated in front of them, a line of elderly Lincoln Center patrons occupied the extra-leg-room row, dressed like they had just arrived from Martha's Vineyard to see the new Almodóvar or Lonergan. (Their wardrobes improved as summer turned to fall.) Among them was Howard Stern, wearing enviably fashionable sneakers. Whether he was there as a member of the press or as a patron I never knew, but I was surprised to learn he was a fan of contemporary art-house cinema. Maybe next time he has Donald Trump on his radio show, they'll discuss Paul Verhoeven's *Elle*.

THIS YEAR'S FESTIVAL opened with a documentary, Ava DuVernay's *13th*, about the racist legacy of the clause in the Thirteenth Amendment allowing involuntary servitude as punishment for crime. *13th* was made for Netflix, where it debuted a week later. Not only was this the first time in its history that the New York Film Festival opened with a documentary, it was the first time it opened with a movie that was essentially made for TV. When Quentin Tarantino said, without having seen it, that DuVernay's *Selma* was more like a TV movie that would have been made in the 1970s than an actual work of cinema, he could not have predicted how DuVernay would turn the opportunity to make a movie for Netflix into an act of defiance.

DuVernay cites Griffith's *The Birth of a Nation* (1915) as the original sin in American filmmaking, contrasting its violent racism with the power digital media has to expose police brutality and other state crimes directed at people of color. Smartphone video cameras and streaming media, in *13th*, are explicitly positioned against the cinema, which, starting with Griffith's white-supremacist epic, encouraged the racism that continues to echo in Hollywood a hundred years after his film. The radicalism of opening a film festival with this message (while also ceding the streaming future by handing Netflix this honor) was acknowledged by DuVernay, if no one else. In her press conference following the screening, she was frank about it. If digital media can keep the police from killing innocent people, it can also make Hollywood rethink the entrenched racism of the film industry, which has made money for decades by depicting people of color as less worthy than white people.

Catalan filmmaker Albert Serra's *The Death of Louis XIV* exemplified a different kind of cinema. Serra's film was designed as a performance piece for a museum. The French monarch is bedridden, almost immobile, occasionally wheeled about—a near mummy. Jean-Pierre Léaud, adolescent face of the French New Wave, now 72 years old, plays the king. (Coincidentally, seventy-two years is how long Louis XIV reigned as king of France.) Noble, sick, pampered, and weird, Louis, as played by Léaud, becomes a stand-in (more of a sit-in) for the European art cinema of the second half of the 20th century. The film's majesty and stateliness are undercut at all times by illness—deathbed scenes turn a museum into a hospice.

Serra self-consciously removes his film from the assaultive world of media. Its slow pace and dark, lush setting require attention but also a forgetting or abandonment of the world outside. Incompetent doctors minister to the king, watching over the decline of this body politic, offering many theories and no solutions. In their desperation to keep Louis alive, they resort to quack remedies sold to them by charlatans. Léaud's presence brings with it our collective memory of his former glory. We watch with these doctors as it fades out of existence.

Léaud, who is not known for his warmth or for setting foot in the US, appeared in person with Serra after the screening. His presence was a thrill—something I realized I had been waiting for since I was a teenager and saw Léaud in Godard and Truffaut films at the university near where I grew up. During the Q&A, he quoted Cocteau, one of his early mentors at the time of *The 400 Blows* and the birth of the French New Wave: The cinema is the only medium that shows death at work. Léaud gave the impression of understanding that quite well. The guy sitting next to me, not so much. He checked sports scores on his phone while Léaud and Serra talked, staving off death one ballgame result at a time.

Like Serra, Eugène Green is a foreigner working in French cinema, an American who added a grave accent to his name and makes films more French than the French do. *Son of Joseph*, about an abandoned son (Victor Ezenfis) planning an elaborate revenge on his father (Mathieu Amalric), takes place in a literary milieu and in churches that hark back to Christianity's formative years. Vincent's father, Oscar, is editor in chief at a publishing house and a mean-spirited philanderer. His office is in an underfurnished 19th-century hotel suite, where, when he is not editing manuscripts or trying to find France's next top novelist, he can be found on a couch with his executive assistant, a leggy bondage enthusiast. If it weren't so cartoonish, this setup could be the envy of cube-bound male book editors everywhere. The literary setting points to a recurring theme of the festival, one that competes with smartphoning-it-in and museumification as a trend in the postdigital cinema: the merging of movies with literary fiction.

PEDRO ALMODÓVAR'S *Julieta* is based on three interrelated Alice Munro stories, which the screenwriter-director moves from Canada to Spain. The film takes place over three periods in the life of its protagonist (Adriana Ugarte as young Julieta, Emma Suárez when she's older), a classicist and translator. The moody plot traces her guilt and depression through her relationship with her lover, Xoan, his death at sea, and her estrangement from their daughter.

The first part of the film, with Ugarte as a 1980s New Wave Julieta during her grad-student days, is mysterious, colorful, and exciting. The Suárez sections, while typically stylish, are at odds with the usual Almodóvarian melodrama and drain the film of emotion until it abruptly ends before the moment of reconciliation. The ending, though Hitchcockian in its unexpected cutoff and mountain-road setting, still belongs more to literature than the movies. Almodóvar plants a foot on each side of the gap between the two, which is fine, but the film, like Julieta herself, seems lost on the road.

Kelly Reichardt's *Certain Women*, as its title's pun suggests, does not have that problem. This adaptation of three loosely related stories by Maile Meloy surefootedly treads its Montana landscape even when it seems to be meandering or concentrating on emptiness. Its sparse dialogue and observational style erase its literary origins the same way Antonioni erased Cortázar's in *Blowup*. The film takes place indoors as much as out, even in the middle of nowhere. Laura Dern's lawyer character deals with childish men in offices, in a motel room, across conference tables, and in prison, while Kristen Stewart and Lily Gladstone meet in a classroom at night or across a table in a diner. Gladstone's young ranch hand, the Native American in this western, pitchforks hay in a barn before dawn and drives her truck to town at the same hour of morning, with little landscape visible through the windows.

The ground here is frozen and hard. Stewart and Gladstone's brief semi-encounter takes place in public but away from men, while Dern has to deal in private with an uncommunicative married lover, an "authentic" type (James Le Gros). As one of Dern's clients, Jared Harris commits to a disturbing performance of confusion and longing that underscores the film's cold rage and loneliness. He's a woodworker with brain trauma who takes a hostage in an office building, an act he can barely commit to before running away. Everything in *Certain Women* is carefully constructed and potentially deadly, but Reichardt rejects the spectacle of violence associated with the American West, replacing it with silence and dark pity.

CYNTHIA NIXON, as Emily Dickinson in Terence Davies's biopic, *A Quiet Passion*, is paradoxically louder and more insistent than Dern, Michelle Williams, Stewart, and Gladstone in *Certain Women*. Davies creates a full society around Dickinson, in great detail, making her housebound nonconformism hard to understand. One by one, her friends and family drop away, through marriage and death, leaving Dickinson nothing but her visions and her poetry. It is tragic but not romantic. Dickinson stiff-arms everybody, and Davies refuses to sentimentalize her as the Belle of Amherst, making her off-putting every chance he gets.

Nixon's performance is a self-conscious tour de force of buried fury. Dickinson's essential attitude, as Nixon and Davies take pains to point out, is bitterness ("not despair"), and at the end of her life, as she lies on her deathbed aware of her obscurity and her sacrifice, she asks why the world has become so ugly. The only cinematic comparison is another masterpiece, Mikio Naruse's 1962 film *A Wanderer's Notebook*, about the life and struggle of Fumiko Hayashi, a Japanese writer who, like Dickinson, died in middle-age.

Naruse's film is considered minor among his works, but it looms over Jarmusch's *Paterson*, too. All three films present poetry as text over images. *Paterson*, the least of them, is *A Quiet Passion* in reverse: the happy story of an obscure young man, a bus driver played by Adam Driver, who is named Paterson and lives in Paterson, New Jersey. This double cuteness is spread all over the film, like the frosting patterns Paterson's girlfriend, Laura (Golshifteh Farahani), carefully applies to the cupcakes she sells at the farmers' market the film unfortunately never visits. It would be good to see a Jarmuschian farmers' market, or maybe a flea market—then Jarmusch could catalog all the knickknacks he loves without the encumbrance of a plot. It's a saccharine film, sometimes relieved during Paterson's walks through town on the way to the bar he visits every night while walking his cute dog.

Like the shrine to writers and hepcats in *Only Lovers Left Alive*, the tribute nook to Patersonians behind the bar reveals Jarmusch as a talent obsessed with explaining what's cool. This has marred his work. He sneaks in Iggy Pop, a non-Patersonian, via faded newspaper clipping, a digression that's a shill for *Gimme Danger*, Jarmusch's documentary about the Stooges singer that also played in the festival. That film, too, descends into a treatise on cool. We learn that the proof of cool—and its endpoint—is Sonic Youth covering a Stooges song. Jarmusch doesn't mention cool's decay, its half-life: Iggy's "Search and Destroy" is now heard in a commercial for Audi on TV.

PABLO LARRAÍN, the Chilean director, had two films in the festival. I saw them in the order they were made. *Neruda* transforms four years in the life of the Nobel Laureate and communist into detective fiction. Luis Gnecco, the star of the Chilean version of the TV show *The Office*, portrays Neruda as a friend of the workers, an enemy of the police, and a habitué of an urban demimonde where his poetry stirs lost souls, prostitutes, and drag queens. A police detective (Gael García Bernal) and his squad spy on Neruda, then track him through snowy mountains as he makes his escape into Argentina. Bernal, swallowed by his fedora and his 1940s suit, becomes a character written by Neruda in this magical-realist fable reminiscent of the weirder, less accommodating films of Raúl Ruiz. Sometimes *Neruda* beautifies fascism in a nostalgic glow of tertiary color the way *The Conformist* did, sometimes it uglifies it along the lines of Cronenberg's version of *Naked Lunch*. It brings to the cinema the kind of literary biography that traces only a short period in its subject's life.

Larraín's *Jackie* does the same, but concentrates on four days, not four years. Larraín follows Jacqueline Kennedy (Natalie Portman) from her husband's assassination in Dallas through his funeral and a subsequent interview with a reporter (Billy Crudup) on Cape Cod. Portman's performance and Larraín's flowing camera overcome a screenplay that too often seems like a one-act play. Larraín and Portman do more than just move a play outdoors. They explode it into lush, grand visions of American history and chaos. Portman, in Jackie's blood-spattered pink Chanel suit, glides through a pinpoint re-creation of the 1963 White House interior, right down to the George Catlin paintings of buffalo on the walls. Drinking vodka, taking pills, listening to the sound-track album from *Camelot*, she considers or ignores instructions from Robert Kennedy (Peter Sarsgaard), her secretary (Greta Gerwig), a priest (John Hurt), Jack Valenti (Max Casella), the Johnsons (John Carroll Lynch and Beth Grant), each whisked through by Larraín so Jackie can cool them with icy disdain and quiet lisping. Portman's performance is one for the ages because, in its fabulous poise, it is camp. She surpasses Faye Dunaway as Joan Crawford and Glenn Close as Sunny von Bülow because the woman she plays is sympathetic. Jackie is nicer than Crawford and more iconic, and, unlike von Bülow, not in a coma.

Jackie was not on the festival press-screening schedule, but I managed to see it one night at the Fox building on Sixth Avenue. As I left, passing giant posters of Bill O'Reilly and Brit Hume in the halls, the last presidential debate was about to start, the one in which Donald Trump called Hillary Clinton, a former first lady like Jackie, a "nasty woman." No doubt he will see that moment re-created in a film someday. Midtown was quiet as the screens in the Fox windows and the ticker on the building showed pre-debate Trump news, delivering his crude messages onto empty sidewalks. Larraín's film wants us to believe that maybe there really was an American Camelot once upon a time. The blue and red glow from the Fox News building made *Jackie*'s conclusion mournful, and in comparison not tacky at all.

ALISON MACLEAN'S *The Rehearsal*, based on the novel Eleanor Catton wrote before *The Luminaries*, is, like *Certain Women*, an unliterary literary adaptation. It offers serious counterpoint to college musical dramas and pop spectacle like *Pitch Perfect*. In Maclean's film, a group of acting students at "the Institute," a drama school in New Zealand, secretly put on a play based on a teacher-student sex scandal in the local news. A movie of negotiated betrayal among millennials and their Gen X mentors (like Noah Baumbach's *Mistress America*), *The Rehearsal* relies on squirm, eventually letting its characters off the hook by forcing them to solve their problems on their own. Reflecting on the suicide of one of their fellow students, a wealthy member of their acting class who couldn't hack it, they realize his internet obsession can be applied to the theater and their audience.

The film is defined by odd, unexpected touches. The tennis instructor looks like an evil cowboy and too closely resembles the teenage girl he's had the affair with. Kerry Fox, as the Institute's director and main instructor, is harsh and preoccupied, but not a *Whiplash* monster. Maclean and Fox present her as a realistic intellectual who leads her own life away from her charges. Ella Edward's performance as the sister of the girl in the scandal is maybe the oddest thing in the film. Not quite the star in this ensemble cast, her out-of-it, distracted manner shows star quality and places her above the older students, who all want to be actors and are therefore very present. They flit through *The Rehearsal* like the Juilliard students at Lincoln Center, their eyes on something outside their immediate surroundings.

THE TITLE OF Alain Guiraudie's new film, *Staying Vertical*, is a pun that might work in French but in English translates as "audience indifference." That's too bad, because this wild, original film deserves to be seen. A gay screenwriter, Léo (Damien Bonnard), blocked in his writing, travels the Pyrenees, where he meets a farm girl and a country hustler who live with an elderly Pink Floyd fan, a ranter Léo assists in his suicide by fucking him on his deathbed. Scandal, woodland homeopathy, and homelessness follow, until Léo reemerges as a hermit. Employed by his baby mama's brutal gay-farmer dad, who looks like John C. Reilly in a nightmare, the two face down wolves in the mountains, united by their mutual obsession with these predators who kill their sheep and to whom they offer Lèo's baby as bait. Some people will do anything to avoid writing.

Nearby, but in a different movie, a hunky scientist (Paul Hamy) studies black storks through binoculars from his kayak. Later in João Pedro Rodrigues's *The Ornithologist*, this title character turns into a different person *Lost Highway*–style, played by Rodrigues himself. The film obscurely recasts the life of St. Anthony of Padua for modern times.

After rapids wash his kayak away, a pair of Chinese girls, Christian tourist-pilgrims lost in the woods on their way to the Camino de Santiago de Compostela, kidnap the ornithologist and tie him up in his underwear. Like the pixie-fairies from *Mothra*, they are delightful yet sinister and portend worse to come. The ornithologist escapes them, then has sex with a mute gay shepherd whom he kills for stealing his hoodie, and for possibly belonging to a sect of pagan vandals in red costumes who speak an obscure language and seem to be hunting him. By the time a gang led by a topless blond huntress appears, the film has begun to exhaust itself and the audience. These women on horseback bring it back to life as the ornithologist lies dying.

This same fallen world and potential homotopia exist in Dane Komljen's *All the Cities of the North*, a Serbian film set in the woods at an abandoned vacation resort. This postcommunist landscape, with its Brutalist concrete architecture giving way to nature, is populated by male lovers and homeless men who rearrange bed mats, wash themselves with buckets of water, and slice apples with large heavy scissors. We see the film's crew at work once in a while, and passages from Simone Weil's *Gravity and Grace* and Godard's screenplay for *Passion* are read on the sound track. I hoped for a scene in which one of the normcore vagrants placed a chip on another's shoulder while a third, offscreen, read from Thomas Piketty's *Capital in the Twenty-First Century*.

The film's slowness seems rote at this late point in the history of slow cinema. *All the Cities of the North* solidified for me, after Guiraudie's and Rodrigues's movies, that these films are part of a genre, and some genre directors are better than others. The self-conscious, desultory feel of this one underscored the power of the other two.

WILLFUL BOREDOM smothers Natalia Almada's *Everything Else*, the story of Doña Flor (Adriana Barraza), a Mexican bureaucrat nearing retirement who spends her days nitpicking paperwork handed to her by a random assortment of Mexico City residents. Her repetitive job, nightly routine, and hapless attempts to work up the courage to dive into a swimming pool compose the bulk of this film, a *Jeanne Dielman* in miniature. The severe vision of lower-class anomie in Akerman's film is leavened in *Everything Else* by a touch of connection from an obese woman in a gym shower room, another invisible woman in a teeming city. Almada spares Doña Flor a tragic end in a moment of potential violence, involving a fire-eating con man who pours lighter fluid on his victims.

After Doña Flor's cat dies, she leaves it wrapped in a towel on her bed all day while she goes to work in her office. When she gets home, she dumps it in a trash can. This cat is one link between *Everything Else* and *Things to Come*, Mia Hansen-Løve's film about a philosophy professor (Isabelle Huppert) who loses everything in middle age, including the antisocial cat her batty mother left behind after her death.

Huppert's Nathalie leads a decent life with her husband, Heinz, also a philosophy professor. They have two kids and a seaside vacation house; he reads Karl Kraus while she reads *Minima Moralia*. Arguments with her publisher about book-cover design reflect the changing world of the late '00s, in which marketing, it seems, came to dominate German-philosophy-textbook publishing in France. Nathalie's favorite student, a bearded Marxist radical named Fabien who wears ripped jeans and wants to live in the woods, ingratiates himself into her life to get published. A *normalien* in Paris at the time of Occupy Wall Street, he's supposed to be likable, committed, searching. After Heinz leaves Nathalie and she starts hanging out with Fabien and his adjunct pals in the French equivalent of upstate New York, I began to worry. Was Isabelle Huppert really going to sleep with this jive turkey? But it's the film's strategy to deny her comfort. When she goes to a movie theater to see *Certified Copy*, she's chased into the street by a lecher.

Kleber Mendonça Filho's *Aquarius*, from Brazil, is less eventful than *Things to Come*. Sonia Braga plays a woman not unlike Huppert's philosophy professor, a serious, slightly older music critic past retirement age. Clara is the last resident of her apartment building on the beach in Recife, and developers, eager to turn it into condos, have begun the nasty process of making life too unpleasant for her to stay. *Aquarius* is forty-five minutes longer than *Things to Come*, partly because it stops to show how annoying it is when the sound of construction makes thinking impossible. This rare flattering portrait of a critic as an aging, still-glamorous woman does not settle for the reheated comfort of nuclear family like *Things to Come* does. Clara turns the people around her into activists instead of hanging out with the already radicalized. The film's revelation of termite infestation, a metaphor for the crumbling infrastructure of capitalist development everywhere, is more direct and obvious than anything in *Things to Come*, more Zavattinian than the Rossellinian vision of a woman alone in Hansen-Løve's character study.

Matías Piñeiro's *Hermia & Helena* presents a potential future-Clara or future-Nathalie in Camila (Agustina Muñoz), a young Argentinian translator on a fellowship in Manhattan. She's working on a translation of *A Midsummer Night's Dream* for a theater company in Buenos Aires—we see the play's lines as text on the screen—but she also has a secret mission the film waits most of its short running time to reveal. Traveling upstate through bright snow under blue skies, she meets an older man played by the New York filmmaker Dan Sallitt, who is reserved but appealing in this role. He's an agreeable version of the patriarchy, a millennial girl's dream of a lost good dad—the opposite of the demanding, threatening father in Shakespeare's play.

Representatives of the patriarchy are more manipulative and aggressive in Hong Sang-soo's quiet, equally short *Yourself and Yours*, which makes for a wittier, stranger, more hard-assed film. Min-jung (Lee You-young), the object of desire here, may be two women. Clueless, drunken men argue over the "good" Min-jung and castigate the "bad" one in her absence and to her face. The good one is a faithful girlfriend who has promised to cut back on her drinking. The bad one gets plastered in public and makes out with strange men in bars.

Set, like *Hermia & Helena*, in a sealed urban world of young artists and writers who only talk to one another (and, here, bartenders), *Yourself and Yours* depicts rising female fury as it confronts passive, confused men. An older filmmaker, a stand-in for Hong, proves himself to be as boozy and dopey as Min-jung's younger boyfriends. The film's signature line of dialogue could also be the tag line on its poster: "Drink up, you pathetic men!"

A BOLDER CAT THAN the one she inherited in *Things to Come* looks on placidly in Paul Verhoeven's *Elle* as Isabelle Huppert is raped on her dining-room floor—a scene the film replays more than once. Michèle's nonreaction to this attack is as dissociated as the cat's. She looks at herself from outside, a spectator to her violation like the audience watching the film, the actress observing her role as she plays it. She cleans up this crime scene and goes to her office, where she runs a video-game company specializing in perverted fantasy and violence. At a fast-food restaurant, a woman dumps her tray on Michèle on purpose. Strange, since Michèle's father, a mass murderer who dragged her to his homicides, killed people for being rude.

Elle is startling and precise, an arrow to the skull. Mordant wit and twisted joy come with Verhoeven's level of control. In a Parisian gun shop decorated with American flags, Huppert picks up an ax and eyes it coolly before rejecting it in favor of a plain-old handgun. Verhoeven has been hackish in the past. Not this time. So much slow cinema in one festival starts to seem conservative, making a film with a killer screenplay like David Birke's, where everything is in place, look as backward-glancing and futuristic as *Total Recall*.

The festival's other insane crowd-pleaser was Maren Ade's *Toni Erdmann*, which also deals with a daughter (Sandra Hüller) and the resentment she feels for her father (Peter Simonischek). When we first meet him, it's clear Winfried is a tad sinister, a prankster-retiree who likes to greet the UPS guy with fake teeth in his mouth while wearing a wig. But he's a sad clown, and soon enough his dog dies. While Ade makes Winfried pathetic, she really stacks the deck against Ines, a self-involved lean-in-type who wears gray suits, speaks in business English, and works as a consultant downsizing industrial labor. She and the other middle-management Germans she works with are unhappy in Bucharest, hoping for appointments in other, better cities. "I like countries with a middle class," one says. Bucharest, we learn, features "Europe's largest mall and no one with money to buy anything."

Winfried shows up in Bucharest for a visit with his daughter, interfering with Ines's work schedule and ruining her weekend. Then he tries to make things right by giving her a cheese grater, that most anxiety-inducing of kitchen tools. At this point in the film, or maybe the next morning, right after Ines accidently slices open her toe before a big meeting (not with the cheese grater), something about *Toni Erdmann* became clear: no scene could be predicted from the one that came before it.

Toni Erdmann, the title character, is not a real person. He is a persona Winfried adopts to nudge Ines toward becoming what he wants her to be: nice, caring, human. Donning a lame disguise that makes him look like the son of Neil Young and Austin Powers, Winfried shows up at Ines's work events and pretends to be a leadership consultant, embarrassing his daughter into silence about his true identity as she squirms and pretends she doesn't know him. His idea that she just needs a little Merry Prankster in her soul crumbles as the pair tour an industrial excavation site in the Romanian steppe, a second-world wasteland of global capital.

The film is resolutely new and unexpected, yet somehow classical, echoing *Dr. Jekyll and Mr. Hyde*, Jerry Lewis's *The Nutty Professor*, Renoir's Boudu and Dr. Cordelier, and any movie in which someone dons a gorilla suit. The gorilla suit here—a folkloric Hungarian tree-creature getup—contrasts with the thin robe concealing Ines's nudity as she chases Winfried's final alter ego out of a naked work party she's hosting in her apartment. Winfried is a beast who hides, Ines a beauty who learns to bare her soul. The film's moment of apotheosis, a scene in which Ines is forced to belt out the Whitney Houston song "The Greatest Love of All" as Winfried/Toni plinks out the tune on a Casio, is a slow-boil demonstration of comedy's limit.

JEAN-PIERRE AND Luc Dardenne's *The Unknown Girl* takes place in the same despondent Belgium as their other films. More than those, it has a murky New Romanian Cinema feel. Often the Dardennes shoot the film's protagonist, a young doctor (Adèle Haenel), so we can't see her face. They shoot the townspeople the same way, hiding them in murk. This is a town populated by people who don't want to be seen or to look at others. Dr. Davin takes a technocratic view of her patients' plight in this dreary place where people live in shadows and no one gets excited about anything, ever: "If a patient's suffering moves you, you make a bad diagnosis."

One night she fails to answer the doorbell in her clinic, refusing to admit a young woman pleading outside. When the woman, an African immigrant, turns up dead, the doctor realizes she could have saved her. Far from being a lesser Dardenne effort, this dour semigenre film about obdurate, callous people with something to hide is one of their best. The film's genre trappings as dead-girl mystery have led the Dardennes to bore deeper into their milieu. Dr. Davin does not appear to have friends or family. People in the film isolate themselves in phone booths in a cybercafé. Nobody likes to talk, and when they do, it's to make threats.

Haenel's self-effacing performance in *The Unknown Girl* is the opposite of Kristen Stewart's star turn in *Personal Shopper*, even though Stewart's Maureen is supposed to be an introvert more attuned to the spirit world than to this one. Also a semigenre film, albeit a far more glamorous one, Olivier Assayas's deconstructed Parisian *giallo* fails to make sense, as *gialli* often do. Hounded by the most unwitty barrage of sexts in the short history of texting, Maureen moves through a disconnected contemporary world in which communication is ghostly, identity slippery, and S&M meets SMS. Every moment of the film's plot is predictable. As Stewart browses racks of clothes to try on in her employer's apartment, the film's big mystery becomes: how long before she masturbates?

In his press conference with Stewart after the screening, Assayas mentioned that he is interested in radical collage. "Of course *Personal Shopper* is not a genre movie," he explained. Furthermore, things have changed in the world of image-making, he said, since he made *demonlover* in the early 2000s. Back then he still had opinions about digital technology and the future. Now he's just a haunted man trying to survive in a world inundated with constant disposable images. *Personal Shopper* is interesting in that it gives so much screen time to Stewart, letting her sit in cafés and flip through art books on Hilma af Klint. She makes the movie work for her. All the other Americans in it seem like extras on *Silicon Valley*, and the Europeans merely members of the international creative class, stylish people with enough time on their hands to have affairs, but not enough to do their own shopping or chase their own ghosts.

COVERING A FILM FESTIVAL is like watching movies on an airplane. You start in one place and end up in another. It wears you down, seeing forty films in three weeks: sitting day after day in the dark, exposed to all that emotion and all those troubled souls. Everyone has their breaking point. Mine came during Mike Mills's *20th Century Women*, with Annette Bening.

The film begins in 1979, that fateful last year before Ronald Reagan ganked Gen X. Dorothea (Bening) is a single mom raising a son (Lucas Jade Zumann) in Santa Barbara, California, in a house she owns and shares with Jamie and two boarders, a New Wave wannabe artist named Abbie (Greta Gerwig) and an ex-hippie carpenter-mechanic who's drifting through life (Billy Crudup). The film opens with songs by Talking Heads and the Clash, and by the time Abbie and Jamie attempt to explain the appeal of the Raincoats' "Fairytale in the Supermarket" to Dorothea—in some pleasing, clunky dialogue that replicates how people really did talk about new music then—I felt like I'd been mugged. I felt embarrassed, as victims of muggings sometimes do, that I wasn't better prepared. I'd let down my guard. I told myself it wasn't my fault; there was no way I could have known Mills and I had the same adolescence and the same mother.

Here are some facts about my mother, which also describe Dorothea in this film. My mother was an ex–graphic designer who divorced my father when I was very young. She owned a Volkswagen Beetle. She smoked two packs of cigarettes a day, and they killed her in her sixties. She would listen to my records when I wasn't around, trying to figure out what I liked about them. She preferred Talking Heads to Black Flag. She was lonely, never meeting any interesting men in our small town, and she was always reading a book from the library. Interested in progress and concerned about the future, she tried to teach me to be decent and kind while the Dead Kennedys and Joy Division were teaching me to be insolent and moody. I, in turn, spent time at a nearby university meeting hip older girls, like Gerwig's Abbie, who worshipped David Bowie, and sneaking out to music shows in bars where they'd let in teenagers with IDs so fake they wouldn't have fooled a blind man.

Like that paragraph, the movie ends up being more about the son than the mother. The easy generational politics of music and T-shirt choice in *20th Century Women* define life in Southern California at the end of the '70s as much as they did present-day California in *The Kids Are All Right* (also with Bening). Mills holds down the keys on these signifiers to sound deep notes of melancholy. His film, in its second half, opens up cultural influence to feminist literature, using passages from *Sisterhood Is Powerful* and other Second Wave writing on the sound track and on-screen. The film's built-in sentimentality put me in the same position as the masses of women who embraced *Beaches* in 1988 or *Stepmom* in 1998. Cinematic melodrama is no longer as mass, and to be taken seriously it has become artier. As melodrama for men, *20th Century Women* reminds the middle-aged that they once evolved, and introduces younger men to feminism at mom's knee. "Forsake not the way of salvation, my boy," sang the Carter Family, "that you learned from your mother at home."

○ ○ ○

BY NOW, DOZENS of articles praising Barry Jenkins's *Moonlight* will have appeared, conferring on it the definite status of New American Classic. Groundbreaking in subject matter and an obvious artistic achievement, *Moonlight* tracks the early years of a man's life over three decades, from childhood, as Little, to adolescence under his real name, Chiron, to young adulthood, in which he's known as Black. Played in turn by Alex Hibbert, Ashton Sanders, and Trevante Rhodes, he goes from Charlie Brown–ish to gawky but tough, finally emerging as musclebound and stoic, a closeted gay drug dealer who has survived teenage beatdowns and juvenile detention.

The film is contemplative and rejects tragedy. A film about a shy person set in a milieu usually defined by ego and confrontation, *Moonlight* exposes violent male competition as sublimated, psychologically wounding, and pointless but survivable. The film's great strength is the way it confronts reality head-on, with cinematic beauty but no mythmaking. Palpably indebted to films by Hou Hsiao-hsien and Terrence Malick, Jenkins and his cinematographer, James Laxton, nonetheless invent a Miami photography all their own, dark blue, yellow, and pink—then orange and brown when the film movies to Atlanta.

Chiron, like Jamie in *20th Century Women*, is raised by a single mother (Naomie Harris), here addicted to crack instead of menthols. Jamie had no male role model; Chiron at least has Juan (Mahershala Ali), a crack dealer with a poetic soul who has learned to hide that side of himself the same way Chiron learns to hide his sexuality. Ali's performance in the "Little" section of the film seems effortless, yet it's so commanding it almost overwhelms the movie. When Juan disappears, something important goes with him.

The immediate, massive, and overwhelming adulation that greeted *Moonlight*, praising it just for existing, left me a little skeptical. Then I spoke with the Oscarologist. I was sitting with a publicist during the festival, chatting about the movie, when he broke in from the other end of the bench. An obese older white man with a cane, he told us he was gay and worked for a website that tracks Oscar predictions. "I'm an Oscarologist," he announced, and then he informed us that *Moonlight* was not going to win any Academy awards. "It's bad for gays, it's bad for blacks, it perpetuates stereotypes with negative role models." The publicist, a young woman, and I countered that Oscars were no measure of a film's quality. "In my business they are! In the film industry they are!" he shouted, adding that *Moonlight* "would not be influential." Right then the film leaped in my estimation. If *Moonlight* was that upsetting to this guy, it had to be a masterpiece.

Up the coast from Miami, in Kenneth Lonergan's *Manchester by the Sea*, Casey Affleck plays Lee, "a janitor in Quincy," calm and patient on the outside, who drinks too much, then gets into bar fights in places with names like Fibber McGee's. After his older brother dies, Lee reluctantly becomes his teenage nephew's official guardian. Lonergan's new film raises Masshole tragedy above the level of *fuckin' tragedy* at which it usually gets stuck. Despite the film's elaborate flashback structure, it does not get bogged down in plot. It reveals each character in his or her own time, meandering into scenes a conventional writer-director would cut. Lee and his nephew, Patrick (Lucas Hedges), spend what seems like twenty wasted minutes (theirs, not ours) looking for Lee's car after they leave a funeral home and can't remember where they parked.

The frozen landscape of *Manchester by the Sea* contrasts with the deadly fire in the scenes of Lee's days with his wife (Michelle Williams) and children. Lonergan gives him Freud's "father, don't you see I'm burning?" dream before allowing Lee to understand he has to get it together enough to be a substitute father to his nephew. The film is deeply melancholy, broken, and painful, as disarming as *20th Century Women* but with fewer gimmicks. Like *Moonlight*, it's a New American Classic, a film bringing movie drama to a high level that quality TV will never reach.

ONE DAY DURING the festival I was sitting in Union Square eating my lunch and reading an email announcement on my phone about a lecture the film theorist Laurence Rickels was giving in New York. There was a photo of Rickels in the email, and when I looked up from my phone I saw a man go by who looked exactly like Rickels: bald, modish eyeglass frames, stocky, well dressed. I got up and stopped him to ask if he was Rickels. "No," he answered. "I am Gianfranco Rosi, the Italian filmmaker."

Rosi's documentary *Fire at Sea* takes place on Lampedusa, an eight-square-mile island in the Mediterranean Sea between Sicily and Tunisia that, according to the explanatory opening title, four hundred thousand migrants have passed through over the past twenty years in order to get to Europe. Fifteen thousand have died on their way, through dehydration and starvation, drowned or lost at sea.

The sea is as important as the island in this elemental film. The fishermen on Lampedusa, fishers of men, rescue migrants from inhumane conditions on crammed boats. Many of the migrants are burned from the diesel fuel that mixes with seawater in the leaky holds. The rescuers wear white hazmat suits, white face masks, and white latex gloves while they work, covering the migrants in gold metallic marathon blankets that glow in the night.

Rosi explains nothing except through images. Half the film is made up of scenes from the life of a boy on the island, Samuele, a native Lampedusan we meet as the platonic ideal of a boy, making slingshots with a friend to hunt birds. As the film progresses, Samuele weakens. He is diagnosed with a lazy eye and has to learn to see all over again and how to row a boat with his eye patch on. He begins to have anxiety attacks. Rosi does not draw a direct line between Samuele and the migrant crisis. The film ends with Samuele alone, making gun-shooting motions with his hands and mouthing bang-bang noises on a dock at twilight.

A crap *Koyaanisqatsi* befitting our time, Eduardo Williams's *The Human Surge*, an experimental documentary from Argentina that takes place there, in Mozambique, and in the Philippines, follows disparate young workers, singly and in groups, in their downtime or engaged in the casual labor of sex work on the Internet, in supermarket checkout lines or stocking warehouses. As with *Fire at Sea*, there is no narration in *The Human Surge*, no voice-over, no explanatory titles. Filmed, I think, with an iPhone, in floating-eyeball style, it follows ordinary people on long treks down flooded streets, into bedrooms, through cane fields, and swimming in quarries. The film all of a sudden looks better when it gets to the Philippines, as if Williams upgraded to a newer iPhone at the Manila airport.

I could not discern a reason *The Human Surge* ended one sequence and began another, but I'm confident there is one. As two men trekked through a field in Mozambique, I left the theater for a minute and came back to close-ups of ants on the screen, a sequence that went on and on and could have been even longer. The film ends in a computer factory, where workers obey the command of a robot voice repeating "OK . . . OK . . . OK" as they complete their tasks. This is post-Costa cinema, slow but chopped to average feature length, puzzling, engrossing, and alienating.

SIERANEVADA BEGINS with an argument about a Disney princess costume. A neurologist named Lary (Mimi Brănescu) and his wife (Cătălina Moga) snipe at each other while looking for a parking space. Cristi Puiu, the film's director, uses this discussion of blockbuster entertainment to move the film into a single apartment in Bucharest, where *Sieranevada*, despite its mountain-vista title, will spend the better part of three hours. Lary's family gathers for a memorial service for his father, awaiting a priest as they argue about 9/11 conspiracy theories, life under the communists in the old days, and the adulterous behavior of various relatives. As each new quarrel swirls around another, a growing sense of disorder and patriarchal breakdown overtakes the ritual they are there to perform. Lary's niece brings a drunk friend to the service, who spends the rest of the film puking and half-conscious while the family argues about whether she's a prostitute and drug addict or just a drug addict. When Lary needs fresh air, he and his wife escape back into the street, where more arguing about parking ensues, the New Romanian Cinema's version of breaking the tension.

Romanian cinema has the special power of finding the murkiest, most desultory way to film petty squabbles and bureaucratic nightmares, to find the worst angles for actors without distorting them and making them inhuman. All the doctor (Adrian Titieni) in Cristian Mungiu's *Graduation* wants to do is make sure his daughter passes her exams so she can accept a scholarship to college in London. After she's attacked in the street, she struggles to concentrate on her schoolwork, so the doctor pulls some strings to make sure she'll pass. His one corrupt act sets in motion a downward spiral in his life. "All that counts," Romeo tells his daughter, "is getting to a normal world." *Graduation* shambles through the same European night as the Dardennes' *Unknown Girl*, shoved along to the sound of barking dogs, breaking glass, and the classical music Romeo listens to in his car. When characters in European films listen to classical music while driving, it's always a bad sign.

The first movie screened for the press before the festival began was *I, Daniel Blake*, Ken Loach's nonmurky exposé of bureaucracy in England. Daniel (Dave Johns), a widowed carpenter recovering from a heart attack in Newcastle, negotiates health-care and unemployment systems while trying to help a jobless new neighbor (Hayley Squires) and her two children, relocated to his town by social services. The film is didactic and focused, placing its most harrowing scene, at a food bank, within a larger context of destructive policies designed by the British government to make life impossible for the poor by robbing them of their dignity one step at a time. There is something thrilling about Loach's dedication to exposing the horror and mind-numbing pointlessness of bureaucracy with as little drama as possible. Audiences are supposedly always looking for something relatable. Loach has identified the last universal subject: filling out forms online. The anger the film generates shuts off delight in entertainment, an exemplary side effect of the film's agenda.

THE EXPECTATION THAT the cinema will delight us with grand adventure while retaining a touch of the metaphysical hobbled *The Lost City of Z*, an epic of Amazonian exploration James Gray adapted from David Grann's book. Gray's admirable sensitivity to the exploitative aspects of colonialist enterprise has produced the first Amazonian epic of British imperialism in which cannibals and piranhas are too respected to be terrifying. A loss of belief defines this film, and in the end, this journey to a destination that probably doesn't exist becomes all plot. The film jumps from one place to the next and one thing happens after another, necessitating supertitles reading "The Atlantic Ocean" so we know where we are.

Gray is also admirably committed to classical storytelling, and *The Lost City of Z* feels out of place among all the festival movies that go out of their way to subvert plot. Charlie Hunnam's Colonel Fawcett is hard to remember after the film, a ghost man as lost in the jungle as he is at home in England. Robert Pattinson's movie-star-erasure of a performance as his sidekick is more interesting, and called to mind Arthur Hunnicutt's performance in Hawks's *The Big Sky* (1952), a better movie about river exploration than this one, made in a less enlightened time.

The Lost City of Z closed the festival and was the last film screened for critics. The press conference after the screening, with Gray and much of his cast, was entertaining. Gray, a supremely witty man, narrated the difficulties a Jewish guy from Brooklyn faces shooting on location in the Amazon. As he put it, he was genetically designed to be an accountant in a Polish shtetl in winter, not somebody yelling "Action!" in a humid South American jungle during crocodile season. I wish some of his verve had been present in his film. Going into the jungle to find truth and beauty is harder than doing it at an uptown film festival, but in both cases you've got to capture that elusive joie de vivre and bring it back alive. +

NAOMI FRY

The Age of Insolvency

Tama Janowitz. *Scream: A Memoir of Glamour and Dysfunction*. Dey Street, 2016.

THIS SUMMER, A MINOR FEUD BROKE OUT IN the press between Tama Janowitz and Jay McInerney, two writers who alongside Bret Easton Ellis were known in the 1980s publishing world as the Brat Pack. This group's fiction, despite its literary, quasi-experimental aspirations, was succinct, digestible, and directed at middle-class young people who were interested in so-called edgy pop subjects like cocaine, light sexual deviance, commodity culture, the lives of artist-scenesters, and the perils and highs of life on the city's fringes. It was a literature that did not refuse materialism, but mined it actively to subversive effect. Though Janowitz, McInerney, and Ellis weren't good friends, they were brought together at readings, photographed at parties, and gossiped about in Page Six. They were at once savage analysts of the Eighties and the era's fizziest exemplars.

But since the eclipse of the decade they appeared to embody—and the aging of the literary generation they briefly headed—the members of the Brat Pack have taken different paths. Janowitz's, by all accounts, has been the roughest. This past August, in an interview with the *Guardian* to promote her new book, *Scream: A Memoir of Glamour and Dysfunction*, she expressed her long-simmering resentment toward McInerney, whose eighth novel had just come out. At the heart of the kerfuffle stood McInerney's suggestion, in an interview way back in 1998, that Janowitz shouldn't have appeared in ads if she'd wanted to be considered a serious writer rather than a "whore." (In the '80s and '90s, following the publication of her breakout story collection *Slaves of New York*, she had done advertisements for Apple and Amaretto, among other brands.) Janowitz said that she was still hurt by McInerney's suggestion and had felt "singled out." Other authors, she said, had done ads. "I just couldn't understand why . . . one author would call another author a whore, especially when that author kept marrying rich women." (McInerney's current wife, his fourth, is the heiress Anne Hearst.) "I needed money and I also didn't want to sit at the desk every day." Asked if she had ever told McInerney or other critics how she felt, she responded in the negative, saying, "It's ridiculous to argue with idiots." When approached by Page Six, McInerney seemed to take the high road, wishing Janowitz luck with her memoir. He claimed he didn't remember censuring her for doing ads but did recall praising *Slaves of New York* in a review for the *New York Times* that, he suggested, "put her on the map."

It's certainly true that Janowitz was on the map, whoever put her there. For a time in the late '80s, she managed to ably straddle the divide between the literary and the truly popular. While several of the *Slaves of New York* stories were published by William Shawn in the *New Yorker* before they were collected in the book, Janowitz's success went beyond the conventional middle-to-highbrow road. As the poster girl of what David Foster Wallace called a CY ("conspicuously young") writer, she was a new kind of literary celebrity. The hype surrounding her was relentless. With her vivid Stephen Sprouse dresses, pouffy dark mane, and bold makeup, she cut a striking figure, attempting with her persona as well as her writing to, as *Entertainment Weekly* assessed, "lure pop-cult fans away from the tube and into the bookstore." The Merchant Ivory film adaptation of *Slaves*, for which Janowitz wrote the screenplay; her friendship with Andy Warhol; her magazine covers and Annie Leibovitz–shot ads; her star-studded parties and multiple appearances on *Letterman* (including one in which she chewed gum and dared the host to open a can of sardines on air)—it all made for great copy, and Janowitz delivered.

Janowitz's ascent, however, proved fleeting. She went on writing novels, publishing a new one every few years, but none achieved the success or the zeitgeisty buzz of that first collection. *Slaves*'s loosely interlinked stories centered on the pressures and boons facing the city's creative circles in the '80s, when artists were still able to emerge from the struggling margins into plush yuppiedom—a transition figured as a threat but also as a hope and a promise, as bohemianism and capitalism became increasingly intimate, increasingly necessary bedfellows. The works that followed, however, told a story of decline, in terms of both their reception (cooler with each passing book) and their narrative themes. To examine Janowitz's life and work is to observe a young, talented writer make a big splash at the onset of her career and then, failing to recapture popular and critical success, continue to write nonetheless, producing works that dramatize her fall from grace. McInerney has been able, to the detriment of his fiction, to become less reflective about the crass realities of material life, which he and his characters take for granted as natural and reasonable. Janowitz has taken the opposite tack: the material circumstances of her protagonists' lives—as well as her own, as we learn from her memoir—do not disappear but become so pronounced and all-encompassing as to verge on lethal.

Unlike McInerney, who recently told the *Paris Review* he prizes "literary heroes Faulkner, Joyce, and Kerouac," Janowitz isn't fond of the kind of stream-of-consciousness modernist narration that once embodied literary quality and a kind of brawny individual agency. As she notes in *Scream* (with no small amount of bravado), books like *Ulysses* and *Look Homeward, Angel* are representative of "an entire first two-thirds of the twentieth century dominated by male writers who were actually pretty lousy but about whom you weren't allowed to say anything." Her work instead owes much more to 19th-century naturalism, which highlights the inescapable entrapment of individuals within the oppressive systems in which they are made to operate, be they familial, economic, romantic, social, or bodily. Some of her later novels are explicitly contemporary versions of classics of realism or naturalism: 1999's *A Certain Age* is an adaptation of Wharton's *The House of Mirth*; 2003's *Peyton Amberg* a take on Flaubert's *Madame Bovary*. Others amplify the menacing animalistic elements of naturalistic fiction into full-on apocalyptic narratives, extrapolating the dreadful fate of individual characters into collective fictions of fantastical destruction.

Janowitz's preoccupation is with portraying the encounter between an uncertain, struggling protagonist and the chaotic, hostile world around her, which can only result in a downward spiral. As she writes early on in *Scream*, "Try as I might, for me, other human beings are a blend of pit vipers, chimpanzees, and ants, a virtually indistinguishable mass of killer shit-pickers, sniffing their fingers and raping." In Janowitz's memoir and in her fiction, the suffering modern subject who must persist in such an apocalypto-Darwinian landscape is almost always a woman. This is not a coincidence.

IN 1981, FIVE YEARS before *Slaves of New York*, Janowitz published *American Dad*, a largely autobiographical novel in which two young brothers experience the debacle of their parents' divorce and their mother's long suffering at the hands of their father, a tyrannical psychiatrist whose will to power oppresses the family with irreversible consequences. Janowitz is the model for the elder brother, the novel's narrator, and the seeds of her later writing are already present in the voices of her main characters. For Janowitz, the patriarchal American family is a prison ("Is there no way out of this family? It's like a thought-form that's taken physical dimensions"), which subjugates and erases brilliant, sensitive women ("No credit for the joke, no credit for designing the house with him, no credit for raising you kids. I might as well never have existed at all," the narrator's mother says of her husband). Upward mobility is a false promise ("I'm not staying in my room until my life improves because I know it's never going to improve"), and human beings are held captive by their animal needs ("nature makes no demands on a person but simply exists, how things grow and germinate and eat and are eaten . . .").

Slaves of New York represented a temporary swerve from this worldview. Many of the stories point toward the possibility of a way out—an ambient shift that likely contributed to the collection's popular success. In "Life in the Pre-Cambrian Era," the painter Marley Mantello walks down to his bank on Wall Street "to take out another dollar or two," a ritualistic stroll to a branch that he has chosen for its distance ("this way I wasn't tempted to spend money as quickly"). On the way, he sees workers leaving their firms for the day, "newly released from their office tombs. Grim faces, worn down like cobblestones, never to make anything of their lives." Next to these *Metropolis*-style zombies, Mantello, as he notes, "stood out. With my long, lanky stride, my scuffed Italian loafers and my beat-up, faggoty Italian jacket": "It didn't bother me, the looks and stares I got. People were angry with me, and why? Because I was some sort of freak, an artist. They were trapped, and I wasn't. So I felt smug, even though I was starving."

Still, from its unequivocal title onward, *Slaves* stresses how artists and office drones alike are ensnared by the ideologies propping up Eighties New York. Janowitz presents an often-satiric assessment of a system in which most people—not least women—are locked in a losing race for notability and achievement, never completely able to bridge the widening chasm between the dream of success and paltry reality. "I was embittered. It was hard not to live in New York and be full of rage," admits the struggling jewelry designer Eleanor, a protagonist of several stories. Her decision to remain in a relationship with her more successful but emotionally miserly painter boyfriend, Stash (short for the Polish Stashua, but in its truncated form suggestive of a meanly squirreled-away reserve), hinges at least partly on his large-enough loft apartment and on her inability to afford her own place while pursuing her as yet unlucrative career. Beyond-reach real estate mixed with the ubiquitous promise of artistic success and a dash of grasping dissimulation and spiritual starvation: this constant drumbeat of life in New York City, now nearing an apex of unlivability, was captured presciently and remarkably by Janowitz. It was the moment to see it: recovering from the 1970s financial crisis, a property boom was fueled by low interest rates, and the city's impoverished aspiring artists could either sink or swim. The breach was enormous, but it could be forged by a single lucky break. As Eleanor has it:

> My mother had warned me about New York, but I was prepared to work hard, and I figured

> eventually I'd make it. I wasn't the only one in my situation. Most of the people I knew were doing one thing but considered themselves to be something else: all the waitresses I knew were really actresses, all the Xeroxers in the Xerox place were really novelists, all the receptionists were artists. There were enough examples of people who had been receptionists who went on to become famous artists that the receptionists felt it was okay to call themselves artists. But if I was going to have to do something like copy edit two or three days a week, I didn't want to lie to myself and say I was a jewelry designer. I figured I should just accept reality and say I was a copy editor.

A copy editor might remain a copy editor forever, and the lucky break might never come. But despite the looming threat of failure, many of the stories in *Slaves* are surprisingly buoyant. These are not Mary Gaitskill's neo-Gothic '80s tales, with self-harming anorexic artists chasing oblivion while stripping, practicing loveless S&M, and snorting speed in East Village dumps. There is, rather, something seductive, horizon-facing, in the way Janowitz presents the lives of artists. Your clothes may be ripped or strange, you may live in a glorified broom closet, you may be on edge and frantic (as Eleanor says at one point, "I consider life itself to be an act of desperation"), but strong feelings, even of hopeless frenzy, can give you agency. People are mad at you for being a footloose parasite, but they're also jealous, enamored. You are potential personified, rejecting stultifying, day-in, day-out labor in favor of a winner-take-all, studio-oriented entrepreneurialism. You wear a zany silver coat, as Eleanor does, and feel "pretty zippy . . . [like] Manhattan was just waiting for [you] to conquer it"—even if immediately after this, a neighbor sitting on a stoop points at you and laughs. And while New York might almost be killing you, it's worth it to stick it out for a while more, because who knows, you may rise to the top of the pile, a gleaming exception to the city's dreary rules. This might be a quintessential instance of culture-industry false consciousness, but seductions of the you're-gonna-make-it-after-all variety are powerful. For all its residents' protestations to the contrary, New York is still very much a part of America, with its outsize promises of worldly bounty. It stands to reason that one might suspend Adorno and Horkheimer's spoilsporty disbelief as long as one still has the chance to win.

When Janowitz is grim about the mercenary New York art world, she performs detachment with a fine knowingness. At a fancy art dinner, Eleanor is seated next to Samantha, the rich wife of an important gallerist and an aspiring rock star in her own right, who wears a rubber dress and keeps getting her picture taken. "I could have strangled her," the half-sneering, half-envious Eleanor says. Later on,

> her best friend, in a feathered tutu, was seated across from us, and when the tutu girl got up to go to the restroom I asked Samantha what her friend did. "She goes out with Fritz," Samantha said. Fritz was a sculptor, famous for his work in lemons and mirrors. "She's only eighteen and a real witch." So much for best friends, I thought.

It's not great to be surrounded by status-conscious bitches always clawing past you, but it is funny to gawk, and Janowitz is a wonderfully astringent observer. The mention of a sculptor "famous for his work in lemons and mirrors" is a nice low-key zinger, suggesting how, with a bit of luck and a good line, very little could be stretched into a lot more—though of course, in the long run, not nearly enough. When Samantha is flummoxed by why Eleanor would want to stay with Stash and invites her to meet her wealthier brother-in-law, Eleanor is tempted. But in the end she decides to go home. "I realized that I really did want to be where I was—with Stash, in this hovel," she says. "At least in this place I had love." Even when Eleanor and Stash break up, there is an optimistic gentleness to the proceedings. The final story in the Eleanor series is sweetly open-ended; she throws a half-disastrous, half-fun party. The life of an artist may be dangerously precarious and relationships may be impossible, but these are facts to be joshed about at a social gathering, not things that might determine, like a gypsy's curse, the path one's story will take. The escape hatch has not yet been sealed; a sliver of sky remains.

The commercial success of *Slaves* and its ongoing status as a pop-cultural touchstone imply that many of us were, and still are, quite similar to Janowitz's trapped office workers, looking with a mixture of contempt and fascination at the outliers. No one was better than Janowitz at delivering this bittersweet bohemian landscape. She was sharp enough to erect a critical scrim between the reader and her often ridiculous, often unscrupulous protagonists, but warm enough to make the youthful fantasy relatable. The built-in awe and nostalgia for that moment can be found even in the epigraph, in a quote from Dorothy as she awakens from her adventures at the end of *The Wizard of Oz*: "But it wasn't a dream, it was a place. And you—and you—and you—and you were there. But you couldn't have been, could you? This was a real, truly live place. And I remember that some of it wasn't very nice—but most of it was beautiful."

FOR THE PAST YEAR and a half, there was some excitement among book people of my acquaintance about Janowitz's upcoming "Eighties memoir." Those who have thought of her as an unjustly forgotten voice of that decade were perhaps hoping that *Scream* would prove the charm and return Janowitz, and by extension its readers, to the imagined Eden of that era, when the drama of artistic ambition was not so certain to end in disappointment.

This, however, was not to be. Since *Slaves of New York*, Janowitz has published six novels and one essay collection, none of which have done as well as that 1986 best seller. (*They Is Us*, her most recent novel, was unable to find an American publisher and was released only in the UK.) As she writes in *Scream*, *American Dad* was also a failure, selling only 1,500 copies "because a cookbook author who was assigned to review it in the *New York Times Book Review* decided to trash it and crush the twenty-three-year-old first-time author."

This kind of narration—weighty with gripes, deeply attuned to slights—marks *Scream* from its earliest pages. A note on the copyright page, to start, is not much at all like *Slaves of New York*'s now-thirty-year-old epigraph, though its general rhythm might at first recall that of Dorothy's soliloquy. "This is a memoir. *My* memories. It is what *I* remember. Except some of the people were a lot worse," the author writes. For a book that slings a not inconsiderable amount of shit, this statement is clearly a preemptive, quasi-legal gesture. Dorothy's reiterated "you" is replaced here with an "I" not at all pleased with what it's seen.

Most memoirs find their raison d'être in the recounting of a life's low points; the fact that the writer has survived to tell the tale throws the climb back up into glorious (or, at the very least, consoling) relief. Janowitz has no interest in this mode, or perhaps no capacity for it. Instead, she describes her life as a series of dreary, chaotic disasters, all barely struggled through, resulting in neither collapse nor triumph but a near-constant, dragging effort. In this context, it makes sense that she would have no true desire to write about her career high point. The glamorous *Slaves* period would have provided, in most other memoirs, a conventional peak (if remembered fondly) or valley (if, say, a crippling drug addiction or a strangling depression was battled against behind closed doors), but not so in Janowitz's memoir. She describes at length the process of sending off the stories that became the book while living in not-quite-genteel poverty outside Boston with her mother. After detailing the weighing of each envelope at the post office, the rude postal clerk, and so on (the literal and metaphoric confinements of bureaucracy—tax paying, litigation, nursing-home-related red tape—take up a large part of the book), this is how we arrive at the turning of the author's fortunes:

> Mailing one story a day slowed me down almost as much as writing a whole book and getting it rejected. But I kept at it. And finally, *The New Yorker* published "The Slaves in New York," and everything changed for me. I moved to New York and found a meat locker measuring ten by thirteen feet that had been converted to an apartment. But I was able to get my second book, *Slaves of New York*, published in 1986. I appeared on the cover of *New York* magazine in an evening dress standing next to meat in a meat locker next to my apartment in the Meatpacking District.

This is as much detail as we get. A mere two paragraphs down: "Ten years after this initial bout of success . . ." The proportions here are so off that I'd argue this is a willful punking on Janowitz's part, as if to say: You came here to read about my life in the Eighties, that decade I helped create, the last time I was truly famous, an "it" girl? Well, fuck you, because now you're going to hear about my crazy father, dementia-addled mother, complicated love life, constant money problems, that time when I was already in my fifties and sewage water flooded the tiny trailer I lived in alone in an arid field upstate with my eight dogs, and all the rest of it.

Janowitz seems to have come by this attitude honestly. Born to a psychiatrist father (who'd "fucked so many of his female patients" he was hardly able to tell them apart, went through multiple wives, was miserly and lascivious and domineering in equal measures) and a housewife-professor-poet mother (brilliant and loving but, following her divorce from her egomaniacal sex-fiend husband, consistently teetering on the verge of turmoil and poverty), she learned how fragile the world could be. Money could disappear suddenly. Relationships that seemed lifelong one moment could dissolve the next. Women could and would be made to feel weak and crazy by men who fashioned themselves as powerful masters.

There is no thrill in this victimhood—not in Janowitz's mother's mistreatment at the hands of her husband or in her difficulty gaining recognition for her poetry, and not in Janowitz's inability to consistently hold men's attention or achieve lasting literary fame (or, crucially, solvency: "I was always so broke," she keeps reminding us). In fact, it probably would have been easier, better, to be a more conventional victim. Then at least there would have been respect, or at least notoriety. This is an option Janowitz raises in jest—it makes for some rare funny moments in this bleak memoir—but there's a core of truth in it, too. When in London in the late '70s as a young woman, she meets the Sex Pistols but fails to grasp their importance and the dubious advantages of hitching her wagon to their rising star. "I missed so many opportunities along the way because of my fears and shyness! If only I hadn't thought the Sex Pistols were so untalented and unattractive, I could have ended up as Nancy Spungen." Rim shot, yes? But a similar riff occurs when Janowitz is selected while a student at Barnard to be a guest editor at *Mademoiselle*, just like Sylvia Plath and Plath's Esther Greenwood in *The Bell Jar*. Sent to help on a photo shoot, she burns a blouse while ironing, and at once, her "life was as ruined as the blouse":

> Would this have happened to Sylvia Plath? She had been a guest editor and went to dance with Yale men during her time at the magazine on the roof of the St. Regent's hotel. There was no mention in *The Bell Jar* of being sent out to iron. But if she had been, she would have ironed beautifully, I am sure.

Janowitz may not know how to iron, or die tragically and remain a frozen-in-time legend, but she also doesn't take things lying down. Writing her boss after the blouse incident, she composes with the help of her mother a "letter-as-performance-art" that begins as a mea culpa ("I'm writing to apologize for the terrible thing I did") but transforms by its second paragraph into a hilariously, almost admirably unhinged justification of her behavior:

> And what if something had happened to me? New blouses can be bought but I am not replaceable. . . . How do you think it felt to me sitting there doing nothing but watch that girl being photographed, simpering away as if she were really *it* instead of a mere nobody whom nobody had ever heard of. And those wretched people, like the photographer who kept saying he would see me again soon and who never called me.

Janowitz may be a drama queen, but the drama, though endless (her on-again-off-again boyfriend is on again and off again; her father names her an inheritor of his property, then disowns her; her finances are in constant disarray; the renovations on her falling-apart husk of a house are a money pit), never really changes the downward slope of her situation. Her anarchic encounters with the world have returned her to the mire. And Janowitz's mother—who is diagnosed with dementia and whom Janowitz moves upstate to nurse—provides a chief example of this biological certainty: "My mother is lying on her side with her diapers full of shit. She was a professor of English at Cornell University and an award-winning poet when she retired less than three years ago." All are of the dust, and all turn to dust again.

This is true, too, of many of Janowitz's fictional women, who are so much more reliant on outside circumstances, and especially on men, than their male counterparts. In *Peyton Amberg*, the titular protagonist grows up in a Zolaesque bog of a Boston childhood—hardship and crime, a mentally ill mother, meager career prospects. But thanks to her beauty and raw allure, she manages to achieve a middle-class marriage to a milquetoast Jewish dentist who refers to her as "sexy princess." This haven, however, turns out to be just another trap, a swamp of boredom and dissatisfaction: "She thought of herself as a sort of girl—woman—who obeyed the rules, who had struggled to pull herself out of a pit—of poverty, lack of options—and had lucked into this prime position only to discover that she was all too ready to toss everything away." The book follows Peyton's attempts to extricate herself from her prison, if only momentarily, through sexual adventuring and a long string of affairs, since "what else was there for women? They trawled for men or they had a man." But as Peyton grows older, these attempts bring her lower and lower, physically and mentally, as the aging female body itself becomes a prison.

Janowitz's writing doesn't just draw on naturalist tropes of decline here; it also recalls, with a bitter twist, popular women's-lib fiction of the '70s. The figure of the seemingly dependable but sexually repulsive dentist/doctor husband appears in two classics of the genre, Marilyn French's *The Women's Room* (1977) and Judy Blume's *Wifey* (1978). He is unsurprisingly, depressingly, named Norman in both, and in both, too, the stuck-in-the-suburbs heroine seeks to break her chains and revolt against her stifling circumstances to achieve greater emotional and intellectual freedom, sexual satisfaction, and a more reflective understanding of her conditions. Unlike French's and Blume's heroines, Peyton instinctively knows an emancipatory arc is out of her reach. Her story is set in stone from the start, because, as she tells herself, "She should have known enough about her own genetic destiny to realize she would manage to fuck things up." And in any case, her life has taught her that a woman is of no use "unless she was young and some man wanted to sleep with her." Sex, even when transporting, is just another trap.

In *A Certain Age*, too, the Lily Bart–like protagonist, Florence Collins, hangs on by the skin of her teeth to what she imagines are her fading looks, her about-to-be-foreclosed-on New York apartment, and her precarious social status. Her constant Darwinian battle for survival determines the downward arc of the book, which describes a world where the only things that matter are beauty, youth, and money. Janowitz doesn't even allow Florence the final release Wharton gave her heroine at the end of *The House of Mirth*—Bart's delicious drugged sleep, sliding imperceptibly into death, "a soft approach of passiveness." Instead, the end of *A Certain Age* finds the debased, crack-addled Florence gnawing at the "cindery edges" of a chocolate bar, trudging "into the darkening gloom, toward the mouth of the Hudson and the Statue of Liberty," like the wretched refuse of a teeming shore making the trip in reverse. "It was the end of the twentieth century, which was to say anyone robbing widows and orphans could find some justification for their actions. Maybe things had never been any different. Yet one would have expected more signs of evolution in the human race by now."

This is the end, but the problem with this sort of end is that it goes on and on—"a nightmare of human waste, filth and consumption," as one of the characters in the dystopian *They Is Us* says, describing life in the toxic swamps and petrochemical wastelands that are New Jersey in the near future. As *Scream* draws to a close, Janowitz's mother has passed away. She is still broke. She is awaiting trial as her brother has decided to take her to court for an alleged mishandling of their late mother's funds. "What happens? What happened," Janowitz writes in a final chapter titled "No Conclusion," an acknowledgment that the past exists only to repeat itself. There are no signs of evolution. There are no signs of revolution either. +

SUPPORTERS

SUPPORTERS

The Baskin Family
Ronald Barusch and Cynthia Dahlin
AJ Brown
Maria Campbell
Christopher Cox and Georgia Cool
The Garrison Family
Jeremy and Rebecca Glick
Jeff Gramm and Susie Heimbach
Eddie Joyce and Martine Beamon
Courtney Hodell
Megan Lynch
Richard Parrino
Chris and Whitney Parris-Lamb
Susie Simonson
Susan and Peter Tortorici
Mark White
Sarah Whitman-Salkin
Scott Wood-Prince

DONORS

Daniel Albert
Brad Andalman
Jonathan Baker
Elif Batuman
Louis Begley
Susie Brandmeyer
Sonesh Chainani
Amanda Claybaugh
Rimjhim Dey
Henry Finder
Melissa Flashman
Andrew and Blake Foote
Aram Fox
Greta Gerwig
DW Gibson
Adam Gunther
Benjamin Heller
Ramsey Hinkle
Kieran and Suzanne Holohan
Elizabeth and Lee Hunter
Peter and Natalie Jaros
Mary Karr
Denis and Rachel Kelleher
Mark Kirby
Nicholas Lemann and Judith Shulevitz
Christian Lorentzen
Allison Lorentzen
Sean Manning
Vanessa Mobley
Cullen Murphy
David Nachman
Leon Neyfakh and Alice Gregory
Bruce Nichols
Edward Orloff
Pamela Paul
Michael Pietsch
Hilary Redmon
Zach Rait
David Rose
Benjamin and Donna Rosen
Mark Rozzo
Christian Rudder
Jim Rutman
Gary Sernovitz
Michael Signorelli
Robert Silvers
Mona Simpson
Lorin and Sadie Stein
Marya Spence
Emily Stokes
Amor and Maggie Towles
Ben Wizner
Stephen Witt
James Wood and Claire Messud

Special thanks to

Andrew Blevins
Deena Butt
Juliet Kleber
Dilara O'Neil

n+1 is published with the support of the New York City Department of Cultural Affairs and the New York State Council on the Arts.

OUR CONTRIBUTORS

George Blaustein is an assistant professor of American studies at the University of Amsterdam. His last piece for *n+1* was "Miracles and Mummeries" in Issue 25.

Thomas Bolt is a writer living in Toronto and West Virginia.

Beatriz Bracher is an editor, screenwriter, novelist, and cofounder of the Brazilian publishing house Editora 34.

Thomas Campbell is a translator, editor, and blogger living in St. Petersburg, Russia, and South Karelia, Finland.

Joshua Cohen is a novelist living in New York.

Caleb Crain is the author of *Necessary Errors*. His novella *Sweet Grafton* appeared in Issue 6.

Kristin Dombek is a senior writer for *n+1* and the magazine's advice columnist. Her book, *The Selfishness of Others: An Essay on the Fear of Narcissism*, was published in August by Farrar, Straus and Giroux.

Sam Frank is an editor of *Triple Canopy*.

Naomi Fry is a writer living in Brooklyn.

A. S. Hamrah is *n+1*'s film critic. His last column, "This Quiet Place Today," appeared in Issue 26.

Victoria Lomasko is an artist, activist, and independent journalist based in Moscow.

Adam Morris has translated Hilda Hilst and João Gilberto Noll.

Aziz Rana is a professor of law at Cornell University and the author of *The Two Faces of American Freedom*. His last piece for *n+1* was "Race and the American Creed" in Issue 24.

LETTERS

Specters of Sanders

Dear Editors,

Namara Smith's "The Women's Party" argues that Bernie Sanders "sometimes seemed to speak to a phantom of the old white male industrial working class rather than to the black, brown, and female service workers who make up the majority of the working class today." But his extraordinary success with women under 35 and his staunch, even militant support from the National Nurses United—a majority black and brown union of mostly women—speaks to just how much he did reach the modern working class.

This is part of a broader discourse in which "what Sanders did wrong" is rarely placed against what he did amazingly right. An outsider with no real bloc within the Democratic Party, he essentially went up against the party itself. No establishment Democratic primary candidate in postwar history had more party support behind her than Hillary Clinton. But for people to whom the establishment was not a given—for, in other words, young men and women of all colors, many of them working class—Sanders opened up new possibilities.

—*Connor Kilpatrick*

Namara Smith responds:

I appreciate Connor Kilpatrick's thoughtful response to my article. I'd like to clarify a few points: I was not disputing that many people were moved by Bernie Sanders's message. Young women, myself included, were among his strongest supporters. My argument was that many of Sanders's campaign proposals rested on unexamined assumptions about gender and race. Take, for instance, one of Sanders's signature initiatives, his trillion-dollar job-creation program. This was presented as a universal program—"putting 13 million Americans back to work." Yet the infrastructure program, like the New Deal–era public-works programs it was modeled on, would have created jobs primarily in the male-dominated fields of manufacturing and construction.

To take another example, Sanders has often spoken about his admiration for full-employment programs. The most ambitious attempt to create a full-employment program in the United States, the Full Employment Bill proposed in 1945, would have guaranteed the "inalienable right" to regular and remunerative work to all American citizens, but it was drafted to exclude all those with "full-time housekeeping responsibilities." This "inalienable right," in other words, did not extend to almost half the population. Any genuinely universal full-employment program would have to provide state-subsidized childcare on a scale far beyond anything we've seen in this country—a subject Sanders rarely brought up.

All these problems are bound up in what Nancy Fraser has called the "crisis of care": the urgent need for a new way of organizing our economic relationship to social reproduction. To do so, it's not enough simply to insist, as Sanders did, on one's opposition to sexism. It requires rethinking our assumptions about the economy from an explicitly feminist perspective.

I don't fault Sanders for not coming out as a card-carrying socialist feminist during the Democratic primaries. I understand that all politics, especially promises made on the campaign trail, involve unavoidable compromises and calculations of expediency. But I do not think the writing done in small magazines should be limited by the horizon of electoral politics.

Dear Editors,

"Canvassing" was a cathartic piece to read. In mid-March I threw myself into the Sanders campaign, and by April I was spending most of my free time in the South Philly office, calling likely volunteers and pushing them to commit to canvassing shifts. I started to canvass despite feeling it was somehow vulgar to knock on random people's doors on a Saturday morning, as if I were a Jehovah's witness. "I'd like to talk to you today about my political lord and savior, Bernie Sanders!"

One interaction I had seemed to characterize the general response. A man about my age with a 3-year-old daughter invited me into his house to discuss the primary. He agreed with all my points about Bernie's policies, his approach to politics, his criticisms of the pay-to-play game. He nodded, then earnestly asked, "But if politics is a horse race, isn't the best candidate one who knows how to buy and sell horses?" I said that horse race wasn't working for the majority of Americans, and that we couldn't afford it—the planet couldn't. None of the things we like about Bernie's policies would get through unless we elected someone willing to fight the system as it is, rather than colluding with or orchestrating it. He shrugged. "I just don't know if it's possible."

The night of the election, I was also at the Gaslight. I shared my disappointment wordlessly with volunteer friends. I tried to fathom the idea that all our work ended here, with all of us alternately watching and avoiding a victory speech that spelled our collective defeat.

I walked home, still without having put words to my thoughts. Ten blocks from the bar I realized I had left my tab open. The next afternoon, after helping pack up the South Philly office, I returned to the bar to get my card. The bartender pulled a three-inch stack of debit and credit cards from next to the register. "You weren't the only one," she said.

—*Kelly Morton*

On the Rhode

Dear Editors,

As a Canadian American who spent three years in Oxford and as a historian of British elite education, I was engrossed and moved by Nakul Krishna's "Rhodocycles." I've been trying for years to write something that mingles Oxford's past with my own experience of the institution, but have never been able to render it as effectively as Krishna does. I recognize his portrait of the institution and all the political pressures it's under, of reactionaries and Rhodies, of what it feels like to be complicit. I have a tendency to tut-tut about erasing history and was never sure what I thought about the statue of Rhodes itself, but as long as the Eton- and Oxford-educated foreign secretary's highest aspiration is to sail round the world on a yacht under the delusion that he is running an empire, it's clear we still have a lot of thinking to do about imperial legacies, the institutions that sustain them, and our complicity with them.

The historian David Cannadine wrote a slim volume called *Ornamentalism* in 2001.

It's a neat little piece of imperial nostalgia, which when it was published was widely mocked by American historians of empire. But one thing it captures is an enduring cultural embeddedness in empire long after formal decolonization. It made me think differently about the Anglo culture my Canadian family inhabits, and helped to explain why I had to go see what the place was all about, too, and why I fell in love with it and had to work hard to push myself out of love and to critical inquiry instead. Which I suppose is all the more reason to take the money while making clear that one reviles what the likes of Rhodes stand for, and to shut up and listen when one's students say they are angry.

—Emily Rutherford

Literally Wasted

Dear Editors,

Tobi Haslett begins an otherwise excellent career retrospective of Gary Indiana ("Modern Love") with a rather partial, misleading representation of the Fales Library and Special Collections Downtown Collection of archives. He writes that if you want to make photocopies of Indiana's papers housed at the Fales, it's going to cost you 50 cents per page; "scans cost $15." Downtown, he intimates, is now nothing more than a diverting freak show for the monied middle classes who can afford to pay such absurd prices and who, in the cruelest of ironies, are actually to blame for making a gentrified Downtown uninhabitable for its artists and writers in the first place.

Leaving aside the fact that anyone can come to the Fales and take photos of items for their own use absolutely free, it's worth pointing out that the absurd $15 price tag pays an archive professional to find the desired item in its collection, box, folder, bring it up from store, scan it, send it, then return with it to the store and put everything back as it was, ready for the next Downtown tourist or *n+1* writer. Viewed this way, $15 is a bit of bargain.

In any case, what really seems to irritate Haslett is perhaps not so much the money as what you're paying for: $15 for a scan of a piece of Downtown paraphernalia is risible because the Downtown Collection is rubbish, comprising the "flotsam of [lives] lived on the so-called fringe." The papers of Downtowners like artist, writer, and AIDS activist David Wojnarowicz are rubbish, trash, junk—dragged out from under beds or pulled down out of lofts by artists and writers once the promise of posterity and a quick buck came calling.

In one way, he's absolutely right: Wojnarowicz's collection is rubbish. Or rather it might have become so had Fales director Marvin Taylor left it in the storage locker on the West Side Highway where he found it, after Wojnarowicz's death from AIDS-related complications in 1992. Without Taylor's intervention, Wojnarowicz's stuff might very well have found its way to the curb like the personal belongings of thousands of other AIDS victims who died without anyone to care for their stuff. Saving it from the dumpster and, yes, as Haslett would have it, "spookily" enshrining it in perpetuity, the Fales effects a radical transvaluation of trash like this by adding it to their archive. Yet, as Haslett observes, the tarnish of would-be garbage is never wholly removed.

In effect, the Downtown Collection at New York University is an archive of waste. In the belly of the beast, as it were, it hoards up the refuse, rubbish, and waste of lives that were quite literally wasted by AIDS or were considered a waste of Lower Manhattan's lucrative space by City-sponsored gentrification.

—Diarmuid Hester